The Polygamous Wives Writing Club

THE POLYGAMOUS WIVES WRITING CLUB

From the Diaries of Mormon Pioneer Women

PAULA KELLY HARLINE

OXFORD
UNIVERSITY PRESS

OXFORD
UNIVERSITY PRESS

Oxford University Press is a department of the
University of Oxford. It furthers the University's objective
of excellence in research, scholarship, and education
by publishing worldwide.

Oxford   New York
Auckland   Cape Town   Dar es Salaam   Hong Kong   Karachi
Kuala Lumpur   Madrid   Melbourne   Mexico City   Nairobi
New Delhi   Shanghai   Taipei   Toronto

With offices in
Argentina   Austria   Brazil   Chile   Czech Republic   France   Greece
Guatemala   Hungary   Italy   Japan   Poland   Portugal   Singapore
South Korea   Switzerland   Thailand   Turkey   Ukraine   Vietnam

Oxford is a registered trade mark of Oxford University Press
in the UK and certain other countries

Published in the United States of America by
Oxford University Press
198 Madison Avenue, New York, NY 10016

Library of Congress Cataloging-in-Publication Data
Harline, Paula Kelly.
The polygamous wives writing club : from the diaries of
Mormon pioneer women / Paula Kelly Harline.
pages   cm
Includes index.
ISBN 978-0-19-934650-9 (cloth : alk. paper)
1. Polygamy—Religious aspects—Church of Jesus Christ of Latter-day Saints—
History—19th century.   2. Polygamy—Religious aspects—Mormon Church—
History—19th century.   3. Mormon women—Religious life.
4. Mormon women—Social conditions.   I. Title.
BX8643.P63H37   2014
261.8'3584230882893—dc23
2013039923

1 3 5 7 9 8 6 4 2

Printed in the United States of America
on acid-free paper

To my Salt Lake grandmother
Anne Naismith Kelly (1900–1998)

Contents

A Note on Sources   xi

Welcome   3

PART ONE *Settling Utah Territory: Polygamous Yet Monogamous*

1   I was perfectly willing...but still it was hard   11

2   I had admired his conduct on the plains   25

3   *Interlude: Justifying Polygamy*   43

4   It is a heart history   51

PART TWO *Making Sense of Sisterhood: Relations between Wives*

5   The drudge and tail of such women   61

6   *Interlude: Sometimes Sisterhood*   73

7   Many nights my pillow would be wet with grief   93

8   I could not say that I loved the man as lovers love   107

PART THREE *Abandoning Polygamy: Weariness*

9   Word came the marshalls were coming, so I skipped out   123

10 *Interlude: The 1890 Manifesto*   153

Contents

11 I grew rebellious   165

12 I heard a voice say you are away from Mr Chestnut   183

Farewell   203

Sources   217

Image Copyright Permissions   233

Acknowledgments   235

Index   237

First Wife Emma Nielson, St. George, Utah, 1889

AFTER I GOT my precious little ones in bed, I took a walk in the moonlight all the while wondering where [my husband] my precious F G was. A sweet response would be that he is in Arizona doing his duty to his other family, but then I often wonder if he is doing his duty to his family [here] in St George. How pleased I would be if he would step in, administer to our wants, soothe the cries of my four little ones and do a fathers part. They have looked forward to the time (so long) that they would see their Pa that they begin to think they have no Pa. I feel heart broken myself. My heart is so sore and who in all this world can heal it except my dear F. G.? One word from his precious lips at this moment could do it. I love him as I do my own life, and when can I linger by his side as I once used to?

A Note on Sources

THE AUTOBIOGRAPHIES AND DIARIES of twenty-nine nineteenth-century Mormon polygamous wives form the core of this study. About half the women wrote autobiographies, and about half wrote diaries (a handful wrote both). The shortest is just three typewritten pages, and the longest are book-length. Fifteen have been published in some form, and the rest are in manuscript. Almost without exception, I retained the writers' original spelling and punctuation. I decided to focus on wives (1) who married between 1847 and 1890; (2) who were not married to high-ranking Salt Lake Church leaders; (3) who were not prominent Salt Lake women's leaders themselves; (4) who did not leave the Church; (5) who did not move to Canada or Mexico to escape prosecution; (6) whose writings have not been widely read; and (7) whose writings were published or archived (or, in the case of Catherine Rogers, offered to me by a descendant) by 1996 when I finished gathering primary sources that fit my criteria. References to all twenty-nine writings are provided at the end of the book, under Sources, and if photographs of the writers could be found they have been included. Finally, the names of the twenty-nine women are italicized in the text at first mention to distinguish them from other women mentioned.

The Polygamous Wives Writing Club

Welcome

FROM SALT LAKE CITY TODAY, the I-15 travels south along the Wasatch Mountain Range leading forty miles out to chiseled Mount Timpanogos, home to Sundance Ski Resort. Late winter afternoons when the aqua sky is turning rosy, and the last western horizontal light is still stretching toward snowy Mount Timpanogos to the east, you might feel that you're standing on the earth but drawn away to heaven—like a clay-footed winged soul yearning for greater purpose. Down in the valley where orchards once dominated the landscape, down in Provo near the corner of 500 North and 500 West where an anachronistic little log cabin goes unnoticed by drivers who zip along State Street, a larger pleasant home used to sit near a stream. Here, starting in the 1860s, a polygamous wife, a little sparrow of a woman, celebrated "Hollidays" that were more work than wash days. Here, she wrote poems (despite her husband's feeling that the world was "so overstocked with literature") and shared her writing with friends during occasional long afternoons when they would get "all tired out talking." Here, she allowed her husband's new wife to move in with her for a year, then eventually banished her from the property. Here, as evening approached, she attended to her chicken pie and children, and amidst her responsibilities felt, "I cannot accomplish the [writing] I should like to do." But when the sun set just so on Mt. Timpanogos, "a spirit" that would "not rest" came over her, and she eventually published her poems herself and wrote an autobiography that showed how "woman is not a stone in polygamy."

After my husband gave me a copy of Mary Jane Tanner's autobiography for Christmas in 1990, I started hunting for more autobiographies and diaries written by women who became polygamous wives between the Mormons' 1847 western migration and the 1890 Manifesto that began the end of mainstream Mormon polygamy. I narrowed my search by choosing obscure polygamous wives who were neither married to Salt Lake leaders nor Salt Lake leaders themselves because I wanted to know how common folk understood and lived polygamy. In the end, I found that Mary Jane Tanner wasn't alone among polygamous wives to believe it was her "duty" to leave a "record of her life," and I turned up a total of twenty-nine who fit my criteria, all married to different husbands. The personal writings of these twenty-nine polygamous wives—who lived from Idaho and Wyoming in the north to various settlements in Utah, Colorado, Nevada, Arizona, and New Mexico in the south—are the heart of this book.

The title *Polygamous Wives Writing Club* suggests that together these twenty-nine women form a special group: their writings were fortunately preserved, and they're all brought together here. I also use the device of the writing club more specifically in each chapter (except in the *Interludes*), as a way to geographically and thematically organize a few women's stories. The idea of writing clubs first came to me after watching seven Mormon Relief Society women in my Utah Valley neighborhood meet monthly to share their personal writings, and I imagined that nineteenth-century women could have done the same. In fact, three women studied here—Mary Jane Tanner, Martha Heywood, and Ruth Rogers—actually mentioned sharing their writings with other women. And according to historian Harriet Sigerman, between 1870 and 1900, a "remarkable movement swept" the nation as women "organized clubs to develop common interests," including "many study clubs" that greatly improved "writing skills." In brief, I lightly employ the writing club as a device to organize, to engage general readers, and to bring the wives' flesh-and-blood nonfiction lives to the forefront.

Although these twenty-nine women are a small sample of nineteenth-century Mormon polygamous wives, their writings suggest some common patterns. The three major sections of this book focus on three. First, Mormons were trying to integrate polygamy into a culture that was overwhelmingly monogamous in practice and underlying attitude. Thus, in general, wives never felt comfortable with polygamy because, despite their efforts to convince themselves otherwise, there still seemed something adulterous about it. This feeling sometimes temporarily abated the longer they were married, the more their families were preoccupied with settling new land, and as they reviewed their belief that the "higher law" of polygamy came from God.

Second, although sisterhood was (and still is) a Mormon hallmark, wives found it hard to treat their husbands' other wives as sisters, and in their writings chided themselves for this lapse and coached themselves to try harder. If first wives' writings had a formula, it would be, "I believed that the principle of plural marriage was from God, but it was still hard—it nearly killed me." First wives, who were sometimes still in their twenties when their husbands entered polygamy, struggled with the initial news that their husbands planned to marry another wife; after the marriage, most wives struggled to share their husbands' time, attention, and resources because there often were not enough time, attention, and resources to go around. Almost without exception, the wives weren't as interested in building relationships with the other wife or wives as they were in building relationships with their husbands—which, again, was typical of a monogamous culture. Nevertheless, the shared domestic routines of some of the wives who lived together are inspiring.

Third, life for these women became especially uncomfortable and inconvenient when the federal government began polygamy raids in the 1880s. First wives could stay in their homes and move about, but they still had to worry about their husbands getting caught and sent to prison for "cohabitation." Second and third wives usually had to hide away from their homes, their families, and their friends, and they hardly saw their husbands—they lived like impoverished single mothers and widows. Under these conditions, and disillusioned with the polygamous system, for the most part the wives studied here didn't mention or mourn the 1890 Manifesto that phased out polygamy in the Church. Aging polygamous wives who lived into the twentieth century (not to be confused with fundamentalist groups that emerged during the same period) usually lived with their grown children or alone.

On average, 25 to 30 percent of men, women, and children lived in polygamous families, and the wives believed that their contribution would help build a solid foundation for generations of Mormons to come. Perhaps ironically, polygamous wives are now rarely mentioned in a Mormon Church meeting. Although modern Mormons take pride in the hard work and determination of their nineteenth-century pioneers, they generally find polygamy, based on Old Testament practices, confusing and controversial and have yet to come to peace with the powerful mythical legacy left by some of their foremothers.

But for better or for worse, polygamous wives remain ensconced in Mormon history. They participated in a controversial religious practice that on a public scale broke marriage rules accepted by most early American Christian religions and on a private scale sometimes broke their own hearts—and yet their voices weren't altogether unhappy. Were

polygamous wives content with their sacrifice? Did the benefits of polygamous marriage for the Mormons outweigh the human toll it required
and the embarrassment it continues to bring? Do Mormons still believe
in polygamy? Although the mainstream Mormon Church washed its
hands of polygamy more than one hundred years ago, you can still hear
the voices of polygamous wives who wrote their stories. And in their stories, the conflict between love and duty—like attempting to float in azure
skies while gravitationally forced to work a plot of land instead—unfold
in Technicolor.

It was the Mormon founder Joseph Smith who first quietly promoted "plural
marriage" among some of his followers. Smith was born in 1805 in upstate
New York to God-fearing parents who, like many Americans at the time,
were more "seekers" among the local churches than "quick to join a particular church." The 2008 PBS series *The Mormons* introduced Smith's setting
as "a place and a time when seers and prophets roamed the countryside
each claiming to profess the truth," and Smith wrote that as a young teen
these circumstances caused him "great uneasiness" and "serious reflec-
tion." He claimed that at fourteen he simply wanted to know which church
to join, went to the woods to sincerely pray about this question, and received
an answer from God and Jesus that he should join none of the churches.
Over time, he felt, like other "Restorationists," directed by God to restore the
original church of Christ, and in 1830, he established what soon came to be
known as the Church of Jesus-Christ of Latter-day Saints.

As Smith studied the Bible during the early 1830s, his far-reaching religious vision to restore "all things" from previous ages made him open to
reinstating Old Testament polygamy. A number of biblical patriarchs had
more than one wife, but perhaps the best known is Abraham, whose first
and apparently barren wife Sarah suggested that Abraham take her maid
Hagar to have children—God had promised Abraham that his descendants would be as numerous as the sands of the sea. Smith began to imagine ecclesiastical and family kingdoms that would persist into eternity.
At great cost, he led efforts to build sacred temples (also echoing the Old
Testament) in Ohio and Illinois where Mormons participated in sacred
marriage rituals—"celestial marriage"—that "sealed" a person forever to a
spouse and children, as well as to ancestors. Smith's biographer Richard
Bushman explains that "like Abraham of old, [Smith] yearned for familial
plentitude" and believed that a piece of the sealing puzzle was polygamy,
or plural marriage.

As Smith secretly began marrying additional wives and encouraging his closest confidantes to do the same, of course Smith feared "wrecking his marriage," his reputation, and his church—and his foray into plural marriage was not without damage. In the end, although there's evidence that Smith seemed most interested in creating an interconnected web of believers that could be exalted together, he "never wrote his personal feelings about plural marriage," and "whether [he] was motivated by religious obedience or pursued sexual dalliances clothed with divine sanction cannot be fully resolved through historical analysis."

Meanwhile, the church he established continued to grow. Smith had many converts who were amazed by the *Book of Mormon* and by the spiritual gifts that accompanied Mormonism, but from the beginning Smith and his adherents also drew criticism from their neighbors on religious, economic, and political grounds. As early as 1832, Joseph Smith was pulled from bed by intruders, stripped, tarred and feathered, and nearly murdered. As time went on, and Mormons congregated in the same area, their swelling population caused fear and resentment as they tended to buy and vote in blocs, destabilizing an area's economy and politics. Along the way, rumors of polygamy also drew enemies. Mormons ended up relocating several times: from New York to Ohio, on to Missouri, to Illinois (where in 1844 Smith was shot dead while incarcerated for ordering the destruction of a printing press), and eventually to Iowa and Utah.

After Smith's death, his successor Brigham Young made the decision to lead his people even farther west. Young wanted his people to settle where they could freely practice their religion, prosper, and grow.

The Salt Lake Valley appealed to Brigham Young at least in part because it was isolated—its expansive desert would be undesirable to enemies and its awe-inspiring mountains to the east created a natural fortress. When he first arrived, he may have stood looking out over the sparsely populated desert as the prophet Abraham once had in an earlier time and place and heard the Genesis God say, "Lift up now thine eyes, and look from the place where thou art northward, and southward, and eastward, and westward: For all the land which thou seest, to thee will I give it, and to thy seed for ever. Arise, walk through the land in the length of it and in the breadth of it; for I will give it unto thee."

Young and the first group of Mormon pioneers entered the Salt Lake Valley on July 22, 1847, and started planting the next day. Within three days, Young had laid out the city that would be "perfectly square, north and south, east and west" with a temple at its center. By December 1847, Young issued notice to newly converted Mormons everywhere—throughout the eastern and midwestern United States, "England, Scotland, Ireland, Wales, and adjacent islands and countries"—to "emigrate as speedily as possible" to join other Mormons.

New converts, such as the future-polygamous wife Jane Hindley born in 1828 on the Isle of Man, headed toward Utah in waves. When Jane Hindley decided to emigrate as a single woman in her late twenties, leaving her parents behind, she explained that she desired to heed the call to "gather" with the other Saints. She wrote, "I believed in the principle of the gathering" and "felt it my Duty to go altho it was a sever trial to me, in my feelings to leave my native land and the plasing associations that I had formed there." Jane felt assured by the Holy Ghost that she should leave Europe and immigrate to America: "My heart was fired I knew in whome I had trust and with the fire of Israels God burning in my bosom I forsoke my home."

Between 1848 and 1852, three to four thousand Saints immigrated each year. As newcomers arrived during the late summer or early fall, they were typically integrated into Salt Lake City wards (geographically delineated congregations) and given work for the winter. In the spring, Young coordinated efforts to settle outlying areas. He may have directed some people to settle particular outlying areas and to settle in compact villages surrounded by farmland, but "people actually settled where they wished" often along "creeks and canals" wherever water was most convenient.

In the meantime, some limited polygamy, or plural marriage, was quietly practiced, particularly among those who had been closest to Smith. Then in 1852, having established a "string of Mormon colonies" and abiding safely in the mountains, Young publically announced that Mormons accepted polygamy on religious grounds—but even at the time, it may have seemed sociologically savvy, too. Polygamous marriage would help Mormons populate the land, provide families for single women, alienate non-Mormons, and connect Mormons to Joseph Smith and their sacred past. Indeed, the Mormon population continued to grow, thanks to missionaries sent around the world seeking converts, and also thanks to the many mothers in Mormondom.

The Mormon's proposed State of Deseret included most of current Utah and Nevada, "the southeastern corner of Idaho, the southwestern corner of Wyoming, a large area in southeastern Oregon, [parts of] southern California, and a strip along the eastern border of California." By 1857, 35,000 Saints lived in the Great Basin; by 1869, 75,000; and by 1877, at Brigham Young's death, 125,000. We're particularly interested in twenty-nine of them here.

PART ONE

Settling Utah Territory: Polygamous Yet Monogamous

Now the Lord had said unto Abram, Get thee out of thy country, and from thy kindred, and from thy father's house, unto a land that I will shew thee: And I will make of thee a great nation.

Genesis 12: 1–2

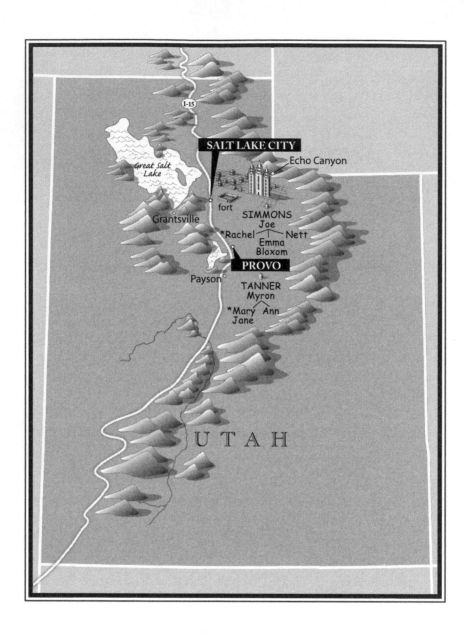

I was perfectly willing...but still it was hard

Rachel Simmons' House: Salt Lake City, Utah, about 1868

If first wives *Rachel Simmons* and *Mary Jane Tanner* had known each other, they probably would have enjoyed spending an afternoon together. Rachel's house was centrally located in Salt Lake City, across from City Hall near the corner of 100 South and State Street, not far from the temple block where the Salt Lake Temple was under construction and just a block from Brigham Young's house. Green and shady locust and cottonwood trees bordered each side of the street, grass on each side of the gutters gave the streets "a fresh appearance," and large gardens at houses on the block included fragrant peach and apple trees. Mary Jane Tanner lived in Provo, forty-five miles south, but she had grown up in Salt Lake and enjoyed visiting her friends there. A visitor such as Mary Jane would have approached Rachel's house via the front path bordered on both sides by grass, near a garden where peas were growing. Inside, Rachel had taken in sewing to try to make ends meet, all the while worrying about growing problems with her husband. Rachel and Mary Jane were fully part of a Mormon society that had tried to adopt polygamous marriage, both of their husbands had taken second wives, and Rachel and Mary Jane were willing—but, truth be told, they were living polygamy in a culture that was still monogamous, and they both felt the resulting personal culture clash.

Rachel's story of marriage started out ordinarily enough. She and her husband, Joe, had lived with Rachel's mother (a polygamous wife herself) during their first three years of marriage. Then in April 1855, they moved their young family into this new house near the Social Hall where Joe was a favorite actor. Not long after their move, Rachel wrote, Joe "began to think seriously of taking another wife." Rachel explained, "I was perfectly willing he should do so, but still it was hard when it came." It was, she confessed, "my first real trial."

Rachel's feelings summed up the complicated response many polygamous wives had when their husbands considered entering polygamy: wives may have been willing on religious grounds but were still troubled by it on cultural, emotional, and personal grounds. It was not easy, even though both Rachel's and Mary Jane's mothers were polygamous wives— Rachel's parents had been among the earliest polygamists in Joseph Smith's day.

Her parents, the Woolleys, had joined the Mormon Church in 1839, when Rachel was three, and they were intimate with Smith, who some evenings came to their home and taught them "very privately" about "celestial marriage"—a sacred ceremony that "sealed" a family together throughout eternity. As Smith taught it, a possible ancillary to celestial marriage allowed men to add an additional wife or wives who could be sealed to the original couple, creating "plural marriage." Taking advice from Smith, Rachel's parents entered plural marriage.

One night when Smith was visiting, Rachel, a curious youngster at the time, remembered sneaking downstairs when she was supposed to be in bed, opening the door "at the foot of the steps" and was "immediately discovered and unceremoniously sent back to bed again." In the "few seconds" she stood there, she "saw several persons standing in the center of the floor as though receiving some rites or ceremonies." Rachel must have briefly seen the ceremony that would add a second wife to the Woolley family.

Plural marriage was hard on her mother, who began staying in her bedroom, where Rachel remembered hearing her cry "as though her heart would break." Her mother "was slower to believe" in polygamy than her father was, Rachel would say, "as was natural." Rachel's mother, "for a change" and in an effort to cope, took her youngest child and went to visit her mother in Ohio but never told her own mother of her "deep sorrow" because the Mormons had not yet admitted to outsiders that some of them were living polygamy. In 1848 when Rachel was eleven, her family, including both wives, traveled by wagon toward Salt Lake.

When Rachel's family arrived in September 1848, her uncle's family was able to serve them "corn, cucumbers, and other vegetables." Her father and brothers "went right to work making adobes for a house" and selected, she wrote, "ninth Ward lots and put up two rooms so that we were very comfortable." They made a floor of torn-apart wagon wood, made a roof of "brush with dirt thrown on," used blankets for doors, and Rachel's mother and the other wife Ellen each had a "bedroom" made from a "wagon set at the door so they could step right into them." A typical wagon was ten feet long, and even non-Mormon Western settlers "who didn't have homes moved into wagons or tents."

Mary Jane's story had many similarities, including hardship and polygamy. She and her parents, the Mounts, arrived in Salt Lake the year before Rachel in 1847, and a few months after Brigham Young. Mary Jane's first impression of the valley was that it looked "barren," with "sage brush and sunflowers, a few small streams of water running through it, and some squallid Indian wigwams scattered about." One member of the original 1847 party had a longer vision of the valley. He wrote, "There is an extensive beautiful, level looking valley" that "extends to the south probably fifty miles where it is again surrounded by high mountains" and "appears to be well supplied with streams, creeks, and lakes, some of the latter are evidently salt," speaking of what would be called the Great Salt Lake.

Soon after arriving, Mary Jane's father helped saw logs that other men brought from the canyon to build houses. Into the winter, the Mounts continued to live in their cold wagon, cooking outdoors, "suffer[ing] so much," until December when they moved into a rustic cabin that was part of a "fort" located in the "6th Ward square," where Salt Lake City's Pioneer Park is today. An example of these early cabins, one that belonged to the Deuel family, was preserved and stands today on the block west of Temple Square, surrounded by tall hollyhocks by summer's end.

By March 1848, in the fort where Mary Jane's family stayed, there were "423 houses and 1,641 souls" huddled together for safety. Outside the fort, thousands of acres of farming fields had been prepared and "875 acres were sown with winter wheat," which was attacked by crickets in 1848. During those first years, the pioneers' situation became so dire that they considered returning East or leaving for California or Oregon.

At the same time in late 1848, Mary Jane's father moved her and her pregnant mother from the fort to a nearby canyon with him to a "miserable shanty" that they shared with other sawmill workers. Then perhaps discouraged, full of wanderlust, and tempted by gold, her father left for California to seek his "fortune," leaving his wife, Mary Jane, and the new baby girl in the care of his partner, who eventually moved the Tanner women back to the Salt Lake Valley. Over the next several years, Joseph Mount, Mary Jane's father, occasionally sent them messages from California, and, although he had financial ups and downs, he sometimes sent money and gifts (including a gold watch and a pet pony that Mary Jane had to part with because her mother couldn't afford to feed it), but her father didn't return after eighteen months as he had promised. The new baby died, and Mary Jane and her mother scraped by.

Rachel and Mary Jane would have nearly been teenagers when they arrived in the valley, and Rachel was interested in boys first. She had several boyfriends, but her mother urged her toward Joe Simmons, a man who had been headed for the gold fields of California (like 25,000 other gold seekers who "tramped through Mormon communities" in 1849 and 1850), stopped in Salt Lake to "replenish" provisions, became interested in Mormonism and was baptized, found work, and stayed. When Joe met Rachel's family, the Woolleys, he pitched a tent in their yard and subsequently boarded with them. Joe later told Rachel that "he loved [her] the first time he saw [her] and came with the determination to make [her] his wife."

Rachel was soon in a love triangle with Joe and a boy named Cal, which made her feel miserable. Although only fourteen and then fifteen, she was pushed by her mother toward Joe but actually loved Cal—until she found that Cal was seeing another girl. After the breakup with Cal, she treated Joe, who was twelve years older than she was, "worse than ever," but he "made no complaint and was just as kind and loving as ever." Then, she wrote, "a feeling of pique took possession of me. I thought I would let Cal see I wasn't going to die for him, so Joe said he caught my heart on the rebound. He was very generous and never made anything of it, except he could never bear to hear me mention Cal's name." Rachel ironically wrote that Joe "was of a jealous disposition, more so than anyone I ever knew."

Mary Jane would not have been surprised that Rachel wanted to marry so young because, as Mary Jane wrote, "it was customary at that time for girls to marry young." During the Mormon "frontier period" between 1847 and 1869 when Rachel and Mary Jane married, Mormon women indeed married young: 27 percent by age sixteen, 83 percent by age twenty. Only 3 percent were single at twenty-four. On average, Mormon women married a year younger than other Western rural women and four years younger than women in Massachusetts. But Mary Jane Tanner, even at age sixteen, "could not think of marrying." She enjoyed school, the "free library," "dancing schools and spelling schools," "rustic beaux," and "walks on Sunday evenings."

On the other hand, Rachel wanted to marry. Rachel and Joe were married by Brigham Young in 1852, just after her fifteenth birthday (Joe was almost twenty-seven), in the Warm Springs Bath House, which was "the largest and best place for parties" and a "fashionable place." Rachel wrote that she had "as nice a wedding as could be had in those days" with a "splendid supper—everything the valley afforded." After supper, Rachel and Joe danced "until next morning" with their guests.

As a young wife in the early 1850s, Rachel almost never missed one of Joe's performances in the Deseret Dramatic Association, and she hated to miss any parties, balls, and "theatricals" at the Social Hall. On the other hand, she would say Joe's acting "took him away a great deal at night to rehearse and get ready to play," which she "did not like" at first. After a while, though, she learned to "go to bed and sleep just as well."

Theatergoers evidently found Joe romantic. Rachel would explain that many times women asked her if she was jealous that her husband could "[make] love so natural as that" on stage. A nineteenth-century critic corroborated the impression that playing a lover came naturally to Joe: "In the plays where the tender romance of love abounded, [Joe Simmons] was nearly always the hero of the love episode." Although Rachel had "confidence" that Joe was loyal to her, she twice told of troubling incidents with other women. One night, "a very good actress" who was "very fascinating with the men" broke her ankle and stayed a few nights, and Rachel wrote it was "unpleasant for [her] to see the solicitations of [her] husband for [the actress]."

Rachel had more tangible reason to feel troubled when Joe started looking for "another wife" in 1855 and began dating a woman named

FIGURE 1.2A First wife Rachel Simmons.

FIGURE 1.2B Rachel's husband, Joe Simmons.

Emma Bloxom. Rachel felt that Joe went overboard and ignored her wishes: "It wouldn't have been so hard if he had not courted [Emma Bloxom] so strong. She was at Horace Whitney's at the time and we were very intimate with them. Joe used to go every other night to see her, and I thought that was too much when he had a family at home, but it made no difference what I thought."

Rachel seemed to have pleaded for him not to go to their friends' house without her. Indeed, polygamous courtships could have the air of an extra-marital affair. Even Rachel's mother, a seasoned polygamous wife, complained to Rachel about Joe's behavior. Rachel wrote, "She used to ask me about it and scold Joe to me, but I used to say, 'Mother, if I can stand it, thee must. It won't always last, he will come back to me in the end.'" Rachel believed that Joe was "infactuated" with Emma, and "like many others" who tried polygamy wanted to try "a new thing."

Joe married Emma Bloxom in August 1855, and Rachel added, "brought her home and gave her my bedroom and the best of everything in the house, and was so infatuated with her that he neglected me shamefully. It was hard to bear." Rachel felt that she bore it patiently, however, and always felt that deep down her husband loved her better (as though it were a competition), so she waited it out: "Sure enough [the end] came, sooner than I expected." Joe and Emma "soon began to disagree and some friend's affairs finished their good feelings toward each other." Luckily for Rachel, Emma Bloxom left with another man and moved to Carson, Nevada.

But Joe wasn't discouraged. He started dating two more women "strong as ever." One was Romania Bunnell, and the other was Rachel's sister Nett. According to Rachel, Romania complained about Joe dating Nett at the same time, so Joe gave her up and married only Nett in 1857. As Rachel reflected on it years later, she wrote, "It was all for the best, I suppose. I mention these things to show that my life has not been all a bed of roses, but I would not, if I could have done by the turning of my hand, had it different." In fact, she and her sister Nett lived together peacefully and almost continuously from the day Nett joined the family.

Mary Jane's experience was just as mixed as Rachel's. In 1852, Mary Jane's father sent a letter from California entreating his wife and daughter to join him there and sent his non-Mormon brother, who believed Mary Jane's mother had been disloyal, to fetch them. When Mary Jane's mother sent word back that she didn't want to leave Utah, her husband Joseph Mount became incensed. It had been four miserable years since the family had been together, and in September 1852, five years after arriving in the valley, Mary Jane's mother finalized a divorce from Joseph Mount in Salt Lake. Not long afterward, she became the polygamous wife of an "earnest, hardworking man." Mary Jane, then sixteen, explained, "it seemed very pleasant to have some one to care for us." Indeed, especially during the early settlement years, polygamy became a way for women who were alone to become part of a family—although this did not always mean that they were well cared for.

After her mother's remarriage, Mary Jane spent some time as a schoolteacher, and then in 1855 at age nineteen, she met her future husband, Myron Tanner. He was a Mormon bachelor who was briefly in Salt Lake selling a band of horses before returning to San Bernardino, California. She explained, "We seemed to be mutualy attracted, and as his time was limited he did not wait for a long acquaintance, but soon asked me to be his wife."

During their engagement, enterprising and ambitious Myron was in California working for the winter, and Mary Jane wrote that she made "the most of her last winter" in Salt Lake attending "many balls and theaters" with a Frenchman named Peter Rouie. A clever letter writer, Mary Jane titillated Myron with social details but made her love for him clear in words that emphasized the monogamous ideal of the time: "how beautiful to see two souls meet joined together in the ties of holy love leaning on each other for that happiness the world cannot give ... shall not our hearts be thus united."

Mary Jane's lines sounded like "Home," a poem published in a popular American magazine in 1863.

> *Two birds within one nest;*
> *Two hearts within one breast;*
> *Two souls within one fair*
> *Firm league of love and prayer....*
> *A world of strife shut out,*
> *A world of love shut in.*

In the ideal nineteenth-century marriage, "home" was established to enclose a devoted couple and "love" was an exclusive feeling between two soulmates. Michael Goldberg explains that as early as the first half of the nineteenth century, women became more cautious in their choice of a spouse because marriage was seen as "more of a partnership," and "courtship became a time to prove the existence of extraordinary compatibility and radiant love." Stephanie Coontz notes that "by the middle of the nineteenth century there was near unanimity in the middle and upper classes throughout Western Europe and North America that the love-based marriage, in which the wife stayed at home protected and supported by her husband, was a recipe for heaven on earth." Assumptions about the normalcy of love-based marriage didn't disappear with the coming of polygamy, and Mary Jane believed this love existed between her and her fiancé Myron.

Four days after Myron returned from California in 1856, Mary Jane and Myron were married at her mother's house. Compared with Rachel's all-night wedding party, Mary Jane's marriage day was hardly a celebration at all. Mary Jane would have liked a "wedding supper," as her friends had, but her California father had not come through with any money for a party, so she was "married privately at [her] mother's house, and made no announcement of the fact until the following Sunday, when [she and Myron] appeared at meeting."

The newlyweds moved to the new community of Payson, sixty miles south of Salt Lake, where Mary Jane noted that in the late 1850s, "the children and many of the women were barefooted," and "not much troubled about the fashions, but looked...like cotton bags with strings tied around them." Settling Payson was not an easy life. The citizens had trouble with Indians (Myron and his brother had sixty horses stolen) and moved into a fort; they were threatened by the arrival of the Utah Expedition—2,500

FIGURE 1.3A First wife Mary Jane Tanner.   FIGURE 1.3B Mary Jane's husband, Myron Tanner.

federal troops sent by President James Buchanan to quell a perceived insurrection; and they experienced famine.

Mary Jane also weathered personal crises: Myron worked in California for stretches of time; Myron's family—his mother, aunt, three brothers, and a hired girl—came to live with her in the little cabin making her feel that she was losing her "individuality"; and in the early stages of pregnancy with her second child and with Myron gone, her fifteen-month-old baby suddenly died. She gave birth to her second child also while Myron was away.

In 1860, Myron and Mary Jane moved from Payson to Provo where she had "always wished to live." Her husband's five freighting trips to California between 1858 and 1860 had been "very successful from a financial standpoint," which she must have appreciated following the financial insecurity of her youth and the famine all around her.

Then came the big change, which Mary Jane explained rather matter-of-factly. On May 19, 1866, after living in Provo for six years, with two living children and a twelve-year-old girl they had taken in because her mother could not care for her, "a change was made in our family by Myron marrying another wife. She was an English girl named Ann Crosby. Of this I will say but little. It is a heart history which pen and ink can never trace." Since Mary Jane believed that polygamy was "a true principle," she "summoned all [her] fortitude to bear it bravely," illustrating that she could accept polygamy as a religious conviction but had to bear it like a burden.

Myron brought Ann Crosby "home to live with me," Mary Jane explained, "and we managed very well," especially when the two wives had babies at the same time. But after awhile, they felt cramped: "Our house being rather small for the increased family [Myron] decided on building a larger one. He accordingly commenced it a few feet back of the old house. He built of brick and laid out what he intended for a kitchen proposing to tear away the old adobie house and build a two story front." Mary Jane would explain that she got the new house: "Myron said I could have the new house and [Ann] might live in the other and keep house for herself. This arrangement made us much more comfortable."

This arrangement started falling apart, however, when Myron did Ann a favor and sent for her mother, her sister, and her sister's son who were in England. Soon after arriving, her sister married and went on her own, but Ann's mother continued to live with Ann. As Mary Jane told it, "They had not been here long before they commenced sowing dissension in the family, which increased until all intercourse between the two houses

FIGURE 1.4 Second wife Ann Crosby Tanner.

ceased. And all friendly relationship between us was destroyed." Mary Jane explained further, "Previous to their coming we had overlooked each others imperfections and tried to live our religion putting all jealousies aside, and had she striven as I did instead of allowing her people to come between us it would no doubt resulted in entire happiness and confidence in each other." Mary Jane felt sure that the practice of polygamy itself was not flawed, only that their situation was flawed.

Of course, it was easier to get along with a polygamous wife who was your biological sister—as Rachel's was. About 12 percent of polygamous husbands married their wives' sisters, and some contemporaneous observers thought that those unions were "among the happiest" and that "the tent [was] more quiet" that way. Although Rachel and her sister Nett were compatible, there were other difficulties. Nett had added five children to the family, and by 1868, the Simmonses had fifteen people living at the house across from City Hall. This alone made it a challenge to make ends meet. Joe's drinking made it harder still. By 1868, Joe had been drinking too much. At first, he had been traveling, at Brigham Young's recommendation, to neighboring settlements to buy paper and rags for a paper factory. But Joe "was of a proud nature" and "thought he was adapted to something better." He switched jobs, and then not long after he began working for the city as an assessor and collector. Rachel remembered, "his wages were very good at that time, ten dollars a day, but we did not get along very well as to money matters, for I am sorry to say that he had taken to drink more than was good for him. His money went in that way, and we got poorer every day. It was this way for several years. He might have been wealthy if he had been careful with his means." Joe continued "playing on the stage" for free, too, putting in long hours, and his health began to fail.

If Mary Jane had ever visited Rachel in 1868, she would have certainly seen her sewing "to help support" herself and her family. Joe had switched jobs again and was working away from home as a "clerk on the railroad in Echo Canyon" and "sent in money every month," but prices were so high that the money didn't go very far. It would only get worse until he died four years later in 1872. Prior to his death, Rachel and Nett moved everyone into one room of the house because they could afford only one fire. Rachel's son Frank, still a child himself, "was helping all he could" by hauling gravel on the State Road in the cold. He boarded out and came home Saturday nights. They had "very little to eat," and "the boys sawed wood for others" and "picked up bits of coal" to heat their home. After Joe's death, Rachel would get $7,000 from the sale of this house, which she considered "our little home," and she would use the money to pay off mounting family debts. She eventually became a successful midwife and lived to age ninety—she died in 1926.

Rachel's and Mary Jane's feelings about polygamy were clearly mixed. When Rachel wrote her autobiography as an old woman, she had been a widow for many years. Her description of her mother's sorrow after entering plural marriage mirrored her own sorrow when her husband courted and married Emma Bloxom. She wanted her readers to know that she and Joe had loved each other and that he was a special person, but he had disappointed her, too—he approached polygamy in what she thought was a rather selfish way and had succumbed to his alcohol addiction. But, in polygamy, he finally chose Rachel's sister Nett for a second wife, a relationship that caused Rachel no problems.

Nett had been a trusted helpmate to Rachel. For example, in 1862 when Rachel went to Grantsville with Joe for three weeks to "make hay," she "left the children at home with Nett." The two sisters and wives also suffered together when Joe got sick: "What Nett and I passed through at that time never can be realized." As Joe got worse, Rachel explained, "We hadn't anyone to help us, night after night we sat up with him." But Rachel wrote nothing about Nett's personality in her autobiography, making her a flat undeveloped character, leaving the reader to wonder if Rachel took Nett for granted and maybe resented her a little, too.

Mary Jane Tanner's ideas about polygamy were also complicated. After Mary Jane's mother was abandoned by her first husband, her mother seemed content to become a polygamous wife to a decent man, and Mary Jane justified her mother's decision. But, in her turn, Mary Jane seemed sad that Myron, who had been called as a bishop in Provo, had married Ann Crosby, and that in the end Ann betrayed her, too, as we shall see in a few chapters hence.

Most polygamous wives' personal writings provide evidence of the underlying tension between the expectations of monogamy and the practice of polygamy. Even while living polygamy, inertia pulled wives back to their cultural DNA—Adam and Eve alone. They would have preferred to have had their husbands to themselves, but this was an unusual time, a time to open the doors: more women than men were gathering to the Mormon West.

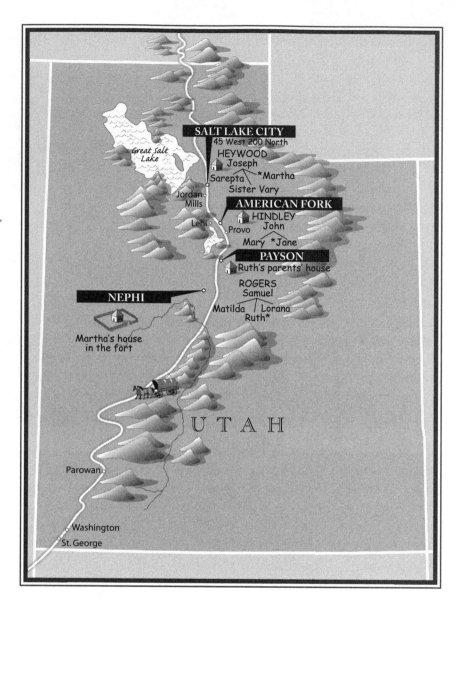

SALT LAKE CITY
45 West 200 North
HEYWOOD
Joseph
Sarepta   *Martha
Sister Vary

Great Salt
Lake

Jordan
Mills

Lehi

AMERICAN FORK
HINDLEY
John
Provo
Mary *Jane

PAYSON
Ruth's parents' house

ROGERS
Samuel

Matilda | Lorana
Ruth*

NEPHI

Martha's house
in the fort

U T A H

Parowan

Washington
St. George

2

I had admired his conduct on the plains

Martha Heywood's House: Nephi, Utah, 1855

Third wife and avid diary writer *Martha Heywood* loved literary societies, which she tried to promote in the small settlement of Nephi, ninety miles south of Salt Lake City, where she had moved four years before. If she had known not-so-different *Jane Hindley* and *Ruth Rogers*, she would have been very interested in what they were writing, too. Jane and Ruth had crossed the plains as older single women, finally married in Utah, and kept diaries—just like Martha. Martha would have enjoyed some company, as well, which helped ward off that peculiar loneliness that polygamous wives sometimes felt. Although polygamous marriage hadn't redeemed them from loneliness or poverty, it had provided two of them with children, and all three of them with the husbands and families that brought them a better social status.

Both Jane and Ruth lived in settlements within a day's distance of Nephi. If they had actually visited Martha, she would have welcomed them into the plastered adobe room that she shared with her only child in the Nephi fort. Martha likely would have told them she wished she could offer them more, but they all knew times were hard in Nephi, as everywhere, and flour was scarce, so that Martha could only dream of making them a "good Christmas Cake all dotted over under & through the middle with little black spots & larger brown ones." Besides, Martha was more of a teacher than housekeeper and cook. Jane and Ruth were not used to being spoiled, anyway, and would have been happy just to be warmed by Martha's fire. And Martha would have been glad to see their diaries—all those beautiful handwritten pages were treasures.

All three of them had been early converts to Mormonism, which would have already given them something to talk about. Martha had been baptized in 1848 near Buffalo, New York, although she was originally from

Dublin, Ireland. Jane converted with most of her family in 1840 at age twelve after hearing Mormon missionaries on the Isle of Man. And Ruth, her parents, and her siblings were taught Mormonism by some missionaries in New Jersey, where they lived before going to Utah. Now all three women lived in fledgling Mormon settlements south of Salt Lake.

Martha's marriage story began when she was thirty-eight years old and still single. That was when she met her husband-to-be, Joseph Heywood, who was almost four years younger than she was, while traveling west to Utah in his 1850 wagon train. If someone would have suggested to Martha at the time that she might marry Heywood, she would have laughed because he already had a wife and family waiting in Salt Lake for his return. While traveling west, she noted in her diary a rumor circulating about polygamy being openly practiced in Salt Lake, but she didn't believe it.

Martha knew she was a spinster—she had once written a friend that she had "many offers & expectations to be married" but had waited for "the Lord to arrange such affairs," and she came to believe that was what happened with Heywood. As captain of the company, Heywood looked out for Martha, who was traveling alone. In return, she took it upon herself to help Captain Heywood's nephew, who suffered from consumption on the trail. Even as part of this large train, though, she sometimes felt alone and wrote in her diary, "how dreadful lonesome it is oftentimes—in the midst of spirits yet feeling all alone." This feeling, she would explain to her new friends, always drove her to God—"him who is greater than all earthly friends."

Jane would have known that lonely longing as well. In 1855 at age twenty-eight, Jane and her half-sister left the Isle of Man "to gather with the Saints." Jane wrote, "It was a terrible trial for me to leave all that I loved, the land of my birth, my dear father most of all. It was indeed stretching my heart strings." She must have longed for both the Isle of Man and for Utah but could not have them both. She trusted in God to lead her and "laid [her] earthly all upon the altar." Full of faith, Jane and her stepsister joined sixty wagons in a train going west. Their wagon train captain had also undoubtedly been asked to help the women who were traveling alone, and Jane was friendly with him, her husband-to-be Captain Hindley. He was thirty-five years old, and, like Captain Heywood, he also left his family behind in Utah. Jane wrote of walking alone with Captain Hindley by a river when the group stopped and of the time she drank wine with him and some other men in a wagon: "we injoyed ourselves in his waggon with the Captain and another Brother has some wine to drink."

At the end of their 1855 trek, Jane was invited to stay at "Bro. Joseph Caine's house" north of Salt Lake. She wrote, Brother Caine "wished me to remain there and make it my home." But in January 1856, Jane "received a note" from the former captain, Brother Hindley, with an invitation to spend two weeks at his home in American Fork, thirty-five miles south of Salt Lake on the west slope of Mt. Timpanogos. Brother Hindley's wife, Mary, picked up Jane and drove her by wagon to American Fork. Jane "did not like the appearance of the place" and found the captain "looking very ill indeed," but at the end of her stay, she explained, "Bro. Hindley was now getting better" and "proposed marriage to me." She wrote, "I told him I would consider the matter and let him know after I returned to Salt Lake." On February 18, Brother Hindley, together with his wife, "called on" Jane where she was living with Brother Caine.

Was her host Brother Caine interested in asking Jane to become his polygamous wife? Brother Caine told her he was "rather opposed" to her possible union with Mr. Hindley because the settlers were "threatened with famine in the land," and Caine didn't know, she wrote, "if Mr. Hindley was prepared to take care of me." Jane continued, "However, I loved [John Hindley] and made up my mind, if necessary to go through poverty and privation for him. I had admired his conduct on the plains and trusted my future life and happiness to him." Jane decided to add that she knew "[i]t was a great step for [her] to take" at the time but that she "never regretted it." Later in life, she would write, "although I have passed through many trials since then," God has "sustained me through them all."

Martha's trek ended in 1851 similarly to Jane's—she also had an invitation to board in Salt Lake, from the already-married man who'd been her guide. Captain Heywood invited her to stay at his home at 45 West 200 North, where the rest of his family awaited him. Joseph Heywood had met his first wife, Sarepta, on a Mississippi River boat. He had been a merchandiser originally from Massachusetts when he saw Sarepta board the boat: evidently, "she was so beautiful that Joseph began courting her at once," and they married in 1841 when he was twenty-six and she was almost twenty. The next year, while visiting Nauvoo, Illinois, Heywood heard Joseph Smith preach and "quickly converted [to Mormonism] and asked for baptism." When the Saints decided to go west, Heywood helped sell properties and trade for "wagons and teams, grain, other supplies" and then joined "the last train of the 1848 emigration from Winter Quarters" to Salt Lake. Sarepta Heywood had also become a Mormon, but she was a "delicate beauty who found frontier life difficult." In 1849 in Salt

Lake, her husband was appointed the "first postmaster of Salt Lake City and soon after was set apart as bishop of the Seventeenth Ward," simultaneously fulfilling both duties. Martha went to stay with the Heywoods, turning down a second lodging invitation, and within a few months was engaged to Captain Heywood.

Ruth would also find a husband soon after arriving in Utah. She could have explained to Martha and Jane that she was twenty-nine when she headed west in 1852 with her parents and siblings, who had all converted to Mormonism in New Jersey. After arriving in Utah, her parents were "living in their wagon near the provo river" that November when Ruth left them to seek employment. She had a feeling she might marry soon and even told her father that she would "be married before he saw [her] again": "He wanted to know who to. I told him I did not know. Mother advised me to hunt up Samuel H. Rogers. Said he would take care of and be good to me." Samuel had been a beloved missionary who preached to Ruth's family years before in New Jersey. The day after leaving her parents, she wrote in her diary, "I learned where [Samuel] lived. Told no one my intention. I thought I would get acquainted before placing my mind upon any one."

Ruth found housework in Jordan Mills, twenty-five miles northwest of Provo and eleven miles southwest of Salt Lake City. She worked for a dollar a week living at the Gardners' house for the winter. In 1849, Mr. Robert Gardner and his brother Archibald had built a solid gristmill and sawmill near the Jordan River that eventually "inspired a cluster of small industries, including blacksmith shops, logging and hauling operations, woolen and carding mills, a tannery, several stores, a shoe shop, and later a broom factory"—today repurposed as "Gardner Village: Established 1853," a quaint outdoor shopping mall.

FIGURE 2.2 Second wife Ruth Rogers.

While working there, two days after leaving her parents, Ruth found an opportunity to make contact with Samuel Rogers. She was getting breakfast at the Gardners' when two men came in "before daylight." Again using her intuition, she said, "it came into my mind that they knew Samuel." As the men waited near the stove before conducting their business with Mr. Gardner, they chatted with Ruth. She found a way to ask "if they knew Samuel Rogers," and "they said they were well acquainted with him." She told them that he was "one of the first Mormon Elders that [she] ever saw and heard preach." The men told her that Samuel lived in Lehi, about ten miles south. They also told her that Samuel "had taken his brothers wife," that is, married her, after his brother died. Ruth wrote that she was impressed that he would care for his brother's widow, and the men commented that Samuel was "slow in getting a wife of his own," which perhaps gave her an opening.

During breakfast, Ruth wrote her name in a letter that Samuel had written to Ruth's father ten years earlier (a letter their family had carried all the way from New Jersey) and asked one of the men to take it to Samuel in Lehi. She explained, "I thought if [Samuel] wished to learn more about me that was sufficient." Not long afterward, she got a note back from Samuel who wanted to know where she was: "your place of residence situation and circumstances I am wholly ignorant of which I would like to know."

As Samuel and Ruth corresponded, Samuel's wife Matilda, who was also Samuel's brother's widow, was full-term pregnant and would soon give birth on December 17. Twelve days after the baby was born, Samuel wrote to Ruth, "I shall be happy in conversing with you. If it is agreeable to you, write on the reception of this." Ruth probably didn't know that Matilda had just given birth when she wrote back to Samuel, "You wrote that you would be happy in the privilege of conversing with me but not more so than I should be to see and converse with you...you must come when convenient." She suggested that he could come some Saturday and go to meeting with her on Sunday.

Then unexpectedly, on Wednesday, January 12, 1853, Samuel appeared at the Gardners' to see Ruth. Samuel was four years older than Ruth, and this would have been the first time she had seen him since he was a missionary in New Jersey. She wrote, "he came. I did not know he was coming. it was almost dark. he said he was going to the City. he heard I was there and thought as we were old acquaintances he would call and see me. I asked him if he would stay overnight." He agreed to this, and after supper they talked of their "travels and what of interest had transpired since he left New Jersey." They evidently enjoyed each other's company because Ruth wrote, "the clock struck eleven before we retired to rest." He told her he was on his way to Salt Lake, and on his way back, he would like her to come home to Lehi with him to "get acquainted with his family." He said he wanted her to stay with them "a week or two."

The next morning at breakfast, Ruth and Samuel had "considerable conversation," and, she wrote, "I agreed to go home with him when he returned." On January 17, he returned for her and they started for Lehi where Ruth wrote that "all appeared very agreeable" and that Samuel's "wife had a son which was born on the 17th of Dec—they had named him Smith Doolittle." Ruth thought it "a very odd name." At the end of her one-week stay, Samuel proposed marriage to Ruth, and she "agreed" if her father was "willing." Samuel wrote her father two letters, but when they heard nothing back, they decided that silence meant they could go forward.

Around this same time, Ruth had also been proposed to by another already-married man, her employer, Robert Gardner. She explained, Mr. Gardner "told me he desired me to become his wife." He told her that if she lived there all winter, she "would know in the Spring" if she was willing. She told him she "ought to by that time." But she turned down Mr. Gardner, a man who could have given her greater financial stability, and instead married Samuel Rogers because she loved him.

Martha could not have said to any guests that she was sure she loved her husband Joseph Heywood when she married him—it had all happened so fast. Polygamous courtships were typically fast—for example, in 1883, Annie Tanner's husband felt that "a long courtship in cases of polygamy was entirely improper." The community preferred short courtships because they minimized the anxiety over a married man out with another woman.

Martha explained that at the end of the wagon trek west, after she had accepted Mr. Heywood's offer to stay at his home, she tried to befriend the young pregnant Sarepta Heywood and an older woman who was also living in the house. Martha wrote of Sarepta at the time, "Mrs. Haywood is much reserved in her manner towards me but I admire her very much. She is the personification of a good wife and in such matters I feel very small beside her." The other woman living at the Heywood's was the sixty-eight-year-old "Sister Vary"—a nickname for the old lady because when she was good, she was "very, very good, and when she was bad, she was horrid." Sister Vary was older, but sometimes men married older women like her not because they could bear children but because marriage would give the women a home, social status, and a family to be sealed to.

Within a month, Martha wrote in her diary, Mrs. Heywood's "reserve towards me begins to wear off," and Martha was enjoying "society" with her and Sister Vary. Even though Martha was told by some people that she was lucky to be staying at the Heywoods' home, one day she wrote in her journal that Mr. Heywood had "peculiarities" and, although he was a "good man," he was not "intellectual."

Martha's feelings changed toward him, however, when seemingly out of the blue Joseph Heywood proposed marriage to her and proposed that they do missionary work together. She wrote in her diary at the time, "Today I had a conversation with brother Haywood who hinted at the probability of wanting me to go with him [to the South Sea Islands] which is a new train of thought to me of a very agreeable nature. This field of labor is one that I would delight to act in—that of a missionary and a wife. The former I believe I have a natural talent for and privation would be nothing in the discharge of it." Before converting to Mormonism, Martha had been an enthusiastic Advent missionary in Canada.

But when the pregnant Sarepta Heywood learned that her husband intended to marry Martha and go on a missionary trip with her, she became "more than usually excited." The idea to go on a mission probably came from Brigham Young, who didn't hesitate to call men on missions to increase the fold. Martha looked for a chance to privately talk to Mrs. Heywood when Sister Vary was gone, and when she did, Mrs. Heywood told Martha that she "could not bear" news of her husband leaving with Martha, "in addition to her other troubles and this made the rest appear but light."

Martha admitted that, at the time, she was annoyed by Mrs. Heywood, who seemed to be getting in the way of Martha's happiness. Martha, who had waited so long to marry, and who loved travel, and who had zeal for missionary work—oh! Martha was indignant. In her diary, she wrote that she would take counsel from Brigham Young or Brother Heywood, but not from Mrs. Heywood, and that Mrs. Heywood was "interfer[ing]" with her "affairs."

Martha would have surely chuckled later at her boldness, because it hadn't taken her long to learn her place and to learn that Mrs. Heywood would always be superior to her in their family. But at the time, as Martha was trying to figure out her fate, living in the same house with them, her "thoughts and purposes" were "vacilating continually." Her confusion was understandable—she was on the verge of becoming a wife but not a *wife* in the traditional sense she knew. Her husband-to-be would not be focused on her wishes; rather, she would eventually be one of four wives with no particular priority. Unfortunately for Martha, she was like some other new polygamous wives who instinctively assumed they would have the privileges of a monogamous wife.

As it turned out, to force her point, Sarepta Heywood went on to complain to Brigham Young, who then agreed that after marriage Martha should stay with the rest of the family in Salt Lake, and Mr. Heywood would travel to do missionary work with Sarepta Heywood's brother instead. Martha lamented in her diary, "The faint probability of going south opened a two-fold gleam of sunlight to lighten my dreary prospect." She ended her entry that day with the following sense of reality: "Oh how unpleasant is the prospect before me." She felt "uncommonly oppressed."

Martha went forward with the marriage "sealing" anyway. Maybe it was too late to turn back or maybe she was impressed that Brigham Young was involved, because not long after the missionary argument he performed the ceremony personally in the Heywoods' home. A marriage sealing only took a couple of minutes and could be performed anywhere until (and even occasionally after) the Salt Lake Endowment House and temples were built. Martha may have thought that she was not getting a bad deal: she was marrying a man of some means who had standing in the community. On the night of the wedding at the house in Salt Lake, Brigham Young pronounced the ordinance as the participants stood in front of him: Mr. Heywood, Mrs. Heywood, Sister Vary (about to become second wife), and Martha (about to become third wife). Martha described the ceremony this way: "Brother Haywood stood on the floor, his [first] wife taking hold of his left arm with her right and taking first Sister Vary by the right hand and placing it in that of Bro. Haywood's right hand" and in that way, Sister Vary was sealed to him first for time and eternity with "words most sublime."

When this first "sealing" was done, Sister Vary fell back by taking Sister Heywood's arm. Martha explained, "I then went forward going through the same ceremony." Martha wrote that the ceremony was "solemn and interesting and different from anything the world knows of." Although Martha felt confused in the days leading up to the ceremony and disappointed at times after her marriage, she found the ceremony ethereal—the words transcendent.

But sadly, Martha wrote after her first week of marriage as an official member of the family that while she was calm and had anticipated some "little rubs," it was "trying to a woman's feelings not to be acknowledged by the man she [had] given herself to and desir[ed] to love with all her heart." Had Joseph and Martha not yet consummated their marriage?

Besides being frustrated in her desire to be a missionary, perhaps Martha wasn't sure that she had wanted to marry into the Heywood family at all. Soon after her quick marriage, she engaged in a conversation with a Mr. Barlow, a gentleman who had earlier given her a "valuable ring," about her "connection with Mr. Heywood." In fact, merely a week after her marriage, she met Mr. Barlow for a "prearranged" date at a literary discussion, and he "accompanied" her home. He told her he heard a rumor about her marriage "but gave it no credence. Said his intention was, the first suitable opportunity to make known," she said, "to me his wishes. His manly conduct in this matter has elicited my warmest feeling of friendship." Had he intended to propose to Martha? He told her to keep the ring "as a token of friendship which," she wrote, "I most gladly do." She also accepted Mr. Barlow's invitation to a dance that coming weekend at the Bath House, and Martha, though no longer single, went with him and "enjoyed [herself] very much."

After that, presumably they went their own ways, and Martha started her life in the Heywood family. Within a few months, Mr. Heywood asked Martha to help Sarepta more around the house. Then eight months after her January 1851 marriage, her husband moved her to the new settlement in Nephi, Utah, leaving Sarepta and Sister Vary in the family home with him in Salt Lake. Neither the Church nor polygamists had a set pattern for housing arrangements, but the way that Martha moved around was typical. Historian Jessie Embry finds that when husbands married extra wives, about half these women moved in with the first family immediately after their marriage. These new wives, however, moved out as soon as possible, and only "a small fraction of the wives continued to share homes once they started having children." Wives probably preferred their own homes because they wanted to be like monogamous wives who had their own homes and who could make independent decisions. And extra wives who had their own homes, like Martha, could help their husbands get more land in outlying settlements.

In their peculiar way, well-off polygamous families with multiple houses captured the western American dream of independence and expanding land ownership. In 1848, when Brigham Young parceled out Salt Lake City land plots, for example, he showed his bias for polygamous families by allowing "family heads" to draw a lot for each of their wives. Interestingly, "widows and divorced women who were heads of families also participated in the drawings," while unmarried men could not draw at all.

When Martha first arrived in Nephi as one of its first settlers, she was "delighted" with her building lot along the creek "beautifully adorned with

FIGURE 2.3 Martha's husband, Joseph Heywood.

FIGURE 2.4 Second wife Martha Heywood.

trees." She anticipated that her house would be built right away, but instead she lived in her wagon box until she got a room in the fort a year later. The settlers had to abandon their houses and instead clustered in a fort for protection from Indians and a federal government raid. While living in her wagon, Martha experienced "a sort of melancholy" that she could not "shake off," apparently because her husband visited infrequently and because she lacked comfort and privacy—her first baby was born in the wagon with one Church sister attending.

Still, on her first wedding anniversary, alone in Nephi with her new baby, she wrote, "I am content to have a husband to care and watch over me that I feel reverence, love and esteem [for] and connected with a family that I am proud to be a member of, and realize that I am much happier now than I was a year ago. My child is the consummation of all my earthly wishes."

In polygamy, the abundance and care that a wife might expect from marriage was not always forthcoming—and not infrequently polygamy made a family poorer instead of richer. In Ruth's case, although she loved Samuel, after her engagement, "seeing he was not very well of[f] in wor[l]dly good[s]," she told him that she "was willing to wait one year [to marry] and let him have a chance to make his family more comfortable and [she] could get some things [she] needed by that time." But "he did not agree to that," and they soon married at home on February 21, 1853, about two months after they had started corresponding.

That June, she went with Samuel to Salt Lake City: "He was going to get his sheep." She wrote, "This was my first pleasure trip with him. Uncle Milton went with us. We stayed over night with Aunt Eda Rogers. My husband took me around through the City and to where the foundation of the Temple was partly laid.... He showed me the Seventies hall and where President B Young lived. We went to Father Smith's and he gave us our Patriarchal Blessings." She finished, "This day I thought the happiest day I had ever spent with my husband."

But trouble came soon after. In November, the family was asked by Church authorities to leave Lehi and settle in southern Utah, in Parowan. Ruth wrote secretly in her diary that she thought "her troubles had begun" when she heard this news. She knew that they were "poor in this worlds goods" and could not afford to move and start over, but Samuel "considered it his duty" to go.

Again her intuition proved right. The family (Samuel, Matilda, her two children, and Ruth) left Lehi and that first night stayed with Ruth's parents in Payson. That same evening, Samuel came to talk to Ruth alone in their wagon: "My husband came and asked me if I thought father and mother would be willing to let me stay with them. He said he thought it would be better for me to stay with them if they were willing." Ruth hadn't seen this coming, and wrote, "This made me feel as if my heart was most broke, but I governed my feelings. I saw by his countenance that he was in trouble." As Samuel was standing guard during the night, she went to him and told him her parents had agreed that she could stay. Ruth's father owed her fifty-five dollars, so he paid her with a cow and a calf, which she unselfishly gave to Samuel to take with him the next morning as he left with Matilda and her children. She wrote of that morning, "My husband left me. I did not know when I should get to see him again." She had twenty-five cents left and was separated from her husband by distance, poverty, and perhaps a little discord.

Ruth's brother asked her to come to Salt Lake to help his family because his wife was gravely ill. All six weeks she was there, Ruth anxiously wondered whether her husband might come for her at her parents' house, and she might miss him. When she couldn't stand the uncertainty any longer, she left; her brother's wife died the next day. At her parents' home in Payson, she found three letters from Samuel. One reported that both the cow and calf she had given him were dead, but there was no indication of when Ruth could be reunited with her husband.

During the year that she spent in Payson with her parents away from Samuel, she worked hard and had very little social life. She attended a dinner dance with her parents one evening, but "this was the only party [she] participated in while absent from [her] husband." An afternoon at Martha Heywood's, twenty-five miles south in Nephi, would have been an unusual break from her hardworking routine. Of course, settling new land was not easy, and frontier women, even in times of abundance, worked hard sewing linens and clothing, churning butter, making cheese, raising chickens, planting vegetable gardens, preserving jams and jellies, curing meat, cooking, producing soap and candles, washing clothes, and taking on "nontraditional tasks when necessary," such as helping their husbands on the farm or ranch.

Later Ruth proudly wrote that after she had paid the expenses on her pig, she "had left in cash fifty six dollars means which I had earned while absent from my husband and one hundred weight of pork." When Samuel finally sent for her about a year later, and she joined him in Parowan 150 miles farther south, she found that she was to live in a "log house only one room," and that her husband wished that the money she earned would go to support his other family, "same as his" earnings. At some point during the next year, Ruth moved to her own place. She never had children, but she earned $225 over the next seventeen months caring for two little girls, taking in wash, helping her husband in the fields, and raising animals and a garden.

It wasn't enough to ease their woes, however. In 1856, during the continued famine, Ruth wrote that "grasshoppers destroyed all the crops," there was no grass for the cattle, and "Army worms came in one day as thick as hail" and destroyed her garden. At one point, for three weeks she had barely anything to eat. One day, lying on her bed, she had no flour in the house and no way to get any until a neighbor came to borrow something and saw that Ruth was so weak that she nearly fainted; that evening the neighbor brought "a drawing of tea and bread enough" for her and the girls she was boarding. Shortly after this low point, the girls' father at last paid her "honorably" until harvest came.

Fourteen years later, in the 1870 census, Ruth was sharing a house with Samuel's other two wives (he had also married Lorana, Ruth's younger sister) and seven children (four belonged to Matilda and three to Lorana). When the family later decided to go to Mexico like thousands of others to avoid prosecution for polygamy, Ruth decided to stay alone in St. George where a temple had been built so she could do temple work. Perhaps Samuel's decision years before to leave her behind had given her the implicit permission she needed to stay behind when it suited her.

Martha's later married life ended up as lonely as Ruth's, though her poverty was less grinding. In 1854 and 1855, Martha endured some stinging town criticism of her and her family. Mr. Heywood, who was U.S. Marshal for the Utah Territory between 1850 and 1855, was also a Nephi spiritual and civic leader, or "president of this place," as Martha called him. In 1854, he had enough townspeople upset with him that he was removed from the local position he held for three years. That was embarrassing enough for Martha, and then about the same time, Martha learned there were "considerably hard feelings" against her "as a school teacher," as well.

But Martha was emotionally and intellectually strong and had gradually learned that she would not see her husband for months at a time, anyway. She became quite independent, but could still get her feelings hurt. One time someone told her that her husband had been as close as Provo but hadn't sent her a note. She wrote, "Learned [that] Joseph came as far as Provo and did not send me one single word which hurt my feelings and taught me to think that I was not much cared for....I felt there was no possible reason but he might have sent me a few lines, not having but one letter from him during the whole winter." She tried to coach herself to hold up under the disappointment, thinking that her trials would help "perfect" her "character," and then she quoted Paul: "Afflictions for the present are grievous but afterwards they yield the peaceable fruits of righteousness to them who are excerted thereby." She went on to complain that Joseph had been "lavish" all winter and "so stringent towards" her, even though her health had been "poorly."

Martha probably worked for pay to support herself and the Heywood family throughout her marriage, and she didn't do badly. For example, her husband encouraged her to teach school in Nephi, and in 1856 he advertised Martha's hat-making specialty in the Salt Lake *Deseret News*. The ad read, "in exchange for hats...Firewood, Butter, Eggs, Pork, Lard, Wheat, Lumber, Etc." Martha not only manufactured hundreds (or thousands) of hats but taught other members of the Heywood family to do so, as well. Her husband would later list his occupation as "hatter."

She created a life of her own in Nephi, which her husband wanted her to do but also sometimes criticized. In 1856, she received a letter from him stating his displeasure because she had "gone ahead with work contrary to his instructions." He also criticized her "spirit of writing," though fortunately for us she ignored him. Together these criticisms "troubled" her "so seriously that all other trials and troubles seem[ed] but trifling." He had expected her to be on her own in a small settlement and make money for the family yet still hoped to control her.

But in December 1855 Martha could have confided that she was happy. She explained, "I love my home, I dearly love the first & only home I've had, since I first left my father's house" in about 1834. Although she thought herself an awkward housekeeper who often made blunders, she enjoyed the chances to entertain important Salt Lake guests like Brigham Young who routinely came through the settlements. She was also glad to be a mother.

Martha was conscious of having been an "old maid" for so many years and wrote in an 1855 letter to a friend, "You never was an old maid was you? Well you know nothing about what I once was, or the path I trod. I learned the value of a home, that I now appreciate so highly, [and] the value of belonging to somebody by the years experience of belonging to nobody." Martha had two beloved children, but in 1856 she would lose her little girl and mourn her over and over in her diary. The next year, 1857, was evidently the last year she wrote, or at least the last record that survived.

In 1861, Martha moved to Washington in southern Utah where her husband recovered a "good adobe" house for her that lay vacant. The house had "sturdy thick adobe walls, a solid lumber floor, and a shingle roof." Inside, Martha, who had never gotten the house she anticipated in Nephi, would have been thrilled to see the stone fireplace and two glass windows that would have been a "luxury" at the time. Here she raised her son Neal to adulthood. Mostly still living without her husband, in this southern town, Martha became a "legendary" schoolteacher who earned good wages. In 1873, she died at age sixty-one when Neal was twenty-two; Neal went on to marry into an established family and eventually became a Mormon bishop. In 1881, Sarepta and Sister Vary, who had continued to live together in the same Salt Lake house, both died. Joseph then lived for the rest of his life mostly with his fourth wife, Mary Bell, and their children, and in 1910 died at age ninety-five.

Jane Hindley, the third member of our trio, never waned in her affection for her husband, Captain John. After almost twenty years of marriage, she wrote that perhaps she loved him "too well" and deeply mourned the additional polygamous marriages that brought new wives into the family after her. Jane had eight children and spent twenty-six years in the same house with Mary, the wife who had first come to fetch her to visit sick Mr. Hindley after Jane first arrived in Utah. But living in close proximity could be bruising. Jane wrote in her diary that she and Mary spoke harsh words from time to time, and because they lived together, she could see

FIGURE 2.5A Jane's husband, John Hindley.

FIGURE 2.5B Second wife Jane Hindley.

FIGURE 2.5C First wife Mary Hindley.

Mary take the wagon to meet their husband in Salt Lake—that night she wrote, "how glad I should of been to of had that priveledge." But in 1882, when Jane got her own house, at last, on a farm that was also in American Fork and that would be better for her boys, she had mixed feelings. She wrote, "I shall feel very lonesome at first. I shall miss Auntie [Mary] so, for I have become very much attached to her. Have lived together now 26 years and seen many changes together. And we have grown Old now."

But her generally good feelings toward Mary did not take the place of her husband. Throughout Jane's diary, when Mr. Hindley was gone, she was full of longing to see him again: "My husband is all I could desire." She felt that her home was "not so Happy" when he was not there. After twenty-two years of marriage at age fifty, she still yearned to sleep with him. She alluded to this as she described a stormy September 1878 Saturday night at midnight when she returned to find "all in bed" and "had a little Heart Ache." She coached herself, "It is all right. I don't wish to murmur or Complain, will try and do My Duty well and trust in God who doeth all things well." Eight years later in 1886, her husband, Captain John Hindley, died, leaving behind four wives. In 1907, Jane died at age seventy-nine.

In the 1850s, Mormons sympathized with unmarried women who seemed in need. Although Mormon monogamists generally believed that "plural marriage demeaned women whose economic circumstances permitted them the time to wait for the right bachelor to propose," they sympathized with women "who needed breadwinners in a pioneer economy," especially with women "whose fathers were not in Utah" and with women "who no longer had husbands." Brigham Young was reportedly happy when he heard that "the handcart sisters," who had crossed the plains as single women, were finding husbands.

Martha, Jane, and Ruth arrived in Utah as older single women, and two of them, Martha and Jane, did not have male kin. Martha and Jane were offered housing, Ruth found employment right away, and all three married quickly after arriving. According to Kathryn Daynes, although older single women may have seemed desperate to marry (presumably explaining why they became polygamous wives), they actually may have had opportunities to marry monogamously: "Women entering plural marriage generally wed more quickly than those marrying monogamously, showing the inadequacy of the idea that plural wives were women 'left over' after most other women had married." Both Jane and Ruth seemed attracted to the men they married, while Martha seemed attracted to her husband's community status. But after marriage, neither Martha nor Ruth could count on their husbands to be breadwinners. Martha and Ruth not only supported themselves most of their married lives but sometimes also supported their husbands' other families. In 1860, Martha and Ruth were among the 15 percent of all American women, usually those of poorer classes, who "worked for wages," which allowed Martha and Ruth to trade goods and services.

In the end, Martha was grateful to have a son and a daughter, Jane truly loved her husband Captain Hindley, and Ruth referred to her husband as a "true friend." They were practical women who never mentioned having a special spiritual belief in "celestial marriage." The seemingly sensible situations of "needy" women such as these—good women who were perceived as having "a right to demand a man in marriage"—went a long way in prompting the Mormon people to justify polygamy.

3

Interlude: Justifying Polygamy

THE BIGGER WORLD in which women like Martha Heywood, Ruth Rogers, and Jane Hindley lived was, as already suggested, a rough and tumble place in its early years—but at the same time, under Brigham Young's leadership, the Mormons were steadily crafting a surprisingly industrious and organized infrastructure. At the visual forefront was the Salt Lake Temple block, where, for church and civic meetings, the first pioneers gathered outdoors in the "bowery," an open-sided shelter. In 1851, the bowery was "replaced by a plain large adobe building called the Tabernacle." In the Tabernacle, Brigham Young presided over regular conferences to guide his people, and it was here on August 29, 1852, that Church leaders first publicly preached polygamy as a religious practice. Polygamy was, indeed, a religious practice at its base, and a way to grow their population, but, in retrospect, polygamy also allowed the Mormons to distinguish themselves and overcome social challenges.

During the August 1852 men-only conference session, Apostle Orson Pratt, with President Brigham Young sitting nearby, gave a theological treatise on what Pratt called the "great, sublime, beautiful, and glorious doctrine" of polygamy. In the 1840s, Orson Pratt had had run-ins with Joseph Smith over polygamy and had been temporarily cut off from the Church because of it. Pratt seemed to have returned with the zeal of a convert who, seeing the error of his ways, was ready to convert others. By 1852, he had time to think about the arguments for polygamy and had distilled them to three: first, Mormon men should follow the example of Abraham and build their own "mighty kingdom[s]"; second, since throughout time men had continually engaged in the sin of adultery, polygamy could be a worldwide antidote for this problem; and third, since the Church was growing, polygamous marriage was a way to welcome more quickly all the children waiting in the heavens to be born. Pratt ended by warning that those who rejected polygamy would "be damned" and "lose their exalted privilege forever."

Following Pratt's speech, Brigham Young gave a shorter talk and shared his belief that polygamy was a doctrine much of the world could embrace: he said it would "ride triumphantly" and be "fostered and believed in by the more intelligent portions of the world." Young's sermons, according to biographer John G. Turner, were typically "filled with fire and dreams and theological speculation." Young was, according to another biographer, Ronald W. Walker, "creative and innovative" and "unshackled by tradition, which he hated." Young hoped that Mormonism would "transform society" and seemed unafraid to announce new ideas. For example, two weeks after the conference speeches, Orson Pratt, perhaps rather naively, traveled to the East Coast to distribute the journal *The Seer* that explained "the views of the Saints in regard to the *ancient Patriarchal Order of Matrimony, or Plurality of Wives.*" Early on, Pratt and Young seemed to believe that outsiders would also see the value of polygamy, but, in reality, many average Mormons would not embrace it. When the "Revelation" was read to Saints in London that December, "the man who read it commented that 'No doubt many would be offended and deny the Faith.'" The reader along with "many" others left the Church.

In 1852 Utah, most Saints already knew that polygamy was quietly being practiced by some Church members, even though the practice had never been publically announced. After the announcement, some were disillusioned and left the Church, while some who stayed believed the announcement was "unwise." It's hard to know how seriously ordinary Mormon settlers took their leaders' advice to consider polygamous marriage. According to Carmon Hardy, "we clearly need a better understanding of the dynamics at work between the broad membership of the church and their leaders." At various times, Joseph Smith, Brigham Young, and Orson Pratt all worried that polygamy approached adultery; to become converted to the doctrine themselves, they and other leaders had to learn to see and feel the difference between the two. Because Mormon people naturally felt an aversion to polygamy, their leaders' speeches had to sound especially assuring and promising. Historian Kathryn Daynes notes, "pronouncements from the pulpit made it clear that entering plural marriage could bring a higher eternal reward," but "the principle was clearly not a popular doctrine," and "church leaders had to give the practice their strongest endorsement for it to expand beyond a small group."

As mentioned earlier, Mormon participation in polygamous marriage averaged between 25 and 30 percent if men, women, and children in polygamous families are counted. Those who became polygamists usually believed that "it was essential to their salvation," that it could "bring a higher eternal reward," that "God required it of them," and that it would provide "marriage and motherhood to thousands of women who may have otherwise remained unmarried." Church leaders continued to stress that polygamy "countered various social evils" and was a principle "commanded by God to raise a righteous generation." In 1855, Brigham Young said that the practice was not "to please man in his carnal desires, nor to punish females for anything which they had done" but was to raise a "royal Priesthood, a peculiar people."

Young's focus on building a righteous people encapsulated Pratt's main arguments that polygamy would help the people build kingdoms and bring children to earth. Pratt focused on Abraham, a connection he undoubtedly took from Joseph Smith. Abraham and Sarah's story has both expedient and expansive qualities to it—in their story, polygamy is used as a solution to an immediate problem, and yet, over time, polygamy helped fulfill God's promise that Abraham would be "exceeding fruitful" and "make nations." According to Genesis, since Sarah was old and had had no children, it was she who suggested that Abraham should "go in unto [her] maid," Hagar, saying, "it may be that I may obtain children by her." When Hagar became pregnant, Sarah complained that Hagar became overbearing and proud, so Abraham told Sarah, "Behold, thy maid is in thy hand; do to her as it pleaseth thee." When "Sarah dealt hardly with her," pregnant Hagar "fled from [Sarah's] face" and departed into the desert.

After facing certain death, Hagar was humbled and returned to Abraham and Sarah and bore her son Ishmael. Subsequently Sarah miraculously bore Isaac. As the two boys grew, Sarah was agitated when Hagar's son Ishmael mocked her son Isaac, and Sarah asked Abraham to cast out this "bondwoman and her son: for the son of this bondwoman shall not be heir with my son, even with Isaac." According to the Bible, "this thing was very grievous in Abraham's sight because of his son."

Abraham tenderly prepared Hagar and his son Ishmael for their journey: "And Abraham rose up early in the morning, and took bread, and a bottle of water, and gave it unto Hagar, putting it on her shoulder, and the child, and sent her away" in the desert where she and her son almost perished. But "God heard the voice of the lad" and "the angel of God called to Hagar out of heaven," and she was helped, for "God opened her eyes, and she saw a well of water," and they were saved. The story finishes as the angel told Hagar, "Arise, lift up the lad, and hold him in thine hand; for I will make him a great nation." According to tradition, from Abraham's wives came the Jewish and Arab nations, fulfilling God's word that Abraham would be the father of nations.

The Mormons also needed to multiply. However, faithful polygamous wife Annie Tanner eventually questioned whether the Old Testament practice of polygamy justified its nineteenth-century practice. As an older woman, she reasoned that the ancient Israelites were "wandering Nomads of the desert" who lived at a "low cultural and spiritual level." She wrote, "Abraham was making history for Israel by his revolt against human sacrifice. From these low beginnings we find a long evolutionary story lasting through centuries as these desert wanderers settled down in Palestine to achieve gradually higher levels of culture." Tanner concluded that polygamy in the Bible was a practice of "the very earliest period in Hebrew history," and "in the New Testament it is not even mentioned."

The closest the New Testament gets to mentioning polygamy is Paul's advice to Timothy that monogamy was preferred to polygamy. When Paul was organizing Christian branches of the church after Jesus's death, Paul wrote to Timothy that bishops, deacons, and other holy men should "be blameless, *the husband of one wife*, vigilant, sober, of good behavior, given to hospitality," and have numerous other admirable qualities. Besides Paul's stipulation that bishops live monogamously, Paul discussed with Timothy the care of widows, never suggesting that men should marry widows as additional wives to care for them.

Even the *Book of Mormon*, the Mormons' special book of scripture, teaches that on rare occasion God might allow polygamy, but the Book more emphatically states that God doesn't approve of polygamy because it hurts women. According to the *Book of Mormon*, a group of people left Jerusalem in 600 B.C. and crossed water to a new land to create a new culture for themselves. Over the decades, their men started reverting to the old tradition of adding wives and concubines, but their prophet Jacob chided them for this, saying that God had led their fathers away from Jerusalem and did not want them to "do like unto them of old." He went on, "there shall not any man among you have save it be one wife; and concubines he shall have none." This was to be their law but with a caveat: "For if I will, saith the Lord of Hosts, raise up seed unto me, I will command my people." According to the *Book of Mormon*, the rare and sole purpose for polygamy could possibly be to multiply a righteous people.

Bearing, nurturing, and guiding numerous devout children was essential to Mormon survival. Demographic studies of Mormon polygamy suggest that Mormon participation in polygamy was "on the high end of what is mathematically plausible." As for births, although sociological studies of polygamous cultures mostly find that polygamous wives "fall behind monogamous wives in the number of children they have," in Mormon polygamy "polygamous wives displayed a fertility pattern fully on a par with and in some instances greater than that of their monogamous neighbors."

But Mormon polygamy was more than populating—more precisely, it was shaping a population into a new religious culture. The presence of polygamy verified the Mormons' unusual purpose—they were building the kingdom of God on earth. They were incubating a race, a culture, a church—like Abraham's family when it departed from populated areas to create a culture on vast expanses of land. Brigham Young told his people, "I want hard times, so that every person that does not wish to stay, for the sake of his religion, will leave." Referring to the physical challenges of the mountainous West and the strict commandments God required, Young said, "This is a good place to make Saints."

For Mormons in the sparsely populated West, the isolation and sense of space fomented their self-concept, and polygamy helped enhance their "unique aura of radical peculiarity" vis-à-vis other Americans and other Christians. Mormons united around "the common cause of self-determination." The noted sociologist Thomas F. O'Dea asserts that Mormons are the most "clear" example in the United States of a "native and indigenously developed ethnic minority." The practice of polygamy helped Mormons carve out a unique identity that made them seem insular and, even today, long after its abandonment, sometimes keeps them from being considered fully Christian.

Besides helping create a distinct culture, polygamy allowed a literal shaping of Mormon offspring—genetic control, even if unintentional. Young may have expected all or most Mormons to become polygamists, but, in reality, most polygamous husbands were Church leaders because they were the most willing to demonstrate their faithfulness. Perhaps not surprisingly, "very committed Mormons were much more likely to practice [polygamy] than were others." Louis J. Kern suggests that because "church approval was required before entering upon celestial marriage, selective breeding was largely in the hands of the Mormon hierarchy" who encouraged or even pressured Church leaders—from local bishops on up—to participate in polygamy. Polygamy inadvertently became "a eugenic device" that was meant to weed out the "unregenerate" and gave birth to elite Mormon children—"a healthy, virile, and robust population." The homes of Church leaders and their wives provided expanses of fertile soil to nurture their children's commitment to Mormonism as their children witnessed their parents' faith and sacrifice.

Polygamy also extended the Mormons' connection to Joseph Smith. Although once the Mormons moved West and were physically removed from Joseph Smith's sacred places (the grove where he saw a vision; the Carthage Jail where he was martyred), their embrace of polygamy reinforced their miraculous origins and sustained their connection to his "charismatic legacy." To Mormons, the "stigma" of polygamy was "nothing less than divine," as the practice became synonymous with "celestial marriage" and "eternal progression."

They developed their own form of rugged individualism as they defended their right, as they saw it, to practice their religion. Once leaders started publicly promoting polygamy, not surprisingly, they incensed outsiders, which led Mormons to increase their defensive rhetoric. Their defense of polygamy in response to outside criticism may have done more to shape their self-identity than actually living the lifestyle did. According to Omri Elisha's interpretation, even though relatively few Mormons practiced polygamy, the "daily social, political, and ritual activities involved in defending plural marriage against outside interference were in many ways of greater consequence than the practice itself." Polygamy helped Mormons develop a "group loyalty."

Polygamy also had some practical benefits. Nineteenth-century Church leaders under pressure to "care for their flocks" saw social and economic advantages to polygamy. Even before Mormons moved west, Church leaders felt that the practice of polygamy could help the Church "fulfill its responsibility to the widows, the divorced, and the fatherless and could more equitably distribute wealth." During the 1850s, there were probably slightly more Mormon women than men, thanks in part to single women converts coming from New England and Great Britain. Polygamous marriages rose with the ebb and flow of immigrants into Utah. Statistically, women without male protectors were more inclined to contract polygamous marriages: almost 52 percent of polygamous wives in the Manti area had no living father in Utah when they married and perhaps came to the marriage market in a weaker position either socially or financially. In Manti, "two-thirds of all the plural marriages" included a wife who was "widowed, divorced, or fatherless."

During the outpouring of zeal from the Mormon Reformation of 1856 and 1857, polygamous marriages increased, as well. The pioneers were suffering from famine, and in an effort to help their hungry people and renew members' dedication to the Church, Church leaders not only made practical suggestions about fences and flour rations but also gave fiery speeches and visited each home with a list of questions about the occupants' spiritual state. Historian Leonard J. Arrington explains that "members were called upon to repent and rededicate themselves fully to the work of the Lord and to seal this rededication with rebaptism." Arrington surmises that during this time "Church authorities may have encouraged a number of the more well-to-do members to add plural wives to their households," both to alleviate the effects of the famine and to show their devotion to the Church. During this Reformation, polygamous marriages were contracted at a rate "sixty-five percent higher...than in any other two-year period in Utah history."

Although polygamy had some practical benefits, it caused problems, as has already been seen. It offered new choices for women, but it also required sacrifice because polygamous marriage privileges men. Some polygamous husbands became zealots operating under the perfect storm: living in a patriarchal culture, believing they were doing God's will, continually forming arguments to defend their lifestyle, and relatively isolated from the outside world. Overly sure of themselves, some men may have taken advantage of the system, marrying teenage girls, for example. Some polygamous husbands deserved the same chiding the *Book of Mormon*'s polygamous husbands received for breaking their wives' hearts: the Lord God has "seen the sorrow, and heard the mourning of the daughters" of his people "because of the wickedness and abominations of their husbands." On the other hand, well-intentioned polygamous husbands were in some ways victims themselves, learning to balance righteousness and sin; abundance and drought; obedience and willfulness; passion and awkwardness; convenience and inconvenience.

Although polygamy excised an enormous human toll, in retrospect, polygamy also solidified the Mormons' grip on the land, increased their devotion to their religion, and distinguished them from outsiders, which all together helped ensure their survival and ultimate prosperity.

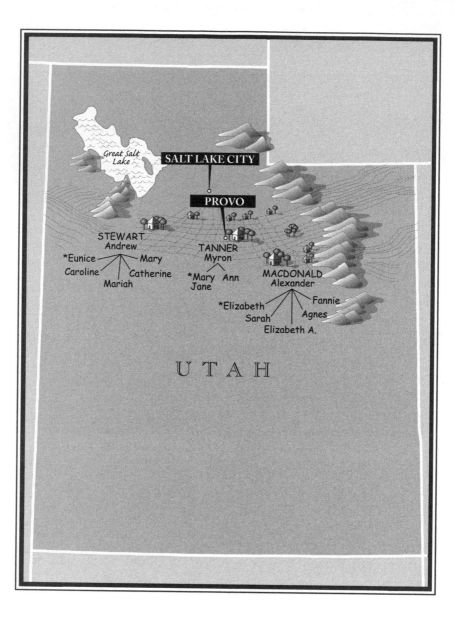

4

It is a heart history

Mary Jane Tanner's House: Provo, Utah, about 1868

Mary Jane, whose story began this book, wrote enough that she had plenty to share. In her hometown of Provo, she would have almost certainly been interested in what *Elizabeth MacDonald* and *Eunice Stewart* had to say about polygamy, too. Mary Jane, Elizabeth, and Eunice were all first wives living in Provo whose lives probably actually crossed: two of them had husbands serving on the Provo City Commission; two of them lived in Payson at the same time before moving to Provo; and all three of them had farmland on the edge of Provo. Together their stories illustrate that first wives considered polygamy a religious burden that was best borne, in their view, by taking charge. Their superior tone and flippant references to their husbands' additional wives betray an underlying assumption that, as first wives, they were their husbands' real wives.

Mary Jane's homestead at 500 North and 500 West in Provo was a "short walk" from the "principle business part" of town. She and her husband Myron had a beautiful property that had an inspiring view of Mt. Timpanogos. The property included a "nice pasture opening out of the corral with a stream of water running through it," a "grove of cottonwood trees in the pasture just a few rods from the house," and a gristmill. The two houses on the property were "shaded with wild rose bushes" and adjoined an orchard. Mary Jane's new two-story brick house included "one square room, three bedrooms, a clothespress and buttry with a porch and low chamber." Her house nearly butted against her old house, where second wife Ann Crosby and her mother had moved last year—but they would be moving soon, thank goodness.

Elizabeth lived near the central part of Provo, too. She was the first of five wives who "lived mostly together, forming one family household," although at that time, she explained, she had only one other wife living with her. The others sometimes went to the farm. Elizabeth believed in keeping busy and

FIGURE 4.2 First wife Elizabeth Graham MacDonald.

FIGURE 4.3 Elizabeth's husband, Alexander Finlay MacDonald.

FIGURE 4.4 Third wife Agnes MacDonald.

FIGURE 4.5 Fourth wife Elizabeth A. MacDonald.

FIGURE 4.6 Fifth wife Fannie MacDonald.

keeping others busy. She explained that she "always had a faculty of creating plenty of work" for herself and had "earned quite a reputation for keeping busy others who happened to be near," so that she and the other wives had "no spare time to interfere with [their] neighbor's business."

Mary Jane would have said "amen" to that, for she had quite enough interference from second wife Ann and her mother. Mary Jane explained that the first six years in Provo before Myron got Ann Crosby as a second wife in 1866 were, despite her longing for their three dead children, "very happy." Maybe Mary Jane saw God's hand in giving and taking away—"the seasons came and went," she wrote, and "we gathered the fruit from our orchard, which we prized highly." Mary Jane also seemed to constantly have overnight guests or people who needed a meal. Her husband had many enterprises, but lately he had been helping establish the Provo Woolen Mills that would become one of the financial foundations of the city.

In 1864, Myron was called as bishop of the Third Ward of Provo City, and this calling probably contributed to his decision in 1866 to marry Ann, since Church leaders expected bishops to show the way. Although Mary Jane's relationship with Ann turned sour, their first year went well. Both women gave birth to baby girls, and Mary Jane explained, "I think we never felt happier or enjoyed ourselves better together than then. We attended each other's babies and got along very comfortably."

But when Ann's mother arrived from England, the wives' relationship deteriorated, and Mary Jane wrote that Myron bought a home "for Ann near the meeting house and central business part of town, about a mile" from her house, and Ann would be moving there. Mary Jane would be glad to have her "premises clear and free from annoyance." Like Elizabeth, she would add, she was always striving to do her duty "before God" and her "fellow man," but the situation had become unbearable for her.

Mary Jane and Elizabeth would have certainly sympathized with the story of Eunice Stewart, too, although they would have been sensitive to the illness that probably often kept her from going out much. At age forty-two, Eunice was about to die, probably of the stomach trouble that had made her so sick ten years earlier in 1857 and 1858 when she stopped keeping her diary. At the time, she hinted at the trouble when she wrote, "I was taken very Sick with a head ache and pain in my stomache. I was not able to work for six weeks." A few months later, she wrote that she ate "a piece of turnip" and it gave her "the cramp" in her stomach and she was "like to die for near three week(s)." During this time, her sister came and took care of her family and, Eunice wrote, "watched with me half of nearly every night.

FIGURE 4.7 First wife Eunice Stewart.

FIGURE 4.8 Eunice's husband, Andrew Jackson Stewart.

Before Eunice got sick, she was a powerful woman characterized by business savvy. She may have had the first store in Provo. Her diary primarily recorded sales, purchases, and bargains she made with Provo and Payson men. Between 1855 and 1858, while her husband was away on missions, wheat flour was scarce, and she was constantly hustling trades to get "flower."

In 1844 at age eighteen, Eunice had married her husband Andrew Jackson Stewart in Ohio, and within a couple of years they joined the Mormon Church; in 1846, Brigham Young witnessed their Mormon marriage sealing. In 1850, Eunice, her husband, and their two living children came to Salt Lake, and Brigham Young asked them, along with two other families, to settle Payson. The Stewarts eventually had homes in Payson, Provo, and Benjamin—all within about fifteen miles of each other.

In 1851, her husband entered polygamy by marrying Caroline, who was eleven years older than he. In 1852, he married Mariah, who was four years older. In the late 1850s while their husband was away on missions, Eunice wrote of sometimes sharing meat and flour with Mariah: "I gave Mariah S. the seventy six lbs of flower that was due of Br Porter."

A couple of days later, she went to see Mariah about using their resources prudently: "I went to see her and told her that I wanted her to make her sons [who must have been from an earlier marriage] take care of our grain and save all that we could. That we must not go in debt and make trouble for Mr Stewart." Unfortunately, when Mr. Stewart returned home, he was in $1,000 debt anyway but soon sold "goods at auction" and "then began to sell land, cattle, and horses and in less than 3 weeks he redeemed his note without one forced sale."

A month after talking to Mariah about being prudent, Eunice wrote that "Mariah sent and got some flower off me this evening 10 lbs"—perhaps not very prudent. The next year, Eunice wrote that she gave Mariah "1 of the cows I Bought. They did not like her and did not thank me for my trouble." A couple of times when Eunice sent word to Mariah to send one of the boys to come work, Mariah didn't do it: "I sent word to Mariah S. to send Rufus S. to help but she would not let him come as I expected. She don't seem willing to help much nor let her children." Eunice saw herself as an overseer and boss of Mariah. She put down Mariah when she wrote that the cows didn't like her and that Mariah wouldn't share. On the other hand, Eunice reported on her own hard work and helpfulness: she wrote, "I went to Mariah's and helped her pick wool."

In 1855, before her husband's mission, at age thirty Eunice had borne her last child. In 1862, perhaps while suffering from the illness that would kill her, Eunice's forty-two-year-old husband married fifteen-year-old Catherine Holden, with whom he had two children. In 1863, her then forty-four-year-old husband married seventeen-year-old Mary Weir, who had her second baby just before Eunice died. There weren't rules against marrying teenage girls, and, in fact, men may have been convinced that the young women and their parents preferred men with solid reputations in the Church and community. Sometimes the parents even encouraged it. It's hard to know what Eunice thought about her husband's new marriages to teenage girls. She had stopped writing in her diary by then, so we don't know if she felt happy that her husband would go on without her or resentful that at almost fifty he was married to two very young women. Mr. Stewart would live to be ninety-two.

On the other hand, Elizabeth made clear what she thought about men in polygamy: she believed, as the *Book of Mormon* taught, that in polygamy men had the most capacity to harm. Elizabeth believed that "to a very great extent" it was "in the man's hands to make his family happy or unhappy." She went on to say that in cases she witnessed when polygamy failed, she had "almost invariably concluded that the failure was in the men," sometimes because they were "as much governed by passion as by principle." With her husband, whom she had always admired and who was "a husband amongst a thousand," she had better luck. Back in 1847 in Scotland when she was sixteen, her husband-to-be Alexander had baptized her and a few years later married her, and soon he was the primary subject of her diary. He was "firm and decisive, he was withal, kind and had a great deal of forbearance," she wrote, and governed himself well in polygamy.

In 1854, they sailed from Liverpool, and after arriving in Utah, her husband Alexander took charge of the tithing office in Provo. In 1857, while living near Provo with three children, Alexander was unjustly arrested and imprisoned by a federal army for "murder, arson, treason and other grave offences." President Buchanan had sent troops "to put down the 'Mormon insurrection' in 1858." Not long afterward, Governor Cumming "made peace" with the Mormons, but her husband Alexander had been caught in the crossfire. Elizabeth explained, "In these trying times, I went twice to Provo [from Springville five miles away] to see my husband [in jail], but was not permitted to see him. I cannot describe the painful feelings I had under these trying circumstances. The last morning I went to Provo, even my little children said, 'Ma, put the gun and pistol in the wagon and we will bring Pa home.'"

When the little family was again denied access to him, Elizabeth said, "My feelings were so over powered that I could not talk to the children." Before the prisoners were transported out of Provo, she was told to try to see her husband at the Provo Seminary building. At last, they were able to embrace each other, and even the guards were softened by the little family's reunion. Her husband's arrest had taken her completely by surprise. He had been asked to "appear as a witness in the District Court" one day, and she had fully expected his "return for supper in the evening." She put her children to bed and kept his supper ready until long after dark, listening for his footsteps. Late at night, her bishop came to tell her that her husband had been jailed. Then Elizabeth concluded, "But I will cease to dwell on this part of heart history."

The MacDonald family later moved to St. George where Elizabeth would remain when in 1879 Alexander moved to Arizona, and then in 1885 to Mexico with his additional wives to avoid prosecution for polygamy. In Elizabeth's autobiography, she chose to emphasize the years that she spent living with her husband rather than the years they spent apart. Her contention that all the wives "lived mostly together" was premature, and she didn't write that in 1903 her husband died without her in Mexico while living with another wife, Lizzie. In 1917, Elizabeth died in St. George and was buried in Provo, perhaps to be buried near the children who preceded her in death.

Meaningful experiences like Elizabeth's husband's arrest and the hours she stayed up waiting for him to return, and the sorrow that Mary Jane and Myron endured together after their children's deaths, or the letters Eunice sent her missionary husband about how she would find enough flour for the family, could not, they thought, be replaced by a new, inexperienced wife. In fact, the presence of someone else would only interfere with and complicate their emotions. First wives must have had an inkling that it seemed strange for a new wife to arrive and assume that she could take what was not hers to take, for she had not helped earn it or build it.

But Mary Jane would have taken exception to Elizabeth's belief that when polygamy went wrong it was usually the man's fault. Elizabeth had said, "While a woman may wander in her weakness and temporarily fail in her part, she affects little else than herself; but with the man who assumes the position of husband and father in the midst of families, what limit can be put to the sorrow and loss affecting those depending upon him when he takes a wrong course."

Mary Jane would have pointed out that she couldn't blame her husband Myron for their own failure in polygamy. She felt badly for Myron because Ann had started drinking and, in spite of all he tried to do, Ann continued to slip. Over time, Myron felt he had to remove the children from that environment, and Mary Jane gradually took Ann's children into her house to raise them as her own.

Although Eunice didn't say one way or another, Mary Jane and Elizabeth both had mixed feelings about polygamy, writing that they believed it for their religion's sake but found it personally challenging. They sometimes undermined their own words in support of it, illustrating how confusing it could be to both want and not want to live in polygamy—and to be living it. Elizabeth felt that polygamy had made her a "far better woman" than she otherwise would have been. Even so, Elizabeth wrote, "I do not wish to have it understood that I have had no trials" in polygamy—"I have had many; and now, am by no means sorry that I had them." Because Elizabeth wrote an autobiography, she had the luxury of reflecting back with distance and perspective. She concluded that she was "thankful" that she had not been "overpowered" by her trials.

Of course, polygamous families attempted to adjust their goals and purposes in order to widen their family circle, but first wives sensed that they had worked for their senior status, and, even as they tried to adjust, and even if years later they reflected back and wrote autobiographies, sometimes they couldn't help their superior writing tone. Overall, private writings show that polygamous wives could not thoroughly or comfortably incorporate polygamy into their lives. Polygamous wives were caught in a major cultural reversal—the attempt to switch from monogamy to polygamy. According to Stephanie Coontz, "Typically, individuals adopt only a few new behaviors at any one time, and old habits hang on long after most people have agreed they should be dropped." Coontz believes that changing the culture of marriage is difficult: "If you've ever tried to alter your own marital patterns you know that change doesn't happen overnight. In history, as in personal life, there are very few moments or events that mark a complete turning point. It takes a long time for ideas to filter through different social groups."

In the end, nineteenth-century Mormon polygamous marriages were polygamous, yet still monogamous in attitude and expectation.

PART TWO

Making Sense of Sisterhood: Relations between Wives

Place me like a seal over your heart, like a seal on your arm;
for love is as strong as death, its jealousy unyielding as a grave.
It burns like blazing fire, like a mighty flame.
Song of Solomon 8:6

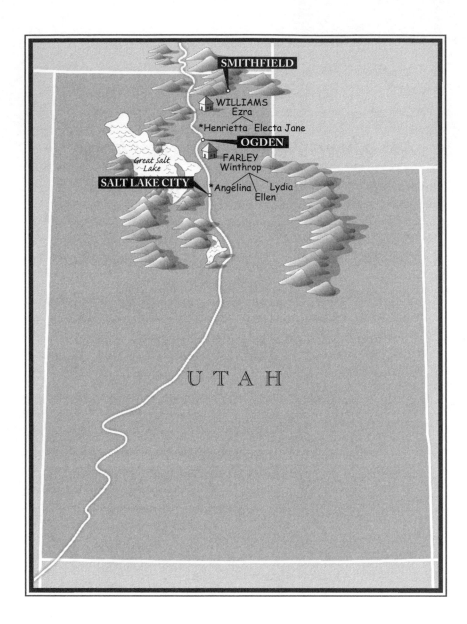

5

The drudge and tail of such women

Angelina Farley's Farm: Ogden, Utah, about 1860

By 1860, *Angelina Farley*, a farmer's wife, and *Henrietta Williams*, a doctor's wife, had plenty of opportunities to cross paths. Both had been born in the Northeast—Angelina in 1830 in New York and Henrietta in 1827 in Boston; both came west to Utah as young first wives by the early 1850s; both lived for a time in Salt Lake; and both eventually left for northern settlements—Angelina forty-five miles north to Ogden, and Henrietta twice that far north to Smithfield, from where she likely would have traveled with her family through Ogden in 1860. And if the two ever had the chance to meet one afternoon to share their writing, then they would have both had this in common, too: their desire to maintain their self-respect and sanity amidst their husbands' decision to marry additional wives. Henrietta maintained her dignity by barely mentioning her husband's other wives in her writing, while fiery Angelina wrote plenty of colorful tales to justify her anguish.

In 1860, Henrietta could have found thirty-year-old Angelina Farley and her large family living in Ogden, probably along a river, in a depressing shack. Although Henrietta, age thirty-three, was a doctor's wife, she was a sympathetic soul who once complained about "the aristocratic element" among her neighbors who didn't "concern themselves about the sick," so she would have gladly listened to Angelina's complaints. Angelina's children were "in dirt and rags," and she wrote, "I am heartsick to look about the room in which I spend my days." On a particularly depressing day, Angelina even wrote that she was "heartily tired and sick of the filthy wearisome life" she lived and could not "avoid."

In 1850, the family had some farmland, and her husband Winthrop had established the Winthrop Farley Shop in Ogden, located on the northeast corner of Twenty-Forth Street and Adams Avenue, where he shoed horses; made wagons, carriages, and tools; and specialized in making zinc-and-tin washboards and threshing machines. In the 1850s and 1860s, Ogden was a "rural agricultural area with small settlements" along two major rivers, but the community remained small until a dam was later built to bring water inland. In the 1860 census, Winthrop Farley listed his real estate value at $1,800 and his personal estate value at $400, a respectable amount that seems to contradict the impression Angelina gives that they were impoverished.

Both the 1860 Ogden census taker and Henrietta would have found Angelina, her husband Winthrop, his third wife Lydia, and seven children (age six and younger) all living in what Angelina felt was a shack. Four of the children were Angelina's, one was Lydia's, and two belonged to Winthrop's second wife, Ellen, who had divorced him and left the previous year.

First wife Angelina had been born in New York, and her husband Winthrop had been born in Illinois, both around 1830. They were both baptized Mormons about 1849 and married the next year in Iowa, where they likely lived with other Saints. In their early marriage, they seemed happily typical. Angelina wrote one evening in her diary of her husband's physical work and her domestic contribution: "Husband hung a door for Mr Watts, chopped wood for me, got hay and straw for his oxen to go to mill, carried David Lewis a pound of butter. I finished his vest and baked bread and pies for him to take along." In 1851, just about the time Angelina got pregnant with her first baby, she wrote almost romantically in her diary, "Went with husband down into the thicket. He (or we) found the tongue and forewheels of a wagon complete, in the river. Heard a lark. Wild geese flying." The day after the baby was born, she wrote, "Husband home all day. Waited on me very pleasant." In 1852, they left the Midwest for Salt Lake City and then went north to Ogden.

In 1853, Winthrop married second wife Ellen, who was five years older than he was. Ellen became pregnant with her second baby in early 1857. By the next January, Ellen had asked for "a bill of divorce," and by 1859, Ellen had divorced Winthrop and married another man, leaving her two small children for Angelina to care for. It couldn't have been easy, and Angelina alluded to run-ins she had had with Ellen. But those were small compared to what she endured with Lydia.

Winthrop was twenty-six years old with two wives and six children when he married eighteen-year-old Lydia in March 1857. Angelina wrote that Winthrop took Lydia to Salt Lake to marry her and that afterward they were "arranging house." Over the next two months, Angelina would complain that Winthrop slept with Lydia every night and that she felt neglected. After three months, Angelina wrote that she was confused about "the real cause" of his neglect and that "the coldness" that existed between her and her husband would "kill" her. She wrote, "O if I knew just what he [scribbled out] desired me to cherish in my heart toward him I would know what course to pursue." Angelina was hurt even more when Winthrop did something that "caused much distress" among them—but she didn't say what it was.

Angelina would have admitted that when Mr. Farley seemed to care more for Lydia, she couldn't hold her tongue. Angelina sometimes even felt that "an evil spirit" was "working on" her, or that she was in a bad mood, as we would say today. She wrote that in July 1857, she and Mr. Farley "had some talk." He told her that he was "much hurt with the spirit" she'd had lately. Angelina knew she was weak and sometimes spoke too quickly. She wished she could ignore the irritations that led her "tongue astray," or that she could, like a horse, "put a bit upon" herself. The day after their talk, she wrote that Mr. Farley was hoeing in the garden, that she and Lydia washed, and that a "good feeling" was "again restored in measure."

However, a couple of weeks later, at the end of July 1857, four months after Lydia came into the family, Angelina saw or heard some lovemaking between her husband and Lydia, and this upset her again. In her diary, she wrote, "I had my feelings woefully wrought up by [what they supposed was] a private act of himself and Lydia which made me act and speak very unbecoming. He is hurt again." Once again, two days later Angelina regretted her actions: "When I consider how I must have appeared and how odious my conduct must have looked, he not knowing the cause, I feel much ashamed." Then a few days later, she wrote, "Mr. Farley and I getting more pleasant again. God grant me grace to continue so forever."

Angelina, Winthrop, and Lydia were an example of an average country family trying to live polygamy together in the same house. Winthrop was not a Church leader, and the family didn't seem to have the strong sense of polygamous "kingdom building" that Orson Pratt had envisioned. Angelina just felt that polygamy didn't work in her day-to-day life. One Sunday Angelina wrote that she went to meeting, but that Mr. Farley and Lydia were "out again," suggesting that she may have attended church without them and that they went somewhere together. Angelina felt that it was "well known" that Winthrop was "always with [Lydia] night and day, at home and abroad" and never with her.

Angelina learned, probably from neighbors, that Mr. Farley's inequitable treatment of his two wives had not gone unnoticed by his "superiors," probably his ecclesiastical leaders: "the difference [Mr. Farley] makes in his treatment of Lydia and myself has an influence on the minds of his superiors detrimental to himself." Angelina didn't blame Winthrop for this; rather she believed it was, like Eve's transgression, "the influence that Lydia [held] over him that cause[d] the Bishop to treat him with so much indifference," and "it sinks him in the estimation of those with whom he ought to stand high." While polygamy was touted as a high spiritual law, Mr. Farley's manner of living polygamy was troublesome enough that it ironically "sunk" him.

Angelina thought it looked bad that a polygamous husband would allow himself to be ruled over by one of his wives. According to Angelina's telling, the bishop and the community had seen that Winthrop had "given up entirely to [Lydia] as far as they can judge" and that she carried "the rule in the family mostly over him, as well as me as far as it is possible for a woman to rule."

Perhaps the bishop of the North Canyon Ward, who would have felt free to counsel struggling families, suggested that the Farleys add more religious feeling to their marriage by receiving religious rites and endowments together. After all, Winthrop already had one wife leave him. About six months after Winthrop married Lydia, the threesome went together to receive their "endowments" at the Endowment House in Salt Lake. Because receiving endowments was a holy ceremony for the devout, the three probably would have had sufficiently tolerant feelings among them at that point.

Their good feelings prompted Winthrop and Angelina to sleep together again, and Angelina became pregnant with her last baby. After this, however, their sexual relations probably halted and their "social communication" waned. Angelina wrote that she and Mr. Farley were living "more like strangers" than like man and wife. Clearly Lydia was Mr. Farley's "favorite" wife and took "quite too much upon herself" in "wife's privileges." Angelina "some times [wished] and [prayed] for some quiet lone retreat" with her children where she could "have the privilege of training them right." She sounded like she might leave like Ellen had—but where would she go? And why would she leave the home that she had helped establish? She could only write that her life was "a cold and dreary waste" and that even her "little ones" could not "warm [her] into life."

Perhaps Mr. Farley tried to improve the situation because within a few months of this comment, the family "[broke] up" the house and "[removed]

south" to Salt Lake where Angelina gave birth to her last child at the end
of May. At the end of the year, she explained that she had made it through
the birth in "pretty good spirits being upheld by the strengthening power
of the Almighty," and that she was "plodding" on her way "with six little
children to take the entire care of including two of Ellen's which have been
with me the last year."

Both Angelina's and Lydia's lives must have been largely occupied with
pregnancy, giving birth, and caring for children in the same house—yet it
doesn't seem they helped each other. Angelina once complained that Lydia
slapped one of Ellen's children. Lydia, in her twenties, was constantly pregnant: a year after marriage, she had her first baby in February, another the
following February, another the following January, another the following
February, another the following March, another the following September,
another the following November—seven babies in seven years. Within
twenty years, she would have carried twelve children, and, unfortunately,
almost half died before she did in 1916, at age fifty-seven. But neither
Lydia's pregnancies, nor her children, nor their deaths, found sympathetic
words in Angelina's diary. The day that Lydia's third baby was born in
January 1860, they must have had a run-in. Angelina wrote, "Well am I all
in the blame and no one else wrong? The devil is up with us again and Mr.
Farley has gone to his room twice without prayer, completely over board
again, and all because I am weak enough to notice and care for his one
sided treatment."

Their dysfunctional threesome limped along, each trying to one-up the
other. One January, Angelina went to "a dance over to Isaac's" with her
father, and as though she meant to gain something with this night out, she
finished her entry—"ha! ha." But, as if Angelina's night out had given
them permission to retaliate, two days later Winthrop took Lydia to a
dance at the Council House, probably in Salt Lake. Angelina reported,
"Mr. Farley and his darling Lydia went to a dance at the council house.
Wonder if he thinks he will always have the privilege of treating me in this
off hand way; if he thinks he can always make me the drudge and the tail
of such women." Had Lydia asked Mr. Farley to take her to a dance?

Angelina even hoped Mr. Farley would take a fourth wife so that
Lydia could see what it was like to believe that you were the focus of your
husband's love and then not be. Angelina didn't like the way that
Winthrop was bonding with Lydia's brother, either. Angelina explained
that Mr. Farley went hunting with Lydia's brother, and Angelina resented
how that relationship put Lydia forward even more. Angelina wrote, "[I]

wonder if they will be as good and clever when he gets another wife, eh? Wonder if he will always hug liars and deceivers to his bosom night and day and make them his bosom confidents. Well, well, the lord's ways are not our ways." Here Angelina suggests that her marriage relationship was fine until Mr. Farley married a second wife; the same could happen to Lydia.

In the midst of these bad feelings, Angelina reported that Winthrop left to find work in Bridger "to procure the necessaries of life for his family" and also to get away from "the contentious spirits of his two women." Angelina confessed that "matters" had come to "a shameful point" between Lydia and herself—"worse than ever [existed] between" her and Ellen.

Angelina used her diary to make a self-improvement plan. She resolved to not "quarrel in [Mr. Farley's] absence" so that Lydia would have "no just grounds of complaint." She resolved to keep an "every day account of doings of both" her and Lydia, on paper, because she thought Lydia sometimes lied and exaggerated. For example, Lydia complained that Angelina kept the coffee locked up "when it was lying in the cupboard." Lydia complained that Angelina didn't divide the milk and butter fairly. Lydia also complained to someone that it made her "so devilish mad" that she couldn't "do more as she [pleased]." Angelina ended her entry that day complaining that Lydia had used the garden hoe all day, resulting in Angelina not getting a chance with the hoe!

Although Angelina tried during Winthrop's absence to be "sociable" with Lydia and not "make a fuss," when he returned she couldn't stand the way Lydia received all his attention: "I declare I have not power to stand calm by the way she tags him from place to place and sticks as tight as though she could not get a part from him while I must stand back like a whipped dog. I fear I shall not stand it." Although no photographs of the two women have been found, they might fit two opposite female stereotypes described in an 1878 *Atlantic Monthly* satire: Angelina as the stereotypical "New England Woman," and Lydia as the stereotypical "French" (or Italian, in this case) woman. According to the stereotype, a married "New England Woman" valued work, her family, and Puritanical religious exactness; hated "cheating"; and "flirtation would give her a headache." On the other hand, a "French" woman loved to flirt and "be coquette in every movement and action" but could still be a "comforting, good woman in her way." Although two stereotypes, a reader can imagine the Puritan versus European culture clash that sometimes filled the Farleys' little place.

Eventually, Lydia got her own house, and Angelina didn't complain as much when she couldn't witness Winthrop and Lydia together, but Angelina never recovered her place in her marriage. Like some other first wives, she missed the "oneness" between husband and wife and would have preferred "a whole husband" because "try as I might," as one first wife wrote, she couldn't help but feel like "the neglected wife, the sap who was left to work her life out so that others might enjoy their life together." But Angelina had been right about vacillating affections—Winthrop married two more wives, which might have changed his relationship with Lydia, too. Angelina died in 1901, at age seventy-one in Ogden, having spent her later years helping her children and grandchildren.

Just as a visit from someone like Henrietta would have been therapeutic for Angelina, so must have writing also helped her cope. Angelina coached herself sometimes in her diary. Once after writing critically about polygamy, she reminded herself that she'd been counseled to overlook injustices and "rejoice always in the [daily] blessings" she received. Remembering this, she felt "unthankful" for not noticing more beautiful things. Perhaps she was so harsh in her writing because writing was a way to release the anger and confusion that she didn't want to blurt out. Women who wrote from the margins of official discourse could use their diaries as a way to "talk back" to their culture. Her refreshing candor was a quiet, acceptable way to have the last word.

Of course, Angelina told her story from her viewpoint, and that's why scholars read autobiographies and diaries as "literary texts" rather than as "documentary histories." Autobiographical writing is, according to bell hooks, a "unique recounting of events not so much as they have happened, but as we remember and invent them." When hooks wrote her own diary, for example, she discovered that as she wrote, she felt that she "was not as concerned with accuracy of detail as [she] was with evoking in writing the state of mind, the spirit of a particular moment." In Angelina's case, certainly her mood and voice help us understand what it felt like to be her at the moment when she "selected, deselected, [forgot], rearranged, blurred, emphasized, or de-emphasized" certain details from all that she could have written.

Angelina, as all autobiographers purposefully or accidently do, created herself as a character in her own story. She chose to transgress cultural expectations that would have dictated that she represent herself as the "ideal woman who embodi[ed] the characteristics and enact[ed] the roles assigned her in the fictions of patriarchal culture." Rather, Angelina came across as a shrew but also as a woman with self-respect. She was fighting to hang onto who she knew herself to be and not what Winthrop and Lydia wanted to make her.

By keeping an emotion-packed diary, she took the risk of alienating any potential reading audience, who would discover that she was violating unspoken Mormon women rules that she always defend her faith and, in a way, also violating Christian women rules that she be more self-effacing. But in some ways, Angelina *was* the good Christian woman who wouldn't put up with the excesses of polygamy and who would "go tell it on the mountain." She seems unconstrained from tattling on the Mormon system or at least tattling on Winthrop and Lydia, who she believed weren't playing fairly.

Besides asserting her self-respect and telling the reader that she was the only woman Winthrop ever had whom he could trust, Angelina sounds curiously fragile. She would sometimes admit to having demons in her head, and even the belief that the devil was getting power over her, as Arthur Miller wrote of the early Salem Puritans, would be disturbing. In 1874, still troubled, Angelina wrote, "I fear I shall break down in mind as well as body. It is terrible. Unaccountable fear and terror creep over me. Strange things and vague fancies flit through my mind. My head aches."

Polygamous marriage was obviously too much for her, and if anything, she needed stability rather than the constant instability and insecurity that came with settling a new place—raising too many children in a dirty house—and sharing her husband with four wives who came and went throughout her life. As her children got older, she learned to forge her primary relationships with them. Angelina later wrote that she spent every "nerve and sinew" to exhaustion raising her children and helping with her grandchildren.

Angelina's raw perspective is all the more pronounced because she kept a diary in which she immediately recorded what she was feeling, rather than an autobiography in which she might have more calmly reflected in her old age. On the subject of polygamy, Angelina's "loud" personal *diary* provides a contrast to Henrietta's "quiet" *autobiography* that was meant for a larger audience—Henrietta wrote very little about her experience as a polygamous wife.

The more even-tempered Henrietta could have told that three years previous in February 1857 her husband had married "our wife Electa Jane," as she called her, but then would offer no details about how the marriage came about or what the effects of that marriage were. In 1857, Henrietta's husband Ezra was thirty-three, Henrietta twenty-nine, and Electa Jane seventeen.

FIGURE 5.2A First wife Henrietta Williams.

FIGURE 5.2B Henrietta's husband, Ezra Granter Williams.

Henrietta and Ezra had arrived in Salt Lake City in October 1849 with their baby girl and Ezra's widowed mother, Rebecca Swain Williams, who never remarried, probably by choice. In Salt Lake, Henrietta and Ezra first lived in a log cabin and then, Henrietta explained, the "Doctor," her husband, "built a seven room adobe house." As "emigrants rushed in," she said, and the doctor's "large practice" increased," the adobe house became a hospital, and the family moved "to the block north of the temple block."

In February 1857, when Ezra married Electa Jane, the settlers were suffering from famine and Church leaders were pushing polygamous marriage as one way to care for all their people—perhaps this situation motivated Ezra to marry Electa Jane. But the Williams family sometimes experienced need themselves. Once when Ezra was about to depart on one of his missions, he cried because his family hardly had any food. While he was gone, Henrietta tried to collect on medical services her husband had performed. Henrietta wrote that when Ezra returned, he was "glad to find his family happy in trying to do the very best they knew how and not complaining." Perhaps Henrietta was cheerful by nature, and perhaps she was influenced by Brigham Young's preaching against complainers—Young felt "he had given everything to the church and expected everybody to do the same."

At first the Williams intergenerational and polygamous family lived together. Henrietta explained that she, her husband Ezra, their wife Electa Jane, Ezra's widowed mother Rebecca, Henrietta's six children aged one month to eleven years, and Electa Jane's two-year-old had been living to-gether in Great Salt Lake Ward 14. In 1880, twenty years later, the census takers would find husband Ezra living in Ogden City with Electa Jane and next door to her only son, Hyrum Royal, a married carpenter. In 1883, Electa Jane died at age forty-three, and nine months later, Ezra probably married a third wife who was never mentioned in Henrietta's autobiog-raphy. In 1900, at age seventy-two, about the time that Henrietta finished her autobiography, she was living with Ezra in a house attached to a farm that they owned. In 1905, Ezra died, and in 1922, Henrietta died at age ninety-five, outliving her husband by seventeen years.

Henrietta probably wrote her autobiography around 1900 when she was seventy-three and when Electra Jane had been dead for seventeen years. It is, again, most notable, for what it does *not* say about the younger wives. She mentioned Electa Jane only a few times. Two of those times, Henrietta briefly compared her experience with the easier one of Electa Jane's, letting the reader know that she, Henrietta, had not always had the advantage. For example, Henrietta wrote that when she had her son Joseph in 1858, she "was alone." She compared this to Electa Jane's baby son's birth a month later: Electa Jane had "her mother, sister, and her husband Dr. Williams, her father, and brother-in-law...to administer to her." Henrietta also wrote of her subsequent annoyance that "some officious person" had told Electa Jane that "the first son born in polygamy ruled the father's house...as though," Henrietta facetiously wrote, "the father was to turn imbecile and could not rule his own house." Evidently, someone must have congratulated Electa Jane for having the first son born in po-lygamy, and Electa Jane took it to heart. Henrietta wrote, "what rubbish some people can invent, giving it for a principle of the gospel."

In a second example, Henrietta wrote that Electa Jane had brought whooping cough from Salt Lake and unfortunately given it to Henrietta's children: "Our wife Electa Jane Barney Williams spent the summer in Salt Lake with her parents returning late in the fall with her only child, Hyrum Royal starting out with whooping cough." Henrietta sarcastically con-tinued, "She loaned it to my young family which was a great favor to me," and the house rang with coughs "all those long winter nights." Henrietta lost one of her little twins that winter to whooping cough because they couldn't get medicine "that time of the year in that snowy country and no travel out of the valley to relieve them from their distressing situation."

Henrietta probably wrote about Electa Jane's birth and delivery of her only boy because Electa Jane had received so much attention compared with her, and Henrietta probably wrote about the whooping cough trouble to show how much she endured that winter. But Henrietta also referred to Electa as "our wife" and shared a humorous vignette that showed Electa Jane could bring fun to the family, too. One April Fool's Day, Electa Jane made a "candle out of a turnip": "The black end was its nose. She handed it to Dr. Williams to light. He could not think what was the matter with the candle." They had a good laugh and shared the "candle" with the neighborhood.

Henrietta's use of occasional humor and sarcasm to portray stories about Electa Jane was mild compared with Angelina's "transgressive writing." Polygamous wives who produced this kind of transgressive writing were willing to expose what they really felt compared with what they believed their audience wanted to hear. Angelina attempted to "write [her] way *through* and *out of*" the complications of "theological, social, and personal dilemmas" when they ran up against "Mormon culture and doctrine." Sitting by that river on her dirty farm, she wrote stories about her messy world, quietly undermining those Salt Lake women.

6

Interlude: Sometimes Sisterhood

DURING THE LATE 1860s, obscure polygamous wives such as Angelina Farley and Henny Williams undoubtedly attended local female Relief Society meetings and may have been caught up in the female suffrage movement that was gaining momentum. In the 1860s in the Utah Territory, the women who headed women's rights campaigns were mainly polygamous wives who had been galvanized by the federal government's efforts to end polygamy. They wanted to defend their religion, show they weren't oppressed, gain the right to vote, and—like Church leaders—gain statehood. At a rally in 1870, a polygamous wife proclaimed before 5,000 Mormon women in the Salt Lake Tabernacle, "Were we the stupid, degraded, heart-broken beings that we have been represented to be, silence might better become us." They argued that the polygamous lifestyle actually promoted feminist ideals, such as independence and opportunity. Considering their rhetoric, it's tempting to see Mormon polygamy as a utopian moment—a seemingly oppressive situation for women that was actually liberating because women outnumbered men in polygamous families and could presumably operate autonomously yet with united purpose.

Indeed a feeling of sisterhood developed in the nineteenth-century Church partially thanks to polygamy. In 1844–1845 before the western migration, some of Joseph Smith's widows "formed the nucleus of women" who nurtured "one another spiritually." Then during the winter of 1846 in Nebraska, a few of Brigham Young's companionable wives lived harmoniously in a "comfortable little log house" and became part of an extended "intimate and intensely spiritual 'female family.'" These elite wives "laid hands on each other to cure illnesses, mourned with mothers who lost children, pronounced blessings upon each other, and cultivated the gift of speaking in tongues." Brigham Young's biographer John Turner believes that for some women "the shared bonds of a social and spiritual sisterhood compensated for some of the disadvantages of polygamy."

A core group of these women took their good feelings with them to the Salt Lake Valley, and according to Jill Mulvay Derr, "out of this early sisterhood of plural wives the female elite of the church would emerge." Polygamy helped create and solidify Mormon sisterhood because polygamy "required both spiritual commitment and emotional suffering, and those who took on the role entered a sisterhood that assumed common aspiration and commiseration." Mormon sisterhood continued to develop as women "who had been separated geographically or emotionally from their families" poured into new settlements in the West and developed "kinship relations" with each other.

Beginning in 1867, Mormon women belonged to the all-female Relief Society, whose members met throughout Mormon settlements; they organized local help for the sick and needy, collaborated on worthwhile community projects, and taught and blessed each other. The Relief Society supported the suffrage movement, and between 1875 and 1896, there were active chapters of the National Woman Suffrage Association throughout the territory. Women in the Utah Territory had gained the right to vote in 1870, making them the second women in the United States to do so (after Wyoming), but they soon had that right rescinded because of antipolygamy campaigns in Washington.

Antipolygamy campaigns escalated Mormon political activism. Brigham Young supported suffrage, and although his "attitudes toward women and marriage elude simple interpretation," he was correct to hope that the suffrage movement would give "Mormons a national stage upon which they could demonstrate that polygamous wives were intelligent beings capable of thinking for themselves and therefore willing participants in plural marriage, not the downtrodden slaves painted by lecturebureau circuit riders." He probably read with satisfaction a 1870 *New York Herald* article reporting on a women's rally: "It will not be denied that Mormon women have both brains and tongues. Some of the speeches give evidence that in general knowledge in logic and rhetoric the so-called degraded ladies of Mormondom are quite the equal of the Women's Rights women of the East." Young realized that a strong society needed the talents of women and believed that women should "enlarge their sphere of usefulness for the benefit of society at large." His daughter Susa Young Gates, a polygamous wife and businesswoman whose endeavors included correspondence with Leo Tolstoy, summer school at Harvard, and a speech at the International Women's Congress in London, wrote of her "divine inheritance of perfect equality with man."

Between 1872 and 1914, Mormon women published their own periodical called the *Woman's Exponent* that early on went to several thousand women throughout the United States and Great Britain and prompted exchanges with other women's journals—sometimes sparring over polygamy. *Exponent* editor and polygamous wife Emmeline Wells addressed topics such as the false notion of the pedestal, equal pay for equal work, and equality in athletic programs. In 1879, Wells was invited to speak at a National Woman Suffrage Association convention. After Wells's trip to Washington, she reported in the *Exponent* that she and a widowed polygamous wife had "bossed" President Rutherford B. Hayes by personally asking why the federal government was ignoring territorial laws and tearing women and children from their husbands. The two explained to the president that "Mormon wives were happy, wanted to live with their husbands, religiously believed they were right in so doing, and objected not to other women having a share to [their] husband's names and property."

Ten years later in 1882, a similar sentiment was expressed by a woman correspondent to the *Exponent* who wrote that polygamous wives would defiantly defend polygamy against interfering outsiders: We will uphold "every doctrine of our Church, Plural Marriage included, and we will say to our sisters 'come share with me, my husband and home and we will love each other, and labor for each other's welfare as we do for our own.'"

Not just in theory but in reality, at age twenty-eight, polygamous wife Ellis Shipp entrusted her three small children to the care of the other three wives in her family and took the train East to become a doctor at Women's Medical College in Philadelphia. Although she loved her children, she wrote that she was "tired" of her life of "uselessness and unaccomplished desires." In 1879, Shipp founded the School of Nursing and Obstetrics in Salt Lake City, which over the years trained 500 midwives from all over the West.

In 1872, an important outsider seemed to confirm that polygamous wives did not seem unhappy. An open-minded non-Mormon Pennsylvania woman, Elizabeth Wood Kane, had the unique opportunity of traveling through Utah with her lawyer husband (who was a friend to the Mormons) and Brigham Young. She kept notes and originally wrote *Twelve Mormon Homes Visited in Succession on a Journey through Utah to Arizona* for her father back home. Although she couldn't help being amused by polygamy, she surprised her audience with stories of harmony between polygamous wives.

According to Kane, the travelers' first stop was a Provo homestead where the singular occupant of the house, a polygamous wife whom Kane called

"Miss Lucy" (her real name was Margaret Smoot) heartily welcomed the group "with many a quip and merry jest." They shared an elaborate meal embellished by nine pieces of china and glassware for each guest. The quick-eyed "active" Miss Lucy ran the homestead herself; her husband and his other wife were guests at the meal. The mealtime conversation included questions from Brigham Young and Lucy's husband directed to her concerning the state of affairs at this homestead, including information on the cows, calves, sheep, hired boys, winter provisions of wood and coal, and the results of the summer's husbandry.

A little farther south in Nephi, Kane sat by a fireside with polygamous wives "Sarah and Mary Steerforth" (also disguised names) and discussed polygamy after Kane attempted to guess which of the children in the house belonged to which mother. The two wives laughed as Kane got it all wrong, suggesting a natural affection between the children and the two mothers. Mrs. Mary, the more talkative one, elaborated on the bond that existed between "sister-wives": "Even sisters by blood are parted, when they marry, by new interests independent of each other." But, according to Mrs. Mary, in her polygamous home, each of the wives had "a friend whose interests are identical with her own, who can share all the joys and troubles of the family, and to whom she can impart her feelings regarding its head [the husband] without fear of violating that sacred confidence which may not be shared with any outside friend."

At another home Kane visited, "Mrs. Jane" spoke affectionately of Helen (by then, dead three years), who had been "like a mother" to the other two younger wives, and Mrs. Jane reminisced about the well-organized days when Helen "regulated the family affairs." Jane spun, weaved, and worked in the dairy; the well-educated and literary Helen took charge of the children's education; and a third wife assisted in other ways. All in all, Kane was not unimpressed with the polygamous homes she visited.

In sum, the polygamous wives who defended their lifestyle before thousands or only before a few visitors in their homes had tried to reconstruct their understanding of marriage. They tried to think of marital love differently: rather than "finding one's soul mate," they sought to accept "a righteous person" who "shared their beliefs," and "cultivat[ed] a love for that person." They tried to move past the "love-based marriage," foster an environment of inclusiveness, and undo the assumption that their husbands were the center of their lives. One seasoned polygamous wife, Vilate Kimball, reportedly advised an unrelated struggling wife not to think about what her husband was doing when he was away, to be pleased to see him when he came as she would be "to see any friend," to "simply be indifferent" to her husband if she wanted to be happy, and to find comfort "wholly" in her children. In times of trouble, Brigham Young also encouraged polygamous wives to control what they could control, focus on their children, and not worry about their husbands: "Are you tormenting yourselves by thinking your husbands do not love you? I would not care whether they loved a particle or not; but I would cry out, like one of old, in joy of my heart, 'I have got a man from the Lord! Hallelujah! I am a mother! I have borne an image of God.'" Some Mormon women, their publications, and their leaders attempted to decenter the patriarchal structure of marriage, encourage women's independence, and praise strong female friendships—and, of course, encourage women to be happy polygamous wives so the system could continue.

As I read these examples of emerging Mormon women's history as a Mormon graduate student in the late 1980s, I was proud of what I learned about my feminist foremothers. In this state of mind, one fall afternoon, a longtime instructor at my university asked me to meet him. He explained that he was the editor of the local literary journal that enjoyed a large distribution in our town and beyond, and then invited me to write an article on any Mormon topic—he was in a bit of a bind because he'd recently published an anti-Mormon story in the journal. I accepted his offer and wrote a short piece titled " 'Fire in My Bones': The Powerful History of Mormon Women." When it was published, the line "The writer recalls her Mormon, and feminist, heritage" appeared under the title.

Although seemingly at peace with polygamy, during the next term in my Nineteenth-Century Women's Literature class when another student told the class that he wanted to research Mormon polygamous wives, I was simultaneously embarrassed and curious. In a twist, a week later, our professor suggested that I take the polygamous wives topic since the other student had dropped it. Perhaps referring to the journal piece I'd written, my professor said, "It's surprising... you'd think polygamous wives were oppressed, but they seem strong—the women helped each other and the husband was pushed to the periphery." I took her advice and wrote a research paper for her class titled "Nineteenth-Century Mormon Women and Polygamy: Feminist Ironies." My thesis statement read, "The ultimate irony of polygamy is that it actually promoted feminist ideals such as independence, female community, opportunity, and power."

After my initial foray into the topic of Mormon polygamous wives, however, I started realizing that there was another side to the story, as just epitomized by Angelina Farley. I learned that not only obscure women like her but also some prominent polygamous wives married to men in the Salt Lake Mormon hierarchy—including some who participated in political rallies—privately acknowledged that they did not like polygamy. For example, Dr. Martha Hughes Cannon, third wife of stake president and hospital director Angus Cannon, wrote that she did not receive enough time, attention, or financial help from Cannon. She came to admire the exclusive relationships of good monogamous marriages which, she wrote, were a "joy and comfort to witness."

In 1874, *Woman's Exponent* editor Emmeline B. Wells wrote in her diary that it must be "an exertion" for her husband to visit her since he was not "in want of me for a companion or in any sense, he does not need me at all." She went to his other house hoping to see him—"O how I want to see him"—and realized that his other family was "plenty ready and willing" to attend to his every "wish caprice or whim." Reflecting on her marriage on her twenty-second wedding anniversary, she wrote, "how few thoughts I had then are realized, and how much sorrow I have known in place of the joy I looked forward to." Her husband did not realize how "weary" she grew for "one sight of his beloved face one touch of his dear hand." To her surprise, however, her husband "manifested" an "intense love" toward her in "late years." As she wrote, "Such a remarkable change from the long ago, when I needed him so much more, how peculiarly these things come about."

In four more examples, Phoebe Woodruff, first wife of future Church President Wilford Woodruff, felt pressured to publicly support polygamy, but when a good friend asked about polygamy, she reportedly responded, "I loathe the unclean thing with all the strength of my nature." Zina Young, wife of Brigham and a strong public advocate of polygamy, told a suffering polygamous wife that her feelings were not her fault and that "the system" itself was to blame. Sarah Pratt, the first wife of Orson Pratt, who in 1852 publicly introduced polygamy in Utah, left her husband in 1868 when he told her he would only spend every sixth week with her. Sarah grew tired of his fanaticism for polygamy and of watching him court young women. Artemesia Snow, wife of Apostle Erastus Snow, wrote her husband that she was convinced that a house full of mothers and children was "no way to bring up children." She explained that she would like him to be there to help soothe four crying babies and the noise of other children.

Yes, elite wives who publicly supported polygamy but in private resented it were probably duplicitous, but it's more complicated than that. Some extolled polygamy at times and hated it at other times; some believed in the ideal but couldn't manage the reality; some felt that by defending polygamy they were defending their religion and their self-respect; some put up with polygamy for an eternal reward and because it had originated with Joseph Smith; some enjoyed the public adulation of being married to a Mormon leader. Historian Richard Van Wagoner finds that "positive testimonials [about polygamy] are most often seen in public or retrospective accounts" and that "contemporary diary and letter accounts of polygamous relationships generally present a less-than-glowing picture of polygamy."

In retrospect, prominent nineteenth-century Mormon political activists who promoted the feminist virtues of polygamy may have ignored the plight of their polygamous sisters who weren't as well off educationally or financially or politically, not unlike American feminists of the late twentieth century who in some ways encouraged female independence at the price of impoverished single mothers. In most political movements, there's a gap between the ideal and what can really be achieved; in these situations, sometimes the weaker members of society become the victims of the promoters' zeal. Feminism and polygamy, perhaps like feminism and pornography, have a tenuous relationship—it's not clear whether either endeavor gives women more choices and power or automatically further oppresses them since men pull many of the strings.

As I began reading the twenty-nine diaries and autobiographies of obscure polygamous wives, I noticed first that the writers rarely provided evidence that they were friends with their husbands' other wives. Wives of the same husband generally didn't confide in each other or seek each other's company. Although most wives tried to get along, they were generally indifferent toward each other—in other words, there was minimal female friendship in the same family. Married women, as they were accustomed, generally continued to privilege the husband and instinctively drew on their Christian backgrounds and their Relief Society sense of charity to treat other wives respectfully, but kept their distance. Second, I noticed that polygamous wives were sensitive to division of labor: the empowered wives were the ones who got other wives to help with hard work and drudgery. If wives could not strike a fair division of labor, resentment could creep in. Perhaps that's part of the reason that most wives preferred to live on their own. All in all, I found in accounts of the day-to-day living of polygamy little of the exuberance I expected.

For example, second wife *Hannah Nixon* wrote superficially about her husband's other wives by logistically mentioning their location or situation but left them undeveloped as characters. In her autobiography, she emphasized how much she helped the first wife "Sister Nixon" (Johanne) but never wrote of receiving help from her or any of the other wives. In 1876, after thirty-one-year-old Hannah Nixon married forty-year-old "Bro. Nixon," they returned to St. George where she stayed in "a little adobe room at [her] father's." Not long afterward, Brother Nixon "requested" that she help "Sister Nixon," whose health was "quite poor" as she awaited her "confinement" in childbirth, and so Hannah went and "stayed until after her confinement." A few months later, Brother Nixon wanted to take Sister Nixon to their property farther south in Mount Trumbull, so Hannah "kept house" for Sister Nixon while she was gone.

After Hannah had her first baby, and the baby had teething trouble, Hannah joined some extended family in Mount Trumbull, Arizona, and helped by "sometimes tending 2 or 3 babys at once." At one point, "Sister Nixon took sick with gathering in her head," so Hannah "had [Sister Nixon's] baby day and night until [Hannah] weaned her." One time, Hannah became sick and weak, but she didn't mention whether anyone helped with her baby. Later, Sister Nixon requested that Hannah "take charge of the cooking" for the family and their hired men. And so it went. Hannah emphasized how she fulfilled Brother and Sister Nixon's requests and humbly stated, "[I] helped what little I could," but Hannah never

FIGURE 6.1 Second wife Hannah Nixon.

FIGURE 6.2 First wife Johanne Nixon.

mentioned having a special relationship with Sister Nixon. Hannah mentioned the third wife Zephyr only a couple of times when Hannah stated where Zephyr was living. When Brother Nixon died six years after Hannah married him, she inherited part of his estate and went her own way.

In another example, second wife *Florence Dean* seemed just as neutral in her feelings about her husband's first wife. Florence wrote in her diary one weekend of the "bedlam" caused when her husband's first wife and her two children came to visit. In 1893 near Salt Lake City in Mill Creek in her "happy little home," she tried "patiently to wait the birth" of her fifth child, while her husband could come "on the car" only briefly in the evenings, because he was worried about being caught for practicing polygamy. After the baby was born, the first wife, Sally, "came down" to stay with Florence. Sally brought her little boy Harry and her daughter Lilly who was supposed to watch Harry.

Florence's story about the weekend emphasized how the visit didn't benefit her or help her rest, and she implicated Sally. She wrote that Sally's son Harry "had not been here two hours before he got to the hot stove and burnt himself in a terrible manner. Great blisters on both wrists, and on the ends of four fingers, and the poor little fellow cried awfully for two hours." By the time everyone got to bed that first night, Sally "was completely worn out and sick" and Florence "felt nearly crazy" herself. As she explained, "What with my sympathies being worked up so, and the noise and confusion I felt," and besides, she had the baby and little "Wilfie" in bed with her—perhaps so guests could have their beds. She continued, "The next day things were no better as little Harry cried all day long for his mama and Lilly made more noise with the children than any sick person could stand without becoming worn completely out." Further, "Sally had some dress she brought down to finish," a flippant comment that suggested that Florence felt that Sally was more worried about her own project than about helping Florence. She finished writing about Saturday by saying, "we had perfect bedlam all day long." She wrote that the next day, Sunday, "was a little better...but not much." At 5 p.m., their husband, Harry Sr., came "to bless and name the baby."

Besides this story, Florence didn't write much about Sally. In contrast to the excitement and stress of that weekend, Florence would sometimes write that she was lonely. After going on the underground for a couple of months to protect her husband from prosecution, when she returned home, she wrote, "No place like Home if it is sometimes lonely." She was not necessarily lonely for Sally's company, though. She wrote in her diary that she had just missed some friends who came to visit and "sat down and cried with disappointment" when she found out that her friends had been there. She explained, "I had been feeling very lonesome and blue and forsaken all the previous week and then to think when we went for our first step out and only for so short a distance we should miss seeing such dear friends." Like many polygamous wives, Florence longed to be with her husband. She wrote of an upcoming event, "I can hardly think of anything else with longing so much to go with Harry."

In a third example, first wife *Laura Thurber*'s writings gave the impression that she genuinely cared about second wife Annie, who was seven years younger, and yet their wife-wife relationship was clearly subordinate to the wife-husband relationship. In a gracious writing style, Laura explained that in 1884, after eight years of marriage, when she was twenty-five years old, a girl named Annie came to their town of Richfield to teach school. Laura's husband considered getting Annie for a wife and, Laura wrote, "spoke about it to me." Laura explained that she overcame her hesitation by remembering that she wanted to "[fear] God more than man." Laura and her husband Joseph "thought her a good girl" and "felt like the time had come for us," she wrote, "to enter into the law of Celestial Marriage."

After the marriage, for a while Laura and Annie "lived together all the time except a few weeks at a time when [Annie] went over to see her folks." Laura had twins and two months later Annie had a son, but rather than describing what the mothers experienced, Laura chose to report on their husband's reaction: "our husband felt double blessed, in having 3 babies to tend, as he liked babies." In many entries, though, Laura mentioned Annie, reporting that she heard that Annie was going to take another class (perhaps to enhance her teaching); that she and Annie rode home together after their husband was taken to jail for polygamy; that she and Annie "got a nice dress alike"; and that Annie intended to get a shawl. Laura finished, "so we both think we are fixed" and then added, "that is I do and I expect she thinks so to." In other words, Laura assumed that she and Annie would feel the same satisfaction after shopping together.

As sweet as Laura was, as the diary progressed, second wife Annie seemed less enthusiastic about their relationship and, while their husband was in jail, kept going home to her parents' house for longer periods of time. At times like those, Laura would write, "O! I dread sickness when my Husband is not here and I have to stay alone of nights, and so much outdoors chores to be done." Laura wished that Annie would stay with her more often: "it seems verry queer not to have her come here." Another time, Laura wrote that she didn't know how long Annie "will stay with me" because "she gets very lonesome, and I do to since Joseph left." Sadly, Laura later wrote that Annie was staying away because "it is a great trial to Annie to be deprived of [their husband's] company so much." Thus, while Laura wanted Annie to help her and keep her company, Annie went home to her family because their husband was gone.

In a fourth example, in 1878 at age nineteen, *Caroline Hansen* "went to work for," Caroline wrote, "the one we now call Aunt Bengta durring confinement"—to help out after Bengta delivered her third (or fourth?) child. The man of the house, Andrew, and his first wife, Bengta, were both twenty-five at the time and had emigrated from Denmark, as had Caroline. Caroline wrote that "a short time after" she started working for Bengta, she "became ingaged to her husband." Caroline wrote that she "had known [Andrew] for many years," and they left for Salt Lake to be married in the Endowment House.

Caroline and her new husband spent a "happy" wedding day: "we were happy that day in our inosence never dreaming of the trials we [would have] to indure trying to live together in two small rooms" with his first wife. Caroline continued, "Aunt Bengta was a good woman and wanted to do right. But it was hard for her. She had a quick temper and jelous disposition and I a young girl inexperienced coming in to share her Husband."

FIGURE 6.3 Caroline and Andrew Hansen family.

Caroline would write that she was glad that she had endured the situation: "Thank the Lord we staid with it and we got along, & in fall conference our Husband was called on a mission to the states." By then, Caroline and Andrew had only been married two months, but Caroline suggested that his mission call was well timed. Taking him out of the equation probably helped the wives' relationship; however, the two women were so impoverished that Andrew had to return home after seven months to take care of his debt.

A month after his return in June 1880, Caroline had her first child, who lived only one month, and by that winter, she decided she should move out. She was so desperate to find another place that she prayed that God would help her: "I felt like it would be better for me to find a place somewhere & move to myself. I had no Idea where for there were no houses for rent around there. I decided to go to the Lord so that if it [were] right & best for me to find some other place to live that He would open up a way for me." Perhaps she felt like an intruder in Andrew and Bengta's family. After praying often and looking hard, she found herself a place— a "little house," and "with in another year [her] father gave [her] a piece of land," and they "built a small house on it." She wrote, "I shall never forget how thankfull I was as soon as I was moved. I closed the Door & knelt down & pourd out my soul in thankfulness to my heavenly father for a home of my own." After three years of polygamous marriage, Andrew, Bengta, and Caroline achieved some family goals: "we were now out of debt and we each had our own home." Under these circumstances, Andrew was able to accept another mission call and left for Denmark. Caroline "got along fine" living with the one child she'd had while he was gone. She did not mention seeing Bengta or even being near Bengta, but she did remark that her parents were "living close by." Caroline was "happy in the thought that [her] husband was counted worthy to go and preach the Gospel."

When Andrew returned from his mission fall of 1884, polygamy raids by the federal government had accelerated, and their family decided to flee to Mexico. Then Bengta and Caroline changed their minds: "now we both had small babys & could not undertake the journey, so we consented for him to take another wife and go and find homes so we could come later, but for some reason they did not get into Mexico, but came back and settled in Cannonvil, Southern part of Utah." The family had geographically broken up, and besides the new third wife, Andrew married a fourth wife a year later. Caroline wrote that their family "moved around a good deal," but she suggested that the Lord blessed them for living polygamy: "we were 4 familys a good deal of the time. We lived among a poor class of people. We were never without bread while some of our nabors were where there were only one family or one wife came to us for flour. My husband of coars worked very hard to support us and I want to bear my testimony that the Lord did bless us."

In 1900, the census taker found Caroline living with Andrew (and no other wife) and their seven children in Panguitch, Utah, where he was running a sawmill. In 1904, Caroline moved up to Idaho. In 1910, she told the census taker that she was a widow, although her husband was alive. When Caroline's boys were teenagers, Andrew wanted them to come and work on his dry farm in Salem, Idaho, so Caroline moved near him again: "he needed my boys to help him, and the boys wanted to be with their father, so we moved there to and done well for a year or two. After that our crops blowed out for two years in succession," and Andrew had rheumatism, so they gave up farming. By 1920, Andrew was working as a police officer in Rexburg, Idaho, and living with his youngest wife Mary and her fifteen-year-old son. In 1920, Caroline lived in Oakley, Idaho, and again told the census taker that she was a widow. In 1928, Caroline and Andrew celebrated their golden wedding anniversary with a "trip down Southern Utah to Tropic our old home and to see Bryce Canyon," and she "enjoyed the trip very much."

Writing in 1931 at age seventy-two, Caroline ended her autobiography by referring to her polygamous family and the efforts they had all made to "live an honest upright life." She acknowledged that they "had some hard times" and "ups and downs" but that all "turned out to be for our best good." She ended by writing that she hoped her children would "try as hard to live right all their lives as there father has" because he had "tried hard to live right and do his duty in the church." Throughout her autobiography, Caroline mentioned the other three wives infrequently—she never mentioned the third wife by name and never mentioned the fourth wife's existence at all.

The previous four examples illustrate some of the domestic realities of sharing a husband. Women who told their stories show what they were willing to do for their Church. But some wives found writing about polygamy a minefield they couldn't negotiate. In personal writings, what is *not* said can be as valuable as what *is* said—"gaps and silences in texts" tell a story, too. Neglecting to write about their husbands' other wives tells readers that those relationships did not have a significant effect on them, or that they didn't know how to write about them, or that they refused to be defined by polygamy—taking ultimate control over their stories.

For example, first wife *Ellen "Nellie" Parkinson*'s detailed autobiography barely mentioned her husband's other wife. Nellie explained that she married her husband after he had been smitten by her performance in a church-sponsored musical. When they married, she was fifteen and he was twenty-three. After the couple had children and put down roots, in 1884 Church leaders called William to be a bishop in Preston, Idaho, and asked his family to relocate there. The new town was only seven miles away but seemed like it was on the edge of nowhere—"a desert sand ridge." Nellie wrote that neither of them wanted to go, and both "felt [they] had reached [their] limit of sacrifice" for the Church, but they decided to heed the call anyway. As bishop, William called George T. Benson as one of his counselors.

A few years later in 1887, William decided to marry a second wife—one of George Benson's daughters. A week before Nellie's twenty-fourth birthday, when she was eight months pregnant with her fourth child, her husband told her that he was going to marry eighteen-year-old Louisa Benson. In retrospect, Nellie wrote that she felt "hurried into it before [her] mind or faith was prepared." Years later, remembering how the news affected her, she wrote, "Just before Irene's birth,...William married Louisa Benson and it nearly killed me." Looking back, she felt she had no choice: "Since the Church urged it and the family all approved there was nothing to do but make the best of it." In the rest of her detailed autobiography, she didn't provide any detail that would help the reader get to know Louisa. She did not say where Louisa was living, nor did she mention any of Louisa's fifteen children, even though family lore had it, as does much Mormon family lore about polygamy, that she and Louisa got along.

During Nellie's busy life in Preston, she wrote that she tried to "[overcome] the trials of polygamy." William and Nellie's home became "the gathering place for everyone," their "business grew and flourished," and she mentioned many friends. Nellie later wrote, "But for the trial of

FIGURE 6.4 First wife Nellie Parkinson, from *Samuel Rose Parkinson: Portrait of a Pioneer* by Lester Parkinson Taylor.

FIGURE 6.5 William Parkinson, from *Samuel Rose Parkinson: Portrait of a Pioneer* by Lester Parkinson Taylor.

FIGURE 6.6 Second wife Louisa Benson Parkinson, from *Samuel Rose Parkinson: Portrait of a Pioneer* by Lester Parkinson Taylor.

polygamy, life would have been very good. I see of late years how foolish I was. I could not escape it so should not have grieved, but caught all the happiness I could." While still not mentioning Louisa, Nellie wrote, "William was always willing to be kind if I did not interfere." Nellie even went so far to say that polygamy could be a "far better" system than "what we have now" (presumably monogamy) "if people could be converted and be able to take a greater outlook on life and eternity." But as she wrote her autobiography as a widow living with a daughter in Salt Lake, she mentioned nothing about Louisa who was also living with a daughter in Salt Lake. Nellie only gave her readers two words about her husband's other wife: her name, Louisa Benson.

Some women wrote even less. *Mary Ann Maughan*'s autobiography and *Josephine Chase*'s diary gave no indication that they were polygamous wives at all. Mary Ann explained that as a young widow she met Mr. Maughan who had been left a young widower after his wife Ruth's death. Subsequently, Mary Ann and Mr. Maughan married, but she never indicated that her husband later married two more wives. Similarly, the diary that second wife Josephine Chase kept later in life never mentioned that she'd been a polygamous wife. In her case, her husband's first wife, his only other wife, had divorced him, which might help explain why Josephine wrote nothing about her.

Like Josephine Chase and Mary Ann Maughan, *Ellen Draper* didn't mention her husband's other wives. Ellen started her very short autobiography

with stories about her deceased first husband's experiences as an early set-
tler of Draper, Utah. Ellen was his third and youngest wife, and, after his
death, she wandered from place to place trying to make a living; along the
way, she remarried and then divorced. Writing her autobiography in about
1900, her last paragraph started thus: "Well, I must say what I think about
polygamy. I went into it in 1862 and no one has ever heard me say I did not
think the principle was true. I know in my heart it is, but it was abused, and
that was why it was allowed to be put down." She referred to polygamy being
put "down" around 1890 when the Church officially stopped the practice.
She went on to say that she knew of polygamous families that were "just as
happy" in polygamy as "in monogamy," and she mentioned one—a family
by the name of Decker. Ellen said she had visited with the older Decker wife
many times, and the woman "always had good to say" about the younger
wives who allowed her to "sit in her room and sew or knit." Curiously, Ellen
didn't explain how she and the other two Draper wives had managed in her
own polygamous family!

It's disappointing to learn that the polygamous wives in this study (with
a couple of upcoming exceptions) did not enjoy rich relationships with their
husbands' other wives. In retrospect, polygamy thwarted female friendships
in several ways. First, women generally did not choose new wives—their
husbands did. Age difference between wives may also have felt threat-
ening to existing wives. Perhaps wives would have been more compatible if
they had more of a voice in the process. Second, husbands had exclusive
one-on-one relationships with their wives.
Thanks to the privacy of sexual intimacy
and bedtime, women were either alone
with husbands or excluded. Doors of privacy literally and metaphorically closed out
other wives. And third, women were suspi-
cious of other women interfering in their
marriages. Their long-held assumption
about marriage was that a husband and
wife should be faithful to each other and
that interference from another woman
could cause trouble and result in jealousy.
The simple word "wife" was loaded with
cultural messages, and, in their culture,

FIGURE 6.7 William Draper
and his wives—Ellen at right.

"wife" meant being an only wife. According
to C. Lévi-Strauss, family positions "exceed

the individuals who temporarily occupy them," because each person is "inserted" into an "already defined symbolic system." Even thinking of an additional wife as a "mother" or "sister" was problematic since mothers and sisters don't have sexual relations with one's husband. Although, as time went on, the presence of polygamy in their communities may have seemed increasingly normal, its very presence might have heightened a woman's private fears that another woman could disrupt her marriage.

Traditional stories along these lines were imperceptibly woven into polygamous wives' collective memories starting with the Bible. The Old Testament canonized jealousy between Sarah and Hagar and later between Leah and Rachel. Leah and Rachel's story began when Abraham's grandson Jacob left home to find a wife among his mother's people. Jacob saw Rachel, the younger daughter of his mother's brother, at a well tending her family's sheep. Isaac was smitten by Rachel, and, as it was written, "Jacob kissed Rachel, and lifted up his voice, and wept." In time, Jacob told Rachel's father Laban, "I will serve thee seven years for Rachel thy younger daughter" because, the Bible explained, "Jacob loved Rachel."

However, after seven years, Laban was not willing for Rachel to be married before her older sister Leah. As Laban explained, "It must not be done so in our country, to give the younger before the firstborn." So Jacob first married Leah, who was "tender eyed," but, according to the Bible, by comparison "Rachel was beautiful and well favoured." After promising to work seven more years, Jacob then married Rachel, and Jacob "loved also Rachel more than Leah."

Since Rachel was temporarily barren, Leah believed that bearing sons would please her husband Jacob, and she said, "Surely the Lord hath looked upon my affliction; now therefore my husband will love me." After bearing yet another son, Leah said, "Now this time will my husband be joined unto me, because I have borne him three sons." Leah continued to yearn for Jacob's love but was continuously second to Rachel. At one point, Leah implored callous Rachel to understand: "Is it a small matter that thou hast taken my husband?"

When Leah's son Reuben found "mandrakes in the field," a narcotic plant, and gave them to his mother, Rachel begged Leah for some. When Leah expressed her resentment at all that Rachel had already taken from her, Rachel suggested a trade: "Therefore he shall lie with thee tonight for thy son's mandrakes." When Jacob returned from the field that evening, Leah met him, and said, "Thou must come in unto me; for surely I have hired thee with my son's mandrakes." The story finished, "And he lay with her that night," and she conceived a fifth son, still hoping this would please Jacob. After bearing her sixth son, Leah hopefully said, "God hath endued me with a good dowry; now will my husband dwell with me, because I have born him six sons." In Leah and Rachel's story, the two wives competed for attention from their husband. Despite the older wife's accomplishments and devotion, the callous younger wife continuously won the husband's love.

Despite the competitive nature of polygamy and negative under-lying assumptions about other women interfering, nineteenth-century Mormon polygamous wives usually tried to get along with their hus-bands' other wives. But in reality, only a small portion of these wives may have personally benefited from the polygamous system by ignit-ing feminist ideals, although perhaps our postfeminist culture wishes they all did. For example, one Mormon woman recently wrote me this idyllic e-mail that explains her understanding of nineteenth-century polygamy—that it benefited women by providing career opportunities and female friendship:

> It worked just great because each day was something different that each wife was in charge of. And each wife was allowed to follow her dream as far as worldly ambitions went also. The other wives would pitch in to make it possible for each other to spend time on educa-tion or projects, etc. One became a doctor, one a teacher, one a singer, one a politician. Each carried their load, but they had an un-derstanding that allowed each to support the others in their per-sonal goals. Each of them became great in their own way—besides raising great families.

The e-mail's emphasis on the link between polygamy and female em-powerment reminds me of my first graduate school paper on the subject when the possibilities of polygamy seemed oh so alluring. But in reality, sister wives didn't always feel very sisterly, as the three wives discussed in the next chapter demonstrate.

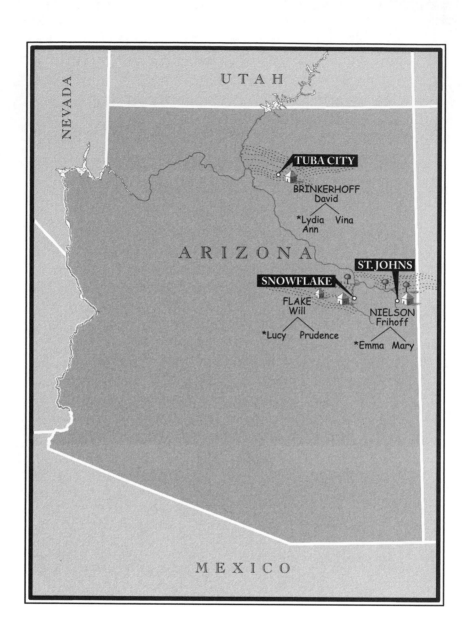

7

Many nights my pillow would be wet with grief

Lucy Flake's House: Snowflake, Arizona, about 1899

Near the foothills of the White Mountains, the Petrified Forest, and the Painted Desert, three southwestern settlers—*Lucy Flake, Lydia Ann Brinkerhoff,* and *Emma Nielson*—could have gathered around 1899 to describe how they felt about their relationships with their husbands' second wives. Lucy was twenty-six when her husband married eighteen-year-old Prudence; Lydia Ann (who lived in Tuba City, Arizona, 180 miles north) was thirty-one when her husband married sixteen-year-old Vina; and Emma (who lived in St. Johns, Arizona, fifty miles east) was twenty-eight when her husband married twenty-three-year-old Mary. None of the three first wives complained that the second wives had any character flaws, and at least two of the three made grand efforts to help the younger wives; yet, after the second marriages, all three first wives wrote of mental anguish and even physical pain that may have been related to polygamy. Two of the three felt so overwhelmed at times that they wanted to die, and the third died of a mystery illness at age fifty-seven. Although raising a frontier family was a lot of work in itself, their stories show that Mormon frontier wives who added the worry of triangular polygamous relations to their load sometimes took on an unhealthy burden.

The best place for the three to gather would have been at Lucy Flake's house in Snowflake, Arizona, a small farming town that Lucy and her husband had settled in 1878. For years, their four-room adobe home was the stopping place for strangers traveling through Snowflake, and court was even held there. Although Lucy doesn't say, the second wife Prudence probably lived there for many years, too. Lucy's frontier life was a busy one: she carded wool to make the family clothes, blankets, and mattresses; incubated chickens and sold their eggs; milked nine cows and raised ducks and pigs; kept the family garden; made seventeen pies for Christmas about a month before she died; and worked in the Relief Society as first counselor, often worried about the sick; and later traveled the region as president of the Primary, the Church's organization for children.

In 1858 at sixteen years old, Lucy married nineteen-year-old Will Flake who had come Utah via California where both his parents had died during his young teens. Will and Lucy settled outside Cedar City in Beaver near Lucy's widowed mother and "had verry little to keep house with but," she wrote, "we were just as happy as could be." They "loved each other and loved [their] home and felt truly thankfull." Lucy confided that early in the marriage the one thing on which she and Will were not united was prayer. Not having grown up with prayer, Will was not as religiously inclined as she was, and this was "somewhat of a trial" for her. From girlhood, she'd had special faith that her prayers would be answered, and they were. Lucy would "pleade with [Will] to pray in the Familey but he would not." When Church visitors asked if Will "tended prairs," he would say "no" and that "he was going to be religious when he got old." A few years later, Lucy got Will to pray for the first time, but until then, Lucy prayed on her own, especially in 1861 before their second baby died. She explained, "it seemed like my prairs did no good but still I kept trying to get my Hevenly Father to here me." The death of her two-month-old son who had been born healthy was the first great sorrow of her life.

Ten years later in 1868, when Lucy was twenty-six, "William concluded to take another Wife," and Lucy wrote that she was "quite willing." She traveled 200 miles by wagon with her husband Will and eighteen-year-old Prudence to Salt Lake so they could be sealed in the Endowment House. She briefly wrote, "9th of Oct Prudence Kartchner was sealed to [Will]. I was there."

In contrast to this brief factual note, Lucy expounded on the chance encounters she had in the Endowment House that day with Church Relief Society President Eliza R. Snow who asked her how she felt about living in polygamy. Lucy wrote, "Sister E R Snow asked me was I willing. Said yes. She asked, do you think you can live in that principle? I said am quite willing to try. My Mother and sister live in it and I think can do as much as them and besides I wanted my Husband to go into that principle before I was old because I think it right." President Snow told Lucy that her "reward would be great" because, Lucy wrote, "I was willing and she said Sister you never shall get old and she gave me a great blessing and every time she saw me that day she blest me." Lucy's confident reaction to

Snow's question was not unusual. According to Linda Wilcox DiSimone's study, when a new wife joined the family, the first wife often hid "her true feelings rather than let her jealousy or hurt show." Lucy also told Snow that she thought it "right" that her husband marry another wife while she, Lucy, was young. Curiously, Lucy did not want to be old when her husband took another wife, or perhaps she thought it not right for a husband to take a younger wife when he and his wife were old.

Lydia Ann also consented to plural marriage. Like Lucy's husband Will, Lydia Ann had also come to Utah via California. About 1870 also near Cedar City, she first noticed her husband-to-be David as he passed by her family home "on a load of hay." Lydia wrote, "I never knew just why, but I always took special notice of him wherever I saw him, for I really admired him and it seemed that as I grew older, my admiration grew. I decided that no other man would be my sweetheart but him, and for two years he really was."

They went for sleigh rides in the snow and were engaged to be married when, one Sunday, David suddenly broke off their relationship. Lydia Ann explained that after returning late one night from a dance, they were in

FIGURE 7.2 Lydia Ann and David Brinkerhoff family.

her house when her mother awakened and, not realizing that David was there, scolded her for not taking her sister to the dance with them. David "went away quite offended," and Lydia never told her mother how much pain her scolding had caused. The next Sunday, David told Lydia Ann that he "did not care to marry the whole family and 'we better quit.'" Lydia Ann wrote, "He took me home and left me broken-hearted, for we were then engaged to be married, and it was a very sacred affair with me. I couldn't understand why a few words from mother need to break into our affairs." She continued, "It was some time before David and I met again; in the meantime I had had several proposals for marriage, but there was only one for me."

In 1876, David and Lydia Ann renewed their "friendship," and David gave Lydia Ann ten dollars to buy her "wedding outfit," which she sewed herself. Taking the calico she'd bought, she "slipped off into the big pine trees behind brush and made [a dress and bonnet] by hand" because, even though her parents accepted her decision to marry David, she didn't want her mother to know that David had given her money. The couple left to be married, and her parents sent the two on their way "in an old wagon which had a board laid across the wagon-box for a seat with a quilt spread over that to make it a little more comfortable." Lydia Ann's mother said, "Well, David, you are getting the girl but not much with her." David replied, "That's all I'm after." After their wedding supper at David's brother's house, the newlyweds spent the night in Upper Kanab among the orange rocks, intermittently interrupted by the "cow bell" tied "under the wagon" by David's younger brother. Then, "for a tour," David and Lydia took a barrel of butter to sell in Salt Lake for David's mother, which took ten days, "and," she wrote, "we were happy."

Lydia Ann's husband David probably decided to marry a second wife after he was called as a bishop. She wrote what the other two southwestern women already knew, that "in those days a man was hardly considered eligible to be a bishop until he had more than one wife," and David had been a bishop for a couple of years before marrying a second wife. Church leaders had asked him to be a bishop the same time they asked him to move his family to Tuba City, Arizona. So ten days after Lydia Ann's fifth baby was born, the family made the trek over a river and "on over Lee's Back Bone, one of the worst roads on earth, and camped for the night." Her brother had helped them that far, but from there, Lydia drove one of the two teams, sitting "up on the spring seat," while David drove the other, and their boys "drove a small herd of cattle." The seventy-mile "tiresome journey" took ten days. In Tuba City, Lydia would confide, "I found myself an invalid with female trouble, brought on, no doubt, from overdoing myself while my babies were so young; I suffered greatly, but in time I rallied and was able to care for my family with a little extra help."

The extra help brought in for Lydia Ann's seventh baby was a hired girl who became David's second wife, Vina. Lydia Ann explained it this way: in January 1888, "my daughter Eliza Jane was born, a beautiful black-eyed girl. [Vina] was helping at our home at that time; with my consent, [David] decided to go to St. George and make her his wife. With my help in preparing her clothes, for she had no experience in that line, she was ready to take the trip with my husband." Lydia Ann's description emphasizes her motherly efforts to prepare Vina, along with Lydia Ann's humiliation as she watched the girl leave with her new clothes and with, as she wrote, "my husband."

When David and Vina returned from being married in St. George, Lydia Ann struggled to adjust. She evidently didn't want to cause trouble or show her sorrow, so she secretly grieved. She wrote, "I tried to be a mother and sister to her, but, oh, it was hard. Many nights my pillow would be wet with grief." She continued, "I had seven children when she came into the family, and had seven afterward," suggesting to the reader both the fatigue she must have felt and the toll childbearing had taken on her body. And then, after writing of her suffering and appealing to the reader to understand her loss, she attempted to explain the reason behind her suffering: "I was only human, though I knew that principle (Plural Marriage) had been revealed to the Prophet Joseph Smith and that it was true and sacred, it was almost more than I could endure; it came nearly taking my life."

In this statement, she encapsulates the internal conflict, the human complexity, and the religious sacrifice required of her. She did her best to be well-behaved, yet inside it was killing her. The way she describes it, a point of doctrine is weighed against a young mother losing her life. Lydia Ann may have been sincere in her scant words about the "true and sacred" nature of polygamy, and she could have been repeating what she heard at church. Jill Mulvay Derr believes that public testimonials on the truth of polygamy among Mormons "became so conventional and ritualized that one wonders to what extent women shared personal and not merely institutionalized feelings about the practice."

As for Lucy Flake, although she doesn't explicitly tie her own suffering to polygamy, her husband's comings and goings with Prudence are associated with Lucy's struggles with depression. Will and Prudence's movements are hard to detect because Lucy rarely mentions Prudence even though Lucy and Prudence lived in the same house or near each other. According to Lucy's grandson Chad J. Flake, "Lucy's not mentioning Prudence at family gatherings, church meetings, parties, and other such functions, leads one to feel that she largely ignored Prudence." Yet Prudence evidently had an effect on Lucy. One of the only times Lucy mentions Prudence was to write that Will "took Prudence with him to spend the summer in the fall they moved home." Afterward, Will left to work on the St. George Temple, and Lucy hardly got out of bed for four months and wrote that she was so sick that she "never washed dishes or swept the floor and felt so despondent it seemed it was hard work to live." Here she doesn't mention any physical symptoms but explains that she felt "despondent" and didn't want to live. She also wrote, "just as soon as I could walk around a little," Will and Prudence "moved on a ranch three miles from town." Lucy seems to feel neglected by them.

The third first wife in the trio, Emma Nielson, elaborated on the symptoms she associated with polygamy: the emotional weight, the confusion, and the insomnia. Emma kept a diary that expressed her day-to-day feelings about a second wife coming into the family. In February 1887 when Emma was twenty-eight, three weeks after the birth of her fourth baby, her husband Frihoff married twenty-three-year-old Mary, and then early that summer left with Mary to settle land in St. Johns, Arizona. Intelligent and even-tempered Emma stayed in St. George with her four children, including the new baby. Perhaps she and Frihoff, or FG as she sometimes called him, saw that he might be arrested for polygamy if he stayed in St. George, because she wrote of the federal marshals who were prowling the town. Perhaps Emma's new baby was too delicate to travel. Perhaps her husband needed to plant that spring. Whatever the reason, she wouldn't see her husband again for seven months and truly missed him even though she had family and friends in St. George.

While Emma stayed in St. George, she wrote that her new baby became very ill with "tiphoid fever," and this was only one example of the kind of trouble she faced alone—even though neighbors tried to help—while her husband was gone. For weeks, she worked through the night with her baby, trying various medicines from the doctor, and calling for nearby Church men to come and bless the child. She also received visits from her bishop and other Church members who spent time reviewing her circumstances, offering aid, support, and "anything [she] wished." They were "indeed very good to" her, and her baby, Vera, survived. During this time, her husband wrote her letters and sent money.

But the goodness of her neighbors and even close friends could not substitute for her husband, FG. One night, she had a delightful supper with her friend Libbie when "for a short time" they would "forget all earthly cares." But later that lonely night, she longed as much as ever for her husband and questioned whether the separation that polygamy brought made sense. She wrote in her diary that after getting her "precious little ones in bed," she "took a walk in the moonlight all the while wondering where [her] precious F G was." She realized that "a sweet response would be" that he was "in Arizona doing his duty" to his other family, but then, she admitted, she "often" wondered if he was "doing his duty to his family in St George"—her family. She needed his help: "How pleased I would be if he would step in [and] administer to our wants, soothe the cries of my four little ones and do a fathers part." Her four little children, aged seven and under, also missed him: "they have looked forward to the time (so long) that they would see their Pa that they begin to think they have no Pa."

She wrote more on that night: "I feel heart broken myself. My heart is so sore and who in all this world can heal it except my dear F. G.? One word from his precious lips at this moment could do it. I love him as I do my own life, and when can I linger by his side as I once used to?" Then she appealed to God to help her: "O Lord give me strength to bare the trials that daily beset my pathway. My life thus far has been indeed rain and sunshine for which I thank Thee. I feel thankful that I am numbered among those that are tried even to the very core of my heart." Here Emma seems to suggest that the cross she's taken up for her religion is like a refiner's fire.

Later that year in September 1887, Emma and her four children finally started their sixteen-day journey, mostly by train, to reach her husband and his other wife in Ramah, New Mexico. How she longed to be with her husband again, and now she was on her way. When she finally arrived in Ramah, "many" came to see her that night, she had a "splendid time" at a ball a week later, she spent pleasant time with the other wife Mary, and finally nine days after arriving was reunited with her husband: "In the evening our dear husband came." Of her reunion with Frihoff, she wrote, "we was indeed pleased to embrace each other once more, and the dear children was so delighted." The next day, she "spent most of the day" with her husband, "conversing upon passed experiences, in joy and in sorrow, prosperity, and adversity." She also wrote that, after spending time with pregnant Mary, she had decided that FG belonged to both of them.

But over the next two months, October through December 1887, Emma started suffering from insomnia. Frihoff was evidently with Mary on the land he was likely settling in Sunset, Arizona, and Emma stayed in Ramah where they had a mail contract. Emma was trying hard to stay positive but again didn't think it right that she was alone with her sick children in a freezing cold house. Her "little Libbie" was sick, and Emma again had "no husband to comfort" her: "how often I am left alone with my little sick children." Her house was "very cold and uncomfortable," and on December 14, she wrote that everything in the house was frozen "solid."

During the early morning of her twenty-ninth birthday, she wrote, "sit up most of night writing in diary, letters, sewing, could not sleep my head pained me very bad." A month later in December, she revealed that she had had "trials almost unbearable" but, again having called on God to help her, she felt that "with the aid of a Supreme Being," she had "weathered the worst" and hoped to "remain firm and faithful until" she reached "the other shore." Four days later, she acknowledged that she had risen at 4 a.m. and was "severely tried with polygamy." She once again called on "Father in Heaven" to "help" her "bare with trials" and, she wrote, "if it is right I should be bore down with sorrow through this principle I am willing to stand it."

Emma used her diary to coach herself and weigh the complexities of her situation. Emma wrote, "I have lived in the order of Celestial marriage for one year and am thankful I have this privilege. I love my husbands wife and have taken comfort with her. She is a good girl and I know the Lord will bless her and myself if we are faithful. I feel to thank the Lord for the comfort I received at his hands. He is indeed merciful unto his children." Sometimes Emma called the other wife Mary, and sometimes she called her "my husbands wife." When Mary went into labor that month, Emma was called to assist her "husbands wife." Emma "worked very hard with her all night," and at 10 a.m. a nine-pound boy was born. Emma washed and dressed the baby and helped Mary get "fixed comfortable." Frihoff was not with them, so Emma wrote a letter to Frihoff and Mary's mother. At 4 a.m. the next morning, Emma attended to Mary and the baby, and she continued to visit Mary "twice a day." On December 26, Frihoff returned from Arizona, and Emma wrote, "Mary is doing well."

But sadly the baby died. On New Year's Eve, Emma went to a party and "danced until twelve o clock." Before retiring she prepared her "childrens New Years gifts." On New Year's Day, she was with Mary most of the day, and all seemed well, but then the baby started having trouble. On January 2, Emma went again at 4 a.m. to find that the baby had "cramping spells." They called "the elders" to administer to the baby. Emma tried soaking his feet, putting onion drafts on him, and administering tincture of lobelia and oil. At midnight the baby seemed to be resting and nursed well, but just "after day light," Emma wrote, "his little spirit takes flight to a better world he passed peacefully away." Emma could "see the death pang is in its fathers and mothers brest," but, she wrote, "Mary takes the loss of her little one very good." Emma made burial clothes for the baby: "it is layed away very neat and plain." Emma again wrote Mary's mother.

Emma continued to help, and Frihoff perhaps stayed nights with Mary, who was probably alone, and bonded with her in their mutual sorrow. On January 20, Emma "attended Mary's breast"—since Mary no longer had a baby to nurse, her breasts may have been full, engorged, and sore. That same night, Emma wrote, "I go to bed early do not feel well, had a very restless night." On January 24, Emma wrote that she was "borne down with trials but with the aid of my Heavenly Parrent I hope to surmount them."

A week later at a Relief Society meeting, Emma got encouragement from one of the speakers. One of the counselors talked to the sisters about the trials she had endured since being one of the first settlers and also having "been tried in poverty, polygamy, and being deprived of her husband" while he was a missionary away from home. The Relief Society counselor told the group that "having passed through it all she was thankful she had remained firm and faithful to the cause she had espoused and still desired to progress in the Kingdom of God." Emma wrote that the woman "spoke very effecting, and encourageing to the sisters." The next day, Emma made a "supper" for Mary's wedding anniversary (and her son's birthday), but that night again she had a "severe pain" in her "head and heart" and "did not sleep any all night."

Lucy also suffered from chronic headaches, perhaps migraines. She sometimes noted symptoms such as these in her diary: "sick head ache," "pain in my sholders and back," and "sick to my stumick and dizzy could hardly open my eyes and such a head ache." Sometimes while visiting her close friend Mary J. West, the two friends would go upstairs to talk, pray together, and encourage each other: "I put my hands on her head and blessed her and she blest me." At times, Lucy must have felt anxiety over her estranged relationship with Prudence and her four daughters, as well. In 1896 when Prudence died at age forty-six, she left behind four daughters who evidently didn't like Lucy. Chad J. Flake explains: "After the death of their mother, Prudence's four daughters refused to move to the ranch if Lucy were going to live there also. So Lucy remained in town for the first month of the summer. A reconciliation seems to have been accomplished since she did move to the farm later in the year, but both families continued to have separate homes in town, and it is doubtful that the girls spent another summer on the ranch as long as Lucy lived. They were, however, finally included in family gatherings such as that of the Christmas of 1897." The breach that had occurred between Lucy and Prudence's family must have been not only personally disappointing to Lucy but also socially embarrassing to her in Snowflake.

If these three southwestern women actually had met in 1899, within the year Lucy would be dead. On December 9, 1899 at age fifty-seven, Lucy Flake "took sick," but by Christmastime, she had gained some strength and decided to have Christmas dinner for the family at her house. On December 23, she made pies, cooked beets, "done up work and finished Joel mittens"—she concluded her entry by writing, "I think that is good for a person that is called sick." Right after Christmas, Lucy wrote of the "butifull Old Folks dinner" she attended with "Brother Flake," the music, the speeches, and the "very plesant time" they had before going to the theater. Then on January 27, 1900, Lucy died. Her grandson Chad J. Flake explains, "The exact nature of [her] illness is not known." He then states that those who've read her diary have suggested that her death resulted from a combination of things: hard work, the rigors of the frontier, and loneliness; the loss of her adult son Charles who was shot by an outlaw; the "loss of the ministration" of her close friend Mary J. West who moved to Salt Lake; and "her chronic headaches and other health problems." Most of these explanations suggest that, along with hard work, Lucy may have suffered from depression.

Emma also worked to keep depression at bay mostly by spending time with her family, being sensitive to nature, and counting on God to sustain her. She wrote of when she went walking in the fields with Frihoff and when she helped him plant potatoes. On a day that was "quite stormy," she wrote, "Take a walk with my husband into the field" where he had been "very buisy putting in a crop." She continued by writing that a rainbow looked "lovely in the east" and that nature was "slowly decking herself with a lovely robe of green." A few days later, she accompanied her husband to Arizona, but a week later, she wrote again that she had "much work and duties" and "cares" on her mind, and again she was relying on God to help her: "at times it seems almost impossible for me to bear up under the trials that daily beset my path, but by being humble and prayerful the Lord is able to strengthen me to war successfully against the opposing power." Here she sounded like Angelina, who felt she needed to fight off bad spirits.

Lucy, Lydia Ann, and Emma could have all commented that this was the nature of their lives: hard work every day caring for their children, their house, their animals, and their garden; some encouraging moments, accompanied by inevitable feelings of loneliness, followed by prayers to overcome bad thoughts about polygamy and other trials. Emma wrote as much: "I devote ten hours to the comfort of home and family, the remaining four I spend in literature, improving my own mind and that of my children. I am at present thirty two and feel broke down with the hardships of a frontier life in Arizona and New Mexico. I do not feel discouraged but desire to persevere in all that is noble and good that I may win the prize I have set out for." Emma was determined, as in the New Testament Paul's race analogy, to win eternal life.

Emma also admitted her realization that all things in life could be disappointing, save her relationship with God: "I have one source of enjoyment that I can always rely upon and that is the companionship of my Father in Heaven. I find him always a true friend." Through Him, she must have maintained a sense that she was beloved. Similarly, Lucy wrote that at times she was so "lonely" she could hardly "stand it," if not for prayer: "if it was not for the consolation we get in prair we could not stand our trials but our Hevenly Father is so merciful we dont have to call on him in vain." From the time she helped settle Snowflake until her death, Lucy's Church work brought her great satisfaction. Hopefully, Lucy passed away peacefully, remembering Eliza R. Snow's blessing that she would "never grow old."

During midlife, both Lydia Ann and Emma ended up living in their respective small towns taking care of mail contracts, while their husbands and their second wives mostly lived on the family farms that were about thirty miles outside of town. In town, Lydia Ann took in boarders, did laundry for hotels, sold vegetables from the farm, and took care of the mail. Emma sometimes submitted a piece of writing to the *Woman's Exponent*, and she "registered as a student in the Bryant & Straton Correspondence Business College Buffalo, New York." Emma's last lines before giving up diary writing were, "I feel that my Father in Heaven has a hand over me and my family for good. [M]y joys and sorrow have not been few. But I look a head to the time if I prove faithful when our sorrow

and pains will be no more." Her dream for the next world was to be pain-
and sorrow-free—and she seemed to feel that she deserved that.

In later years, both Lydia Ann and Emma independently moved without
their husbands to Mesa, Arizona. There, in 1920 at age sixty-five, Emma
was probably with some of her adult children when she suddenly died of
acute endocarditis that was likely caused by a staph infection that attacked
the smooth interior lining of her heart. As for Lydia Ann, after moving to
Mesa, she ended up caring for her husband David "like he was a child"
after he had a leg amputated from diabetes and then suffered from "pleu-
risy." Lydia Ann wrote that David said to her, "I don't know how I'll ever
repay you for this." She replied that she "didn't expect pay in this world," a
confirmation of her belief that they would continue to be married in the
next life where she thought he could make it up to her. After David died,
in 1936 Lydia Ann wrote that she and her widowed daughter were "happily living" in their "little home" at 119 South Sirrine Street, only a half
mile from the Mormon Temple where Lydia loved to do volunteer work. In
1944 in Mesa, Lydia Ann died at age eighty-seven.

Lucy, Lydia Ann, and Emma sacrificed in the holy way that Christ sacrificed, suffering physical pain and emotional torment while living as perfectly as they could, seemingly suffering for no wrong they had done.
They sensed that they were trampled on, and they cried out to God to raise
them up again. They felt the weight of the greatest commandment "to love
your neighbor"—those second wives—"as yourself," and at the same time,
they ultimately didn't seem to believe that polygamy was a fair rendition of
that commandment. It seemed self-defeating. It seemed to spoil something
good. As former presidential candidate John Edwards's late wife, Elizabeth,
much more recently explained after her husband had an extramarital
affair, "Putting together a home and putting together a family, developing
a family purpose and goal, that's all really hard. And when anyone steps in
to disrupt that, to basically take some for themselves without having put in
the work—it's disturbing." Lucy, Lydia Ann, and Emma seemed to ask,
Why should we be asked to give to the second wife our primary joy as
though forfeiting the love of our husbands and the stability of our homes
were a Godly sacrifice? And furthermore, they wondered, should a commandment of God be so excruciating that it threatens the health of our
minds and bodies?

So without trying to convince their readers that they advocated polygamy, these three women manifested their faith that if they could only
get a little further, they might understand better.

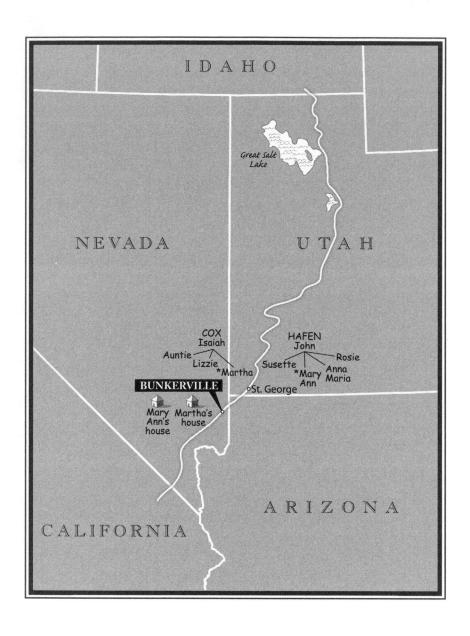

IDAHO

Great Salt
Lake

NEVADA

UTAH

COX
Isaiah
Auntie
Lizzie
*Martha

HAFEN
John
Rosie
Susette
*Mary
Ann
Anna
Maria

BUNKERVILLE

St. George

Mary
Ann's
house

Martha's
house

ARIZONA

CALIFORNIA

8

I could not say that I loved the man as lovers love

Mary Ann Hafen's House: Bunkerville, Nevada, about 1900

In 1900, Utah's largest southern town was St. George. Northwest lay tiny, abundant Santa Clara. To the southwest, just forty-five miles over the Nevada border, was tiny, windy Bunkerville. In 1900, Bunkerville was home to second wives *Mary Ann Hafen* (who emigrated from Switzerland as a girl) and *Martha Cox* (whose family hailed from Kentucky). In a small place like that, they surely knew each other. Besides, Mary Ann was fifty-six years old, and Martha was fifty-eight; when they were girls, both their families had moved south, one year apart; both remembered the well-dressed Miss Romney who had come from Salt Lake to teach at their school; in their late teens, both married older men who were already married; both lived in Santa Clara and St. George for most of their married lives; and both were now in Bunkerville raising their youngest children on their own. Also, for a long time now, they'd both lived more like widows than married women—well, actually Martha *was* a widow, but she barely noticed. Neither of them had ever really loved their husbands and gradually felt almost estranged from them. Martha, in particular, felt more married to her husbands' other wives than to her husband.

Whether Martha was walking to Mary Ann's house or elsewhere in town, she'd see that Bunkerville was "rather inviting" in the late afternoon light with its abundant cottonwood trees along the Virgin River and the town's canals. Martha could have found Mary Ann's adobe house on a large lot with five or six almond trees, three mulberry trees, grapevines, and a large vegetable garden.

In 1891, when Mary Ann's husband first moved her and her children from Santa Clara to the adobe house in Bunkerville, the house had dirt

FIGURE 8.2 Second wife Mary
Ann Hafen.

FIGURE 8.3 Mary Ann's husband,
John Hafen.

floors and a dirt roof. Her husband soon left but promised to return to up-
grade the house. He did, over many years, and with Herculean help from
Mary Ann's oldest son, the house eventually had a wood floor, a shingle
roof, and second-story bedrooms that were accessed from an outside lad-
der. Most recently, her husband had journeyed down from Santa Clara to
help her oldest son add the kitchen and cool cellar she had longed for. It
made her house more comfortable for her four children, ages six to
eighteen, who were still living at home.

Mary Ann's probable sometime visitor, Martha Cox, was curious by
nature. She loved to meet people, to "interview" them, and to find out
their histories. When Martha and her siblings were children, her mother
had rarely gone to church or socialized because she couldn't get all her
children ready at once, and, Martha later surmised, because her mother
was embarrassed about her clothing. Martha was just the opposite—she
didn't care what other people thought. An improvement in her social ma-
turity came in her midteens when she joined the church choir led by a
music professor who was sent to St. George to teach singing. While singing, she learned the "beauty and sweetness" of Mormon hymns and was
able to associate with some of "the best people of St. George." Singing also
"brought [her] out to meeting every Sunday," which she saw as "another
advantage."

By 1900, Martha Cox was living in Bunkerville with her daughter, who
was raising her own two teenage daughters. Since Martha had been forced

to split from her two "sister wives" (as she once called them), life had not been the same. The three wives and their children had once lived "one of the most harmonious portraits" of polygamy ever penned, but that was before federal Marshals Armstrong and McGeary had started prowling around St. George and Santa Clara hoping to ferret out polygamous families and send the husbands to jail.

Mary Ann knew them, too. Oh yes, she wrote, "we hated the sound of their names."

In 1888, threat of prosecution and jail time had convinced Martha's husband to marry a fourth wife and leave for Mexico, which turned out to be a failed idea, and the couple eventually returned. But, in the meantime, the original three sister wives had to split up and strike out on their own. Starting in 1881, their break up "was the beginning of Martha's wanderings as a migratory school teacher on the Mormon frontier," and in 1900 she was teaching school in Bunkerville.

As for Mary Ann, she had a distant relationship with her husband John Hafen. He was still a bishop in Santa Clara and would be for a total of twenty-eight years. He lived there with his first wife Susette and their eighteen-year-old son. The 1900 census listed him as a "general merchant." His second and third wives, including Mary Ann, lived in Bunkerville. His fourth wife, Mary Ann's widowed sister Rosie, lived in Santa Clara. In 1891, after eighteen years of marriage, Mary Ann and John had decided, as she diplomatically wrote, that "it would be best" for Mary Ann to take her "young family" to Bunkerville "where there was more and cheaper land." Mary Ann probably didn't mind leaving John and Susette behind; Susette had never been very cordial, but Mary Ann hated to leave her parents, family, and friends. When Mary Ann's family arrived in Bunkerville, they were greeted and fed by the third wife. Mary Ann's oldest son was there, too, because he had been helping the third wife.

In the "first years" when they were "just getting started" in Bunkerville, Mary Ann's husband had come down from Santa Clara "frequently" and "helped [them] a good deal." But as time went on, "he had his hands full taking care of his other families," so she cared "for her seven children mostly by [her]self." John had provided them with "a house, lot, and land and furnished some supplies," and made some improvements, but they were on their own now. In 1900, Mary Ann was renting out her twenty-five-acre farm up the road—the 1900 census listed her as a "landlord." During some years, she and her children used the farm to grow cotton and sorghum cane that she could exchange at mills for cloth and sorghum sweetener. Mary Ann sewed the family's clothing on the White sewing machine she saved for. They preserved peaches and green tomatoes and ate from their large garden, and they kept a couple of pigs, a cow, and some chickens.

Both Martha and Mary Ann would admit that they'd never been close to their husbands. For example, from the beginning Mary Ann hadn't really wanted to marry John Hafen, even though her parents considered him a "fine man." So she married someone else first. She explained it this way in her autobiography. In 1874, when she was of marriageable age, "the law of Plural Marriage was being practiced in the Church, and the authorities recommended that the men who were able to provide for more than one family should marry again. In this way more persons in the spirit world would have the opportunity to come to this earth and have bodies." Polygamy "would also build up the Church and the country faster." Mary Ann wrote that "many did not want to go into polygamy, but felt that it was their religious duty to do so when advised by the Church authorities."

As a teen, Mary Ann explained, she had taken "interest in parties, dances and different kinds of fun" and "naturally" had "young men callers," but "none of them appealed" to her as much as her uncle by marriage (to her father's sister) John Reber. In Switzerland, her Uncle John Reber had been the first in their family to find the Mormon missionaries and get baptized. She wrote, "He was much older than I, was married to my father's sister, and had four children. But he was kind and jolly and everybody liked him." A second married man was interested in her, too: John Hafen. She explained, "John Hafen called and took me to several dances. John Reber did not dance, so I had not been out much with him, but when he asked me to marry him I was ready to say yes."

Martha Cox would have understood why Mary Ann had been drawn more strongly to a mature man. When Martha was of marriageable age, she didn't like the boys her age because they seemed too interested in the wine outside the dance hall. The boy she liked the most drank too much, she thought. He had "agreeable manners" and "liked to dance and have a good time," but she decided he might make her life miserable. So she considered polygamy, which by this time was more likely to mean marriage to an older man. Martha had "studied out" the pros and cons of polygamy and prayed about it. She "knew the principle of plural marriage to be correct, to be the highest, holiest order of marriage." She felt that entering it was risky, in a way, because it was a harder law to live than monogamy, and she might, like the fear a nun might feel, "fail to live the holy life required and lose the blessings offered." But she eventually decided that she would go into polygamy.

Again, Mary Ann felt the same. At nineteen, it hadn't been hard for her to decide to marry her Uncle John Reber. She explained that his wife was kind, too: "his wife, Aunt Barbara, helped me make my wedding outfit, a simple dress of blue material with little pink flowers and a white petticoat." In July 1873, she and her uncle set out in a wagon, loaded down with dried peaches "for the northern brewery," headed for Salt Lake City to be married in the Endowment House. Mary Ann said that their "ten days of travel to Salt Lake were happy ones," and that it was "interesting to see so much country and the northern towns." She wrote, "In ten days more we were back again in Santa Clara, happy and satisfied with our lot."

The day after returning from their wedding trip, however, tragedy struck. Martha Cox certainly would have heard about this event when it had happened. Mary Ann wrote, "My husband took me and Aunt Barbara and her four children for a ride down to the field to see how the crops looked." On the way back, John was killed: "One of the horses caught its bridle under the wagon tongue, pulled off the bridle, and started running. I jumped off; so did Aunt Barbara and the children. The frightened horses turned down a lane, ran over a woodpile, threw my husband under the wagon, where two wheels ran over him. . . . This was a sad finish to my honeymoon, and I went back to live with mother and father." Her parents told her that times were hard and that she should try to remarry.

Within three months, she did—this time to John Hafen, who "came courting" again. Like her, he had also emigrated with his family from Switzerland. By now, he had already been married twelve years to his first wife Susette. Mary Ann explained, "When John asked me to marry him, I hesitated at first. But my parents urged me to consent, saying what a fine man he was and that by waiting I would probably do worse." There was a major problem, though: "Susette was opposed to his marrying again, but the authorities advised him to do so anyway, saying that she would be reconciled." Mary Ann wrote, "I did not like to marry him under those circumstances, but being urged on by him and my parents, I consented."

She again traveled to Salt Lake, to marry John Hafen this time. But, Mary Ann wrote, the "trip seemed different from the first one" because she wasn't happy. "I cried when I left home, and cried often all the way up and back. John was kind to me and did everything he could to comfort and please me, but somehow I was not happy." Probably still mourning her first husband's death, she also felt sort of "indifferent" toward John Hafen.

When they returned from Salt Lake, they "set up housekeeping" in a "two-room adobe house that had belonged to his father." John stayed one night with Mary Ann and one night with Susette, and they "got along pretty well at first." But perhaps like the original Mormon first wife, Emma Smith, Susette made steps toward polygamy only to regress. Mary Ann explained, "Susette seemed unable to reconcile herself to my coming into the family," and "gradually [John] began to neglect me." Fed up, Mary Ann decided she could not put up with John's unequal treatment. She "doubted whether it was right," but she told him that "if he could not treat" her more fairly, she "would leave him."

John was probably caught between his two wives—he obviously could not please them both. Susette didn't want him to give Mary Ann more attention. Mary Ann insisted that if he didn't give her more attention she would leave. John would later write that he suffered in polygamy, too. Before he died, he said, "I complied with the celestial law of plural marriage in obedience to the Church authorities and because the command was divinely inspired. It cost me much heartache and sorrow and I have shed many tears over it." Mary Ann had given him an ultimatum, and she was suffering for it. For at least three days afterward, he didn't see her. By then, she was likely pregnant with her first baby. To make the serious decision about what was right for her, she humbly fasted for three days and prayed and experienced a small miracle. During the third night, she awakened to find that "the indifference and bitterness [toward John] had gone from [her] heart." She wrote, "I loved him and forgave him for his neglect."

The next morning, she was anxious to tell John how she felt. She finished her morning work and went "uptown" to find him. He was talking to some neighbors, likely not as concerned as she was about their conflict. She told him about what had happened in the night and said she "would stay with him if he would treat her right. He promised to do so, and after that," she wrote, "for several years we lived happy."

Martha Cox would have been curious to learn that Mary Ann's parents had urged her to go into polygamy, because Martha's family had the opposite reaction—they did *not* want her to become a polygamous wife: "My decision to marry into a plural family tried my family, all of them, and in giving the trial I was sorely tried." For Martha, entering polygamy was not so much about the man she was marrying—she rarely mentioned him—

but more about what she saw as a divine lifestyle. Despite her parents' opposition, she made up her mind after praying deeply: "If the Lord would have manifested in answer to my sleepless nights of prayer that the principle of plural marriage was wrong and was not the will of Heaven that I should enter it, I felt I should be happy." But she explained that once she moved in that direction, she felt she should keep going: "Having decided to enter this order it seemed I had passed the Rubicon, I could not go back. Though I fain would have done so rather than incur the hatred of my family."

In her writing, Martha pitted herself against those who disapproved of polygamy, just as the Church pitted itself against outsiders who railed against polygamy. Writing her autobiography as an older woman, she dramatized and justified the significant choice she made. Martha found that her community respected monogamous, romantic love, but she, a maverick, became a champion of polygamy. She was on God's side. When Martha told her family her final decision to become a polygamous wife, "the storm broke upon my head," she wrote. "It was not a marriage of love, they claimed, and in saying so they struck me a blow. For I could not say that I really loved the man as lovers love, though I loved his wives and the spirit of their home. I could not assure my family that my marriage was gotten solely up on the foundation of love for man." Martha said she relied on her strong feeling that God wanted her to take this path: "The fact was I had asked the Lord to lead me in the right way for my best good and the way to fit me for a place in His kingdom. He had told me how to go and I must follow in the path He dictated, and that's all there was to it." Perhaps her polygamous marriage arrangement *was* her best option since she didn't seem inclined to a traditional monogamous life with a husband—she preferred being married to the other wives.

Martha and Mary Ann and other wives who weren't close to their husbands emphasized their independence, both as an advantage and disadvantage. Mary Ann wrote, "I did not want to be a burden on my husband, but tried with my family to be self-supporting." Martha and Mary Ann seemed like the fulfillment of an Isaiah prophecy found in the Old Testament, which predicted that at some future date "seven women" would "take hold of one man," saying, "We will eat our own bread, and wear our own apparel: only let us be called by thy name, to take away our reproach." Martha "could not assure her family" that her marriage was "gotten solely up on the foundation of love for man"—rather, she "loved his wives and the spirit of their home," and she saw the chance to be a third wife there as a desirable life, even though they were poor.

In her autobiography, Martha never called her husband by his full name, and he was so seldom mentioned that a reader would find it difficult to determine when her husband was actually living in the same house. Martha only mentioned his 1896 death of a heart attack because it helped explain why her bishop was reluctant to let her son go on a mission. When Martha described her wedding trip to Salt Lake, she wrote nothing about her husband except that they stayed with some of his old friends along the way, whom she described in detail. And like Lucy Flake, Martha wrote that she met a formidable women's leader, Bathsheba Smith, in the old Endowment House and that Smith had remembered Martha's mother.

Before Martha married in 1869, she'd thought polygamy to be "the leading principle among the L.D.S," so after becoming a polygamous wife, she was surprised to learn that the general community disapproved of polygamy. After realizing this, she "took a survey" in her mind and could locate "very few men, not one in fifty of the whole city who had entered it at all." A friend told Martha, "it is all very well for those girls who cannot very well get good young men for husbands to take married men," but the friend felt that there were young men that Martha "could have gotten." Her former friend "cold-shouldered" Martha and made "uncomplimentary remarks." Martha retreated into her polygamous family and took solace there.

She began to learn the family's routine: "perfect obedience" and to "speak no words when angry." She learned to get up at five, which she found very difficult. At nine at night, the curfew "sounded," and she would "toss sleeplessly there until near the middle of the night." She learned that the family didn't eat much meat, drink tea, or use salt in their salt-risen bread. Martha would explain that the first year of her married life gave her "more experience in the duties of life" than she ever had before.

At their residence, the 1880 census taker found Isaiah Cox (age forty-three) and three wives—Henny (forty-four), Elizabeth (thirty-two), and Martha (twenty-eight)—and fourteen children between the ages of one and twenty-one. Three of the four adults—Isaiah, Elizabeth, and Martha—descended from Kentucky stock.

Martha came to love living there! The three wives' work was "so systemized and so well ordered" that they could "with ease do a great deal." First thing in the morning, one would "superintend the cooking and kitchen work," one would "make the beds and sweep," and another would "comb and wash all the children." At 7:30, they all sat down to breakfast.

FIGURE 8.4 Third wife Martha Cox (right)
and her two sister wives.

The second wife was the "dressmaker," the "best saleswoman," and "generally did most of the buying, especially the shoes" because she was "a good judge of leather." The first wife did all the mending and darning, but never ironed—Martha did most of that. On wash day, "all hands were employed" except the cook. The three wives usually never went out together, even to church, because "one always stayed home and took care of the children and the house." They even shared baby clothes and maternity clothes and helped each other during childbirth.

Even after they split up in 1881, another wife took Martha's little girl so Martha would be free to teach school in another town. Their separation, however, was trying to both Martha and her daughter, and she wasn't sure she had done the right thing.

Martha believed in hard work and that God would make up the rest. During a low financial point after her husband had made a bad investment, the family had to pitch in to pay back the debt. Martha took her teacher pay in produce to help feed the family. Two of their sons had to miss two years of school to "freight ore" to help pay back the debt. And during this time, Martha wrote of experiencing children-of-Israel-like miracles. On Saturday night, the mothers mended, washed, and ironed the children's clothes for Sunday morning church. Martha wrote, "The Lord blessed our clothes as he did those of ancient Israel and we bought few during this trying period." Alluding to the sweet manna that God provided the children of Israel, Martha wrote that their "bread and gravy, the main stock in hand, tasted sweet" to them. In addition, they had "planted an orchard and a vineyard" that both "yielded good returns" in fresh fruit, and fruit to dry and can for the winter. In retrospect, she felt that "the Lord was good to leave us in our poverty that we might learn to cleave together."

While writing her autobiography late in life, Martha saved her sweetest words for her sister wives. She imagined a blissful eternity as one in which she would be reunited with "the two best women in the world." She wrote of many times when they came to her aid. When Martha was newly married and trying to get a job as a schoolteacher in St. George, she found that she wasn't well qualified enough and did not have enough experience. One student's mother told Martha that she had "married into a poor family," that she was "no better than the other wives," that she should go home and help them, and not be "setting [her]self up as a school teacher." When Martha found road blocks at every turn, her sister wives came up with the idea to use a large unfinished room at their house for a school. Their husband was away, and the room didn't yet have floors or windows, but the lumber was there. "With the children's help," they fit together the floor. Then one sister wife got five dollars in the mail and used it to put in windows. They used "boards and blocks" to arrange seats, and "the front yard was given over to the children for a play ground."

This home school jump-started Martha's career. It wouldn't be long until she was contacted by the Trustees, who said that she was required to release her pupils so they could attend their correct schools. While considering if she should acquiesce, she received a call to start right away as a teacher of the "4th Ward" school, and she took it. One time a principal would not supply a blackboard for her classroom, and one of her sister wives suggested that they take their big bread board, paint it black, and use it for a blackboard. Martha was able to use this blackboard for many years, and it reminded her of how much she loved her sister wives.

In fact, when imagining eternity, she left her husband out altogether. Instead, she wrote of her sister wives: "we three who loved each other more than sisters, children of one mother love, will go hand in hand together down through all eternity." In another place, she expressed the same sentiment, writing that "through all eternity" she would "go hand in hand with those two dear women." To really enjoy polygamy, it seemed, none of them could be holding hands with the husband.

Martha Cox may have succeeded at polygamy because she loved her two sister wives more than she loved her husband. Martha had a soft spot for her husband's first wife, "Auntie," who had "buried her last three babies." After their deaths, Auntie took the other wives' babies "to her bosom" and treated them as her own. Martha acknowledged the sacrifices that Auntie must have made when her husband married additional wives. Martha told Auntie that she was sure that "many times she had been grieved and even felt heart broken under her trials of plural marriage and poverty." Auntie looked Martha "squarely in the face" and said, "Whenever my heart comes between me and my Father's work it will have to break." Like many religious women, she subordinated herself to God's work, and she felt polygamy was exactly that.

It wasn't that Martha didn't have any respect for her husband Isaiah. She considered him "the father of the house" and "a good workman." He worked "from seven to seven by the clock." But Martha also told of his lapses in judgment. For example, in 1876 when they were quite poor, he borrowed $700 "to assist in the opening of the Grand Gulch mine." The "manager" of the mine left with all the money, and the Cox family was left with the debt, which was "in those times . . . a large sum of money." Another time, after a failed trip to Mexico, he made the decision to sell the family farm that Martha had "scraped and schemed to buy in Muddy Valley." Martha wrote that she used her best "reasoning power" to convince him to "let his sons have a chance" at the land, but he decided otherwise.

Martha herself seemed to have a whimsical way of making decisions. She found she could move from place to place and get a job as a school-teacher. With feistiness, she would convince administrators to try her out. One time a principal disappointed her when he said the school where she was supposed to teach wasn't finished yet, and she convinced him that she could teach outside "under the beautiful cottonwood trees by the side of the lovely clear stream." At one point, she went and lived in Mexico for ten years, but more often she lived in a place for a year or two. In 1893, while she was living in Bunkerville, she felt badly for the Church leader who was going from door to door to solicit financial contributions for a chapel. She impetuously told him she'd contribute "a month's wages" toward the new building.

Around 1920, Martha moved to Salt Lake City where she worked in the Temple. From age seventeen to sixty-nine, she'd "taught every year but two." During those two years, her sister wife Lizzie's health had been "poor and the home work was so heavy" that she decided to labor more at home. At age seventy-seven in Salt Lake, she briefly taught English at Pioneer Stake's Mexican branch. In 1932 at age eighty, she died in Salt

Lake. Historian Lavina Fielding Anderson wrote of her, "she was the salt of the earth, and she seasoned it."

Unlike Martha, after 1891 Mary Ann Hafen stayed in one place—Bunkerville. Besides work and church, she made education and music a priority for her children. She didn't make her children miss school to work in the fields or watch babies. While the children were at school, she sometimes "picked cotton on shares" to earn money to buy the children clothes. She would take her "baby to the fields" and "never took the children out of school if it could possibly be avoided." Her girls all played the guitar and "the town organ," and two of her boys played violin for town dances. With nine children, her house became a "gathering place for the young people of the town," and "almost every Sunday night," she wrote, "they would gather around our front doorstep and sing songs while one of my girls played accompaniment on the guitar."

When her children reached high school, they had to go away to school, and she missed them. In 1910, she and her youngest son moved in with her daughter Lovina's family for a while, but then moved back to her adobe house. Eight of her nine children settled in Bunkerville, and when her grandchildren came over, Mary Ann fed them the mulberries and grapes she grew, "something they really liked." For a few years, she rented her house and went to work in the St. George Temple. Even though she was alone, she had once been given a blessing that she would have "comforting dreams to cheer and bless" her "in times of need," and she found that had come to pass. Once she dreamed of a "large choir of singers" who created the most beautiful music that stayed with her after she awakened. In 1928, she wrote that she had a sort of "vision" and awakened "sobbing" and "overcome with joy" because she felt she had "seen the Saviour in His glorified body and smiling face." This dream was "such a comfort" to her for as long as she lived.

In 1935 for her eighty-first birthday, all her children, grandchildren, and great-grandchildren came to Bunkerville to give her a picnic birthday party. She wrote, "The many children made the place ring with their shouts and laughter. The big mulberry trees furnished shade for all. At night they played the guitar and sang songs as they used to." Her first year in Bunkerville, her oldest son had gone to the next town to dig up those baby mulberry trees along the river for her. The day after her birthday party, her ninth child, Roy, who lived in Colorado, and his family took Mary Ann to see the Boulder Dam. They "took a ride on the lake in a motor boat and sped over the water with the spray sprinkling [their] faces.

It was so thrilling." She also made trips to his home in Colorado where he was the state historian. Roy's family treated her "royally," and she saw his museum exhibits, the *Colorado Magazine* he edited, and the books he'd written—some about the trail she followed toward Utah as a Swiss immigrant so many years before.

By 1928, her husband John Hafen had died. She wrote that "he was a good man, reared fine children, and did the best he could by us all." Although he thought polygamy was hard and had shed tears over it, he said before he died, "I feel that the sacrifices I made have brought great blessings, and I am satisfied." Mary Ann would finally feel the same way. She wrote, "Trials and difficulties of all kinds often turn out for our own good in the long run."

Both Mary Ann and Martha had learned to care for themselves and their children—to carry on as widows and single mothers do—because for much of their lives they could not depend on their husbands for help. They lived without men. In the New Testament, women in their situation were considered vulnerable, and James explained that Christians should care for widows who are alone and children who don't have fathers: "Pure religion and undefiled before God and the Father is this, To visit the fatherless and widows in their affliction." Mary Ann's and Martha's communities may have given them some support, but, for the most part, they carved out lives for themselves and their children through sheer grit and determination. Although people in their communities may at times have thought Mary Ann and Martha were pathetic cast-off polygamous wives, as the two pressed forward with self-confidence and a sense of dignity, they must have evoked respect, too.

They were among those who saw the end of the Mormon's investment in polygamy and among the last to suffer its disadvantages. Having experienced the breakdown of polygamous marriage, from both outside and inside forces, neither Mary Ann's nor Martha's lengthy autobiographies mentioned the 1890 Manifesto that officially banned polygamy, suggesting that they didn't oppose its demise.

PART THREE

Abandoning Polygamy: Weariness

*To what purpose is the multitude of your sacrifices unto
me? Saith the LORD: I am full of the burnt offerings of
rams, and the fat of fed beasts; and I delight not in the
blood of bullocks, or of lambs, or of he goats. Bring no more
vain oblations; your new moons and your appointed feasts
my soul hateth; they are a trouble unto me; I am weary to
bear them.*
Isaiah 1:11–14

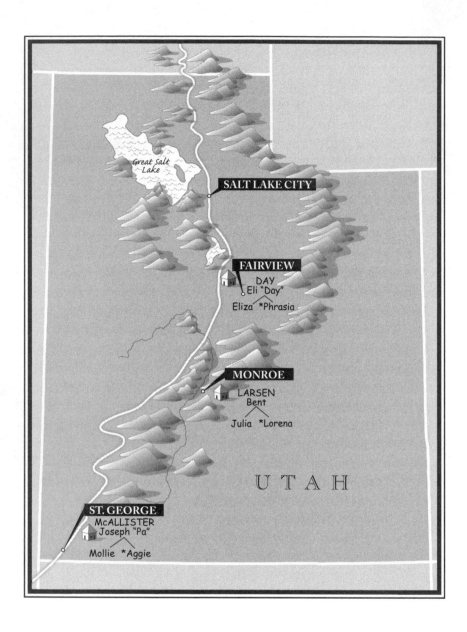

Word came the marshalls were coming, so I had to skip out

Lorena Larsen's House: Monroe, Utah, about 1900

If *Aggie McAllister* and *Phrasia Day* had ever visited *Lorena Larsen* in south-central Utah farm country just before harvest time, the Monroe fields would be ablaze with hay and wheat irrigated by two canals that ran along the Sevier River. Aggie lived 150 miles to the south and Phrasia lived ninety miles to the north. By 1900, Aggie, Phrasia, and Lorena could have comfortably spent an entire afternoon or more sharing tales of the grand efforts they made as second wives during the 1880s and 1890s to disguise their polygamous marriages and to hide from the law. Part of the reason they had been so vigilant was that they had truly loved their husbands and didn't want them to go to prison.

Lorena's "lovely little home" was an 1887 one-story adobe house with a nicely pitched roof. Those entering walked by the shade trees by the sidewalk, went through the front gate, moved up the path bordered by level lawn on both sides, and passed by the sand around the door. Lorena's house was pleasingly simple thanks to its symmetry—door in the middle, window and chimney on the left, and window and chimney on the right. Behind the house, probably behind the kitchen, she had pear, apple, peach, black cherry, and sweet blue damson plum trees. In addition, she had a large garden and a corral.

In the big room, visitors would have noticed Lorena's cleanliness and sense of style. Lorena proudly noted that some of the "town's people and teachers" had told her that coming to her house was like "going to the fair" because so much of the decoration was handcrafted by Lorena: there were "towers and boxes" covered with varnished shells on the mantelpiece and "lovely tidies on every table and chair back." She noted in her autobiography that a salesman who often stopped by to rest "always looked around

FIGURE 9.2 Second wife Lorena Larsen and her children.

the house, and sometimes heaved a sigh, and said, 'Oh what solid comfort a man could take reading the paper in a home like this.'"

Lorena was also proud of her kitchen—the good-sized, south-facing kitchen had a closet, "built-in cupboards," a "splasher" at the back of the wash bowl, and a distinctive white oilcloth tablecloth "hand painted with floral designs" on the table. Lorena was artistic—in her autobiography, she made drawings of the detailed clothing she sewed for her children; she also sometimes painted designs on velvet for girls' dresses and hoods, and her oldest son, B. F., would eventually become a well-known artist.

Lorena's artistic flair would have caught Phrasia's eye because she romantically decorated her diary with swirls and fancy writing—her husband had given her the diary as a present, and she began it in 1889, four years after they married, by writing that she hoped it would "show in truest, clearest light the condition of my heart and soul" and "unerring records of the deeds of those whom I hold dear," especially those of her husband. She would confess that she hoped future readers of her diary ("if any should") would know "something of his goodness and perfections and if there are any, of his faults, and profit by both." Oh, how she had adored her husband.

Phrasia could have told Aggie and Lorena that her name was short for Euphrasia and that she got a lot of attention because of her unusual name— furthermore, her older sister's name was Triphena and her nickname was Pheenie. Her mother loved to call them "Pheenie and Phrasia." Phrasia hailed from Fairview, a small town twenty-five miles north of Manti where in 1900 she was employed as a "Post-Mistress," and where she lived with her four children. She was thirty-nine. Her husband was forty-three, his first wife Eliza was thirty-nine, and they didn't live far from her with their seven children.

Phrasia finally got her first house in 1893 and had been "so thankful for a little home of [her] own," where she could invite her friends and "have them treated" as she wanted them treated. For so many years, even while married, she was without a home. She had lived with her widowed brother, who was sometimes bothered by her children, and she also heard a hurtful rumor that people were saying that he couldn't afford to board her. After that, she stayed with her mother, who she was sure had been "glad to be rid" of her by the time she left.

Phrasia wouldn't have had to explain why she was wandering: not long after each of the women had married in the early 1880s, the polygamy raids began, making their housing situations tricky. Polygamous families could no longer live together openly, and even women living alone with children drew suspicion. Lorena became a second wife in 1880, Phrasia a second wife in 1884, and Aggie a second wife in 1885. All were soon on the run and separated from their husbands.

Beginning in 1856, the federal government had attempted to curtail Mormon polygamy and had finally and emphatically succeeded with the Edmunds Act of 1882, which disenfranchised polygamists and made securing convictions against them easier. Starting in 1885, the federal

FIGURE 9.3 Second wife Phrasia Day.

FIGURE 9.4 Eliza and Eli Day.

government authorized intense prosecution of polygamists by sending federal marshals to raid Mormon towns to identify polygamists, and, during the next eleven years, "over a thousand convictions were obtained under its provisions." Lorena confirmed that the Edmunds Act had the desired results: "thereafter the storm clouds of persecution began to rise, at first slowly, then terrifically, and from 1883 to 1890, the storm raged." In 1890, their Church president issued the Manifesto that officially began a retreat from polygamy. All three women experienced a pre-Manifesto/ post-Manifesto transitional "storm" when they had to leave their homes, go into hiding, watch their husbands go to prison for unlawful cohabitation, and then finally adjust to post-Manifesto life.

But that had been a distant future when they, in good faith, had become polygamous wives in the early 1880s. In February 1880, when Lorena married Bent Larsen at age twenty, she had felt clear-headed about her decision. She had other marriage proposals and "believed that there were several people in the world that a person could love." When she was fifteen, her parents had wanted her to marry their bishop, whom they thought was a "fine man," but Lorena told her parents she felt too young. The bishop, whose ill wife eventually died, told her father, "I love that girl dearly, and will never give her up as long as she is single." Lorena felt close to his family and had helped his sick wife. When Lorena was sixteen, she was engaged to marry a young man from another town but broke it off after once again feeling "entirely too young to become a wife and mother." Lorena could easily have chosen to be a first wife because there were "more boys in Monroe than girls, so the girls could have their choice among them," she explained, and there were "a number of very fine young men." But when she was twenty, she decided to become the second wife of Bent Larsen.

Bent had been a long-time Monroe resident and her older brother's friend. In 1873, the two friends had married their first wives the same day in Salt Lake. When they returned to Monroe, they celebrated their marriages that night with their 200 invited guests. As a thirteen-year-old girl, Lorena had attended the festivities and stayed up until dawn dancing "in the log school house in the old fort": "the house was filled to capacity," and the only way she could rest during the dance period was to "run outside until the floor was filled with dancers," and then go back inside after it was too late to be asked to dance. She talked, straining her voice above the noise of music and conversation, until she was "so hoarse" that she "could not speak a loud word." During the only intermission, between eleven and twelve o'clock, guests were "served wedding feasts at the Washburn and Larsen homes."

Seven years later when Lorena decided to marry Bent, there had been three deciding factors. First, Bent's wife, Julia, who was only two years older than Lorena, approved of the marriage, even if slightly begrudgingly. Lorena explained, "I could not think of hurting a man's wife by marrying her husband, but Aunt Julia told me she would feel much worse if I did not marry her husband than she would if I did. She said that she and Bent had planned for a long time that if they could get my consent, they sure wanted me to be a member of their family." A second factor was a dream she had in which Bent asked her to a dance. She previously had "no thought of marrying Bent Larsen, but," she wrote, "one night I dreamed that we were at a dancing party, and he took me to his home, and pled with me to marry him. A short time after I had dreamed this, it happened just that way," and she took this as a special sign. A third factor was that she was taught that "there was no way of getting into the Celestial Kingdom [except] by plural marriage." Her ambition to reach the celestial kingdom was part of a bigger feeling about education and life experience. She accepted the Mormon belief that earth life was part of an eternal progression. She thought of "life as a great school...to prepare us for the great beyond, that we might there, go on advancing and progressing." She believed that plural marriage was "a capstone" experience, and, like Martha Cox, was "afraid [she] wasn't equal to the occasion" and "went into [polygamy] hesitatingly, reluctantly."

Bent and Lorena decided to marry in February 1880. They had planned to travel south with another couple to the St. George Temple to be married, but when the other couple was held up, Bent and Lorena left without them, double tasking by hauling a load of freight. They expected that the other couple would catch up, but terrible February storms kept them apart. Bent and Lorena camped six nights on the way to St. George. One night was so cold that if another camper's dog had not come to sleep at Lorena's feet in the wagon where the wind gusts were ripping her blanket from her all night, she thought she would have died before morning. Bent had come to the wagon several times during the night "to try and fasten the quilts down, but in vain." The most comfortable night along the way, they "procured a camp house, wood, and hay" and slept in front of a fire in separate corners of the room. After their marriage on the way back to Monroe, they found that the "snows were melting" and that when they arrived home the farmers were "planting grain."

Lorena moved in with Bent and his first wife, Aunt Julia. Between 1881 and 1883, Bent was called to serve a mission in Norway, not only to seek converts but probably also to avoid prosecution for polygamy. Between 1880 and 1887, Lorena and Aunt Julia "lived in the same house" and "ate at the same table" and "never quarreled," though they "were often badly tried with anxieties." They "took turns milking the cows and doing the house work"—one did the house one week, and then they switched. They did "the washings together" and "worked together" to grate fifty to one hundred pounds of potatoes to make "potato starch" every fall.

While their husband was in Norway, Lorena and Julia worked together as leaders in the Young Women Mutual, and the girls who came to their house for meetings admired the friendship that existed between Lorena and Julia. Lorena explained, "[Julia and I] were glad that there were two of us; it kept the home more cheerful. And with Mutual meetings at our home once a week, we had plenty of social life. The Mutual girls thought it was sure an ideal life, and some of them said they would never marry unless there could be two of them, congenial like we were."

After Bent's return from Norway in the mid-1880s, he sensed trouble. In some towns, Mormon hideouts, secret codes, and spotters developed to avoid the new onslaught of federal intervention. In response, marshals sometimes "disguised themselves as peddlers or census takers in order to gain entry into homes and hired their own spotters to question children, gossip with neighbors, and even invade the privacy of homes." Lorena explained that in 1886 when her oldest son was four, she wrote a poem that she liked to recite to him. Part of it went like this: "I am a little soldier / For truth I'm going to fight / We boys will scare bad marshals / and put them in a fright." Evidently not everyone hated the marshals. Lorena wrote, "for years during that polygamous persecution if our neighbors had seen [Bent] come to my home they would have reported to either spies or U.S. marshals."

Bent had befriended the head marshal in town, Andy, who was scouting out Monroe looking for polygamists, and Bent felt confident that the marshal would not bother him. At the same time, Bent realized that "it was no longer safe to have...two wives in the same house," and so he was preparing another house for Lorena. One night at 2 a.m. in the fall of 1887, just before she moved to her own house, their common house was surrounded by four federal marshals who "were peeking in the windows." When her husband let them in, they "looked in every bed and examined the pillows to try to find out who had slept in the beds." Incensed, Lorena threatened one of the marshals that he would "sure reap his reward for his filthy work." She also wrote a poem around this same time that began, "Proud America blush with shame," and continued, "Oh America, where is thy pride / That liberty for which our fathers died / That freedom for which their blood did flow / Little more than a century ago?" Her poem championed the cause of freedom of religion and "the faithful servants of God" who were being "hunted every hour." But because of the raid that night, the marshals succeeded in nabbing them. As a result, in 1888 Bent Larsen went to prison for five months.

As for Aggie, in 1885, when she married in the St. George Temple at age eighteen, temple sealing had become a super-secret affair: she and her thirty-year-old husband, Joseph, were married at night to avoid suspicion. They had met eight months earlier while he was her writing teacher and choir director. During this time, he "sent a note" asking Aggie "to see him," so she "sneaked out," and they started dating. He explained that "he thought a lot" of her and "wanted to marry" her. She said she "couldn't answer him then," so they "kept going out for eight months"—"first twice a week, then every other week, then once a month." She liked his independent demeanor and found it attractive that "[n]o one run him." She wrote that their courtship was "one of the happiest times" of her life and that the time between rendezvous couldn't go quickly enough.

Unlike Lorena, who had been invited to the Larsen's home to discuss a possible polygamous marriage with Bent's first wife Julia, Aggie gave no indication of any contact with Joseph's first wife, Mary Ann "Mollie" McAllister until she had run-ins with her after marriage. If Mollie had known her husband's plans, she would have thought him a fool to marry a second wife with marshals swarming around. Besides, during this

FIGURE 9.5 First wife Mary Ann "Mollie" McAllister.

FIGURE 9.6 Aggie's husband, Joseph "Pa" McAllister.

time, the pressure to live polygamy "was on church leaders," and it was enough for ordinary members—like Joseph—to believe that polygamy was "a righteous principle ordained of God" even if they didn't practice it. And, at least by 1882, Church leaders had realized that polygamy could not "be a practice without limit," because by then there were more males than females. On the other hand, St. George was a special place: the number of polygamists remained unusually high there in the 1880s, at least in part because the building and 1877 opening of the St. George Temple seemed to foster a polygamous environment, and Aggie's family had strong temple connections.

In 1885, Aggie wrote that when she and Joseph decided to marry, the ceremony had been quick. She had already done her temple prerequisites at age fourteen, so at age eighteen when she married, she just needed to be "sealed" to Joseph in the St. George Temple. On the prearranged January night, she left her house wrapped in her sister's big shawl, under which she hid her temple clothes; she was also carrying her father's supper. The setup was perfect because her father was the temple night watchman, her uncle was the temple president, and her fiancé was the temple recorder. When she arrived at the temple door, which was locked, her father and her fiancé Joseph were waiting for her. They went to her uncle's office, and he took her by candlelight to a room where she changed her clothes, and then to the sealing room where she was married to Joseph. Her father and uncle kissed her, then they all went downstairs and left by different doors. When Joseph exited, he carried some papers and one of the night watchmen said to him, "you have been working late," and Joseph answered in the affirmative. Alone, Aggie went along the south side of the temple grounds, she explained, "so if any one saw me they would think I had been" at the gardener's house.

After Aggie and Joseph left the St. George Temple separately that night, the newlyweds were so afraid of being caught that they didn't spend their first night together, but they did meet a block away from the temple near "an old house with large tamarack trees in front." Joseph said "he couldn't go home without seeing" her again. Aggie was crying, and he asked why. She told him, "I don't know. I suppose everyone crys, leaving their dear old name for a new one." In her autobiography, she would confess, "Pa [her husband Joseph] didn't stay the first night and I always felt hurt about it." When she got home, Aggie "hunched by the stove," and her sister said, "same old hunch," as though nothing had changed. Aggie was only beginning what would be years of secret living. Her husband rented a room for her, and her sisters helped move her trunk and bed there—she explained, "we didn't dare ask anyone to take my things for fear they would know."

Polygamists who left home and stayed hidden were said to be "on the underground" and were obliged to secretly find a temporary place to stay. Sometimes they stayed indoors with family or friends, but this might put their loved ones in compromising situations. Polygamous wives sometimes moved to a new community and took on false names and tried to deflect notice.

In 1885, after Aggie had been married a month, she explained, "word came the Marshalls were coming, so I had to skip out." She traveled six miles to a nearby town to stay at her uncle's, since he was a night watchman at a factory. Her uncle was also letting another polygamous wife who was "on the underground" stay "in the other part." Aggie explained that the night she got there, "a friend [of her uncle's] was there and they were laughing and talking about the men hiding." They didn't know who she was, but she told them, "'It may be a laughing matter to you; but I can't see it,'" and then she burst into tears. Another evening while in hiding, her husband Joseph "got a horse and came to see" her. Insinuating that his first wife Mollie didn't approve of his effort, Aggie wrote, "He had to eat breakfast off the mantle at home next morning." Aggie was gone from home for a month until "the scare was over," and she returned home "but wasn't allowed to go out in the day time." She said that "things would quiet down for awhile, then they would come again."

Because they feared trouble from the marshals, Aggie's husband Joseph didn't eat a meal in her house until after her first baby was born; apparently he didn't stay all night, either, until after the baby was born, and then he would "get up before daylight and go." In 1886 after her baby was born, her husband Joseph would "stay with number 1 two evenings," and "one with" her, she said, "for a long time for fear [people] would know we were married."

In 1888, about the same time that Lorena's husband Bent was serving time in prison, Aggie was subpoenaed to court in Beaver on charges that her husband was living polygamy. Aggie had answered an early morning knock on her door and found the marshals there. They asked her if she were Mrs. Cannon, and she said no, and when they asked her name, she told them the truth—"McAllister." The marshals said "oh" and left, and, afraid, Aggie went to hide at her mother's house all day. In the evening, she "went to where [her husband] was hiding" and asked his advice. She was afraid to go back to her mother's house for fear the marshals would be looking for her father there, so Aggie and Joseph decided she should just go back to her house.

But when she got there, Marshals Armstrong and McGeary—the same who were despised by Martha Cox and Anna Maria Hafen—were watching for her. They told her they had a subpoena for her to testify in court in Beaver the next month, which would be a four-day journey, and they also had a subpoena to search her house. When she told them she couldn't go to Beaver, they told her, "It will be a nice vacation for you." Her Uncle John later chastised her for telling the marshals her real name and "getting Joe in a lot of trouble."

So in April 1888 at age twenty-one, Aggie explained, she would take a "vacation" and go to Beaver, Utah, with her baby to testify in her husband's case, and she would be paid $13.50 by the government for her expenses. Her knees had "knocked together" when the marshals had come into her house, and she was "so frightened of going to court." In Beaver, a "brother Judd" coached her and told her "a lot of things to say if questioned." After returning home, she wrote that "things went as usual until November when the Marshalls got Pa [her husband] at Summit," where he was doing door-to-door sales. Probably rather than making Aggie leave St. George, and since he wasn't a farmer, he'd found a door-to-door sales job that required him to travel from town to town, keeping him on the run. But the marshals had finally caught him in Summit, probably about sixty miles north. The marshals brought him to Beaver, then let him go home to St. George for a couple of days before sending him to prison.

His first morning back in St. George before leaving for prison, he "surprised" Aggie by going down to see her. The next day, the day before he left, Aggie went to Mollie's to help sew for him. Before she left to go home, Joseph told her he would come down to say goodbye to her that night, his last night. However, Mollie had invited their friends the Eardleys over to her house that night, and they didn't leave until midnight. Evidently Aggie and Mollie's relationship wasn't close enough for Aggie to be invited or maybe she had to take her children home. After the Eardleys finally left, when Joe finally got to Aggie's, she was "feeling awful." She explained, "He kissed me and said, 'Haven't you got anything to say to me.' I said, 'No.' That was last I saw of him for six months."

When Lorena and Aunt Julia received weekly letters from their imprisoned husband, they decided to each take a turn opening the letter. In contrast, Aggie felt that Mollie always opened the envelope, even though there was a letter for each of them inside. Aggie also felt that Mollie read her letters. When Aggie confronted Mollie, she responded, "I didn't read your letter. Of course, I read about Eardley's. I thought that was for me." Aggie "knew" she'd read it and was "angry" because, as she read her own letter, "there wasn't anything" for Aggie in it—she "crushed it up and threw it in the stove." She wept and thought, "I am only a second, can't even have a letter without she has to read it." Later she felt sorry, but she came up with a plan to have "Pa" send her a letter under a different name, as his "sister," and she asked the postmaster to put it in his drawer for her. This, Aggie felt, prevented Mollie from "snoop[ing] and l[ying] anymore." Aggie even kept for years a special letter Joseph had secretly sent her. It was a "lovely love letter" he sent with a man leaving the penitentiary who "sewed it in the band of his underwear" and then sent it to Aggie—she was "so happy over it."

Six months later in 1889 when Joseph McAllister got out of "the pen," he "didn't dare" go see Aggie, but they arranged a secret meeting through her Uncle John in the temple, and "it was a joyful meeting" that included her little boys. Afterward, husband and second wife went their separate ways, just as they had the night they'd been married, since he "wasn't supposed to live" with her "if he was to obey the law," but they "commenced the sneaking again," and she got pregnant.

At about this same time in Monroe, Lorena Larsen's husband Bent realized that his two wives could not continue to live in the same town. Lorena was pregnant, and Bent was adamant that she had to leave. She would explain, "I had to leave and go into hiding to save my husband from going to the pen again. I and my children had to leave our precious home and hide somewhere, probably for years...but where would we go?" She first went to live in Manti, sixty miles north.

Lorena left Monroe without her children, since her bishop had called her to be a Manti Temple worker for six months and advised her to leave her children with their father. She felt this was "almost more than" she could "endure," and it took a lot of "faith," because her children were "dearer than life itself." Lorena was the kind of mother who sewed for her children, worked with them in the garden, invited their little friends in the house (mopping their shoes first if they were muddy), provided blocks and other toys for them, and would make them all lunch up at the table like she would for her friends. Like many polygamous wives, Lorena was more attached to her children than to her husband, but she realized that "many other women...had to leave their children and go into hiding in obscure farm houses or wherever they could find a hiding place," so her call to the temple was "the best imaginable" opportunity under the circumstances.

Lorena worked faithfully until the temple president realized that she was having a difficult pregnancy and, besides, she longed for her children.

The day after she was released from her commitment at the temple, her husband brought her children to Manti to meet her, and he told her he was taking them to Redmond, Utah, "as he supposed there was no one in that place who knew us," she wrote. To keep their identity secret, Lorena renamed herself "Hannah Thompson," and she taught her children to call their father "Uncle Thompson" when he visited. Her two-year-old Lottie got confused and asked, "Is my daddy my uncle?" Despite her efforts to hide their identity in Redmond, Lorena was taken back when a neighbor woman, Anna Brineholt, recognized her, because they both had a sister married to the same man! Lorena told her "not to tell a living soul" who she was because her husband's "safety from the pen depended on it." Lorena and Anna Brineholt became cautious friends. Lorena and her children had to "keep away from public places," so they didn't even attend church—on Sundays they had their own "little family Sunday School." Lorena also spent many hours with her children on a grass knoll near a small spring that made a waterfall. The children tried to catch the fish there with their hands while Lorena "crocheted tidies and lace."

Lorena's identity was so secret that when her Monroe bishop came through Redmond and tried to visit her, he had a terrible time finding her. Not even the Redmond bishop would say if he knew her. The out-of-town Monroe bishop tried to explain to the Redmond bishop that Lorena was the wife of one of his counselors, and swore that if he, the visiting bishop, was lying, the Redmond bishop could "hang [him] to any of the large trees" in the town. Still the Redmond bishop would only say that maybe a "Mrs. Brineholt" would know something. When the Monroe bishop found Mrs. Brineholt, she said she didn't know Lorena, either. Only through his extended persuasion, saying "she is living somewhere in this neighborhood," and swearing that Lorena would want to see him did he convince Mrs. Brineholt that his intentions might be good. Finally Mrs. Brineholt told him to wait and she would go "find out" if the lady he was searching for was around. When Lorena and her Monroe bishop were finally reunited, they "were sure glad to see each other." She "plied him with questions" about everybody at home. Lorena's mother and her sister Meda also visited her in Redmond once. Later Meda told Lorena that "when she saw what a barren place" they were living in compared to Lorena's "lovely little home" in Monroe, Meda "felt like screaming."

After four months in Redmond, which seemed like a temporary solution, in May 1889 Bent Larsen wanted Lorena to live with her brother, but she felt this would be too much to ask of him, because he was poor and Lorena and Bent had no money to support her. Lorena begged Bent to let her family go home to Monroe, but he refused. Bent instead determined to take Lorena and her family to the San Luis Valley of Colorado.

Here Phrasia's story merges with Lorena's. Phrasia's husband had the same solution as Lorena's husband and took her and her children to Colorado for a while. In both cases—Lorena's trip to Colorado with Bent and their children in 1889, and Euphraisa's trip to Colorado with her husband and their children in 1891—Colorado turned out to be just another temporary solution, and they ended up back in Utah.

Phrasia had married Eli Day, whom she called "Day," in 1884 in the Logan Temple when he was almost twenty-five and Phrasia was twenty—the same age as his first wife, Eliza. At age fourteen, Phrasia started teaching Sunday school. At age fifteen, the Fairview school trustees hired her at twenty-five dollars per month. About 1880 at age sixteen, she took a "two year normal course" at Brigham Young Academy with the money she saved and graduated in June 1882 with a 92 percent average (she received 100 percent in writing). She then taught school in Utah, Idaho, and Colorado. Phrasia and Day became better acquainted while they were both teaching school. After five years of marriage, early in her 1889 diary, she noted, "tonight I take both babies in bed with me. Love." (Underlined twice.) A couple of weeks later she wrote, "I'm happy in my love in its full and complete return, and I thank God that My heart is able to love so deeply and one so worthy."

Because she loved her husband so much, she didn't like to see him hurt. Phrasia would sometimes complain in her diary that Day's first wife Eliza was critical of him and bossy. For example, one day when Phrasia was at Day and Eliza's house, her husband told Phrasia that he would help her with the "Mother Goose Opera" she was trying to produce. Eliza then started, according to Phrasia, "a furious scolding" telling him that he shouldn't be "working for the public," presumably because Eliza wanted him to spend his time working for pay. But Phrasia felt "it wouldn't kill him to help" since he was a public schoolteacher anyway. Phrasia explained that this sort of outburst always hurt her feelings because, she wrote, "I love him and it cuts to know he is found fault with so much." For his part, Day must have felt caught in the middle and unable to please both wives.

Their argument about the Mother Goose Opera may have essentially been Eliza's way of objecting to Day spending more time with Phrasia and her projects, and Phrasia could feel that. Phrasia felt badly that "a disagreeable feeling of some kind" was growing in her heart toward Eliza. In addition, Phrasia sensed that Eliza felt jealous because Day "notice[ed]" Phrasia's children more. But Phrasia argued in her diary that Day noticed them "more than hers for he is with them much and mine but little." She felt badly that her children "seldom" saw their father—"probably averaging a kiss once a week from him." Phrasia also guessed that Eliza might think that Day loved Phrasia more, but another time she worried that her husband was "growing less ardent" for her. She was self-reflective and self-critical and wrote on New Year of 1890 that she hoped to "free herself of some of [her] evils, loud talking and uncharitable feelings for Eliza principally." She also hoped she could get out of debt.

During the polygamy raids of 1889 and 1890, when Phrasia was living with her widowed brother, her heart would sink when Day stayed away from her. She noted, for example, that on the Fourth of July he could not go in the same vehicle as her. She especially hated going to dances but not being able to dance with him! In one entry she wrote, "At night went to the dance for a few minutes for I could not but feel keenly that He dared not dance with me lest it should be 'unlawful cohab' or 'adultry' so when he came to it I stayed only till he danced with Eliza and Sister N. and then came away." She said that she came home and later prayed for comfort: "I had not enough cheerfulness to pray for myself till after dark, but when I did with all my hatefulness the Lord heard me and my breast softened (entirely natural) in about ten minutes." In March of 1890, she wrote that she'd finally had the pleasure of dancing with "Bro Day," her "dearly beloved husband" for the "first time in over a year and a half."

This was about the time that Lorena was living fifty miles away in Redmond before leaving for Colorado. Both Phrasia and Lorena had been suffering over their precarious position as second wives. Once Lorena and Bent had decided to go to Colorado, just the mileage to the border had been grueling. Barely into their journey, they could not find water. While Bent went searching in the rocky hills, Lorena drove the team alone with her three children asleep in the back of the wagon on a "lonely mountain road," once in a while calling out to see if he was close enough to call back. They tried to strain the only water they found because it had tiny worm-like creatures in it, but they finally decided it might not be safe enough to drink. The next morning with no other men around to share the labor, they had to cross a "rock canyon." In order to cross, still without water, Bent had to unload half the weight in the wagon and then return for it in a second crossing. Lorena and the children walked across the canyon but "were helpless as far as making his burden lighter," though they "longed to help him." Lorena disclosed that Bent "gave way to his temper and made some very uncomplimentary remarks before he got the last half of the load across that awful place." Under these circumstances, caring for two families was grueling.

In the afternoon, they found water and continued to the Green River, still in Utah. As they traveled from there, at one point Lorena felt somewhat depressed. She felt that "the future didn't look very bright." She saw 600 miles ahead "in a lumber wagon over rough roads" with lots of "perplexing problems to be solved." Further, she was six or seven months pregnant, afraid to give birth among strangers, had "no money," and an uncertain future.

Along the trail, they soon met up with some friends and other polygamous families who were also seeking a way out of the trouble in Utah. When the Mormons camped, they made "pie, cake, and bread," played checkers, and on Sundays sang while Colorado cowboys came round to listen. A bald-headed man, Brother Harris, had brought his second wife, Lizzie, with whom he was "very affectionate." Hoping to avoid trouble for being a polygamist, the man told everyone that Lizzie was his daughter. One afternoon, Lorena's little three-year-old Lottie "stood right in front of Bro. Harris and looking up into his face" asked him over and over if he was married. Finally he answered her and said, "Who should I be married to?" Lottie pointed to Lizzie and said, "Why that little girl over there." If a three-year-old could tell they were married, a marshal probably wouldn't have had trouble detecting it.

In August 1889, Lorena successfully delivered a fourteen-pound baby boy but "nearly lost [her] life" in the process. Bent and three church sisters tried to help her during her labor and delivery, but she was so sick that they finally made an emergency call for an experienced midwife, whose services they couldn't afford, and Lorena finally delivered. Lorena would explain that she was "crossways on the bed when the baby came and could not be moved nor changed for 24 hours" afterward. The Larsens finally arrived in San Juan County and lived in Sanford for a year in a "one room log house" that Bent built. They then moved to Durango where Bent worked on the railroad. In Durango, Lorena did laundry and earned money to help buy clothes for the family. They were away from Utah a total of two years but could never make a go of it.

In October 1890 on their way back to Utah, the Larsens learned of the Manifesto. Neither Phrasia in her diary nor Aggie in her journal wrote about it when it was issued, but Lorena divulged all the uncertainty she felt. Lorena, Bent, and their children were staying a night with Lorena's niece in October 1890 when her niece's husband opened the evening newspaper to read about General Conference, and "there was the Manifesto which had been given in Conference by President Woodruff." Lorena wrote, "We were all greatly astonished, and we discussed it for some time." She couldn't believe that the leaders of the Church had "given up plural marriage," because "it had been called the crowning principle of the gospel" and had required "such a sacrifice on the part of many young women" who believed it was "the only way that a person could get to the highest degree of the Celestial Kingdom of God." If the news were true, her niece's husband threatened he would go to Mexico and practice it anyway.

Lorena, Bent, and their little children—who were then eight, five, three and a few months—continued traveling west to Moab, Utah, where people returning from conference confirmed the news. One man told Bent that "the first presidency and the apostles were all united on it, and that it should be practiced no more." Lorena explained that when Bent came to their tent to tell Lorena what the man had said, her feelings were "past description." She primarily became a polygamous wife because she thought God wanted her to, and "it seemed impossible that the Lord would go back on a principle which had caused so much sacrifice, heartache, and trial."

After her husband delivered the news, he walked out. She didn't realize that he felt inadequate to comfort her and that he'd gone to "a patch of willows" to pray for her. As he left her, Lorena thought, "Oh yes, it is easy for you, you can go home to your other family and be happy with her, while I must be like Hagar, sent away." They were both praying independently when she "heard a voice and felt a most powerful presence." The voice asked her to consider the trial Abraham had been given to offer up his son Isaac. She felt that if she endured her trial as Abraham had endured his, the "trial would be removed." Feeling a little better, she felt ready to continue their journey.

Although Lorena had refused to impose on her brother earlier, Bent wanted her and her children to stay in Huntington with him until the next spring. Her brother had lumber, and Bent helped him build a room on the back of his house for Lorena's family. During her stay, her brother kindly supplied them with "milk, pork and wood" and "refused" to be paid. She would write that she considered this brother, her father, and her sons "the kindest men" she'd ever met. The three ladies under consideration here might well have wondered aloud, did any polygamous wife consider her husband among the kindest men they knew? Too much was expected of them, and perhaps their good qualities eventually became diluted and divided. Polygamous husbands had never been able to be full husbands, and the Manifesto further complicated their roles.

Yet in January 1891, a few months after the Manifesto had been issued, Phrasia wrote that her husband was not willing to give up his relationship with her: "nearly all the men in polig now are promising to obey the law, but E A Day can't see the point yet, and that's a comfort to me. I don't know what rash act I would do if I was cast off like some poor women are." Within the month, however, while she was teaching school, Marshal Parsons "came in" and subpoenaed her to "appear in the case of E A Day." The marshal told her that they might not need her because Day might agree to "obey the law." Although she felt nervous, she calmly taught until the end of the day. Within a few days, her husband had skipped out on his trial, and she and Day were on their way to Colorado—even Eliza had helped them pack to get away.

So in 1891 Phrasia was preparing to make the same Colorado trip that Lorena had just returned from, and, at the same time, Lorena was fifty miles away staying with her brother under the fake name of "Mary Peterson." Phrasia, her husband, and their children (Orville age five, Earle age four, and Elva age two) headed toward the Green River and crossed it "swimming." Lorena could have told that when they had crossed the Green River, a ferry took them, their team, and their lumber cart, but Phrasia's family was traveling much lighter that spring.

On a Sunday the previous January, Phrasia had written how she longed to spend time with her "own"—her husband—and how if she "could see him once more" that afternoon, she would be "content to die." In a way, her trip to Colorado with Day was the time with him she had yearned for. As they were traveling and she caressed him, Day told her he thought she was "so happy" that she was "selfish," which hurt her feelings. He probably meant that they had left his first wife Eliza in a bad way, without means, so their trip shouldn't be construed as a pleasure trip—their situation called for some solemnity. But after his comment, she decided that "if he did not want my caresses I did not want to give them." A few days later, she told him, "if he did not want me to go with him I would return gladly. He told me he did want me with him." The next month, she was "vexed" that he didn't bathe and wrote, "He doesn't love me as well as I had thought, and I have to hold my expressions of love back all the time till I'm fairly miserable." For more than two months, she held back so that her husband would not think she was selfish.

They'd found a place to live, and her husband made her a "nice cupboard." One Saturday morning, she wrote of her joy, after a long talk in bed, to learn that her husband really did love her as much as he always had. She wrote in her diary at the time, "After we awoke in the morning he asked why I did not act more affectionate; I said I thought he did not want my kisses etc; then he said he believed I was trying to think he did not love me as well as formerly. Then I told him why I had changed and he wanted my affectionate expressions just as I felt them when we were alone."

In reality, Phrasia did think of Eliza and the situation they had left her in. Because Phrasia had often been without her husband and dependent on the charity of others, she could write of Eliza's situation, "I know how she feels." When Phrasia thought of Eliza, her "breast heave[d] with sadness" and "tears very often flow[ed]." Phrasia and Day received letters from home that suggested that Day's mother and sister were stirring things up—they were mad that Day had left Eliza and gone off with Phrasia. His sister wrote saying "she would not blame Eliza if she got a divorce." Eliza had evidently had to move to another town and was in "delicate" health. Phrasia and Day sent some money to Eliza as often as they could, and Phrasia wrote, "God knows we have neither of us done any thing intentionally wrong." In the summer, Eliza wrote them "very blue and almost jealous letters" that made Phrasia "feel so bad" that she "didn't know what to do." She tried to write back to Eliza that her life was not a bed of roses in Colorado: "I nearly starve for something to read, or some association to improve my mind. I have nothing . . . ." Phrasia wrote that her "life seemed more of a nuisance than ever." And around the same time, her only little girl, Elva, died after choking—a continuous heartache for her. By that fall, they had returned to Fairview where Day recommenced teaching school and decided to live the law. Both Phrasia and Lorena would slowly learn that from then on, they would have to do more to support themselves.

Earlier that spring, Lorena's husband had sent word that she could leave her brother's home and finally return home to Monroe. He was to meet her in Manti to take her home to Monroe. He told her which train to take to Manti, but the train had moved slowly through storms to avoid a wreck, and Lorena and her children didn't arrive until 2 a.m. It had snowed and was cold, and when she got off the train, she was hurt that her husband was not waiting for them—she didn't know where he was. She spent her last half dollar on a cab to take her to her friends the Higgs's house, where the cab driver went to the door for her since she had a child asleep on her lap. She was afraid to give her real name, so she asked the cab driver to say that "a lady friend from Colorado" wanted to stay with them. The Higgses told the driver they had no room for strangers. The cab driver said he would take her to the hotel, but she had no money left. Finally the driver took her sleeping child, and Lorena went to the Higgs's door where she was warmly received for the night.

The next morning, she went to the Temple Hotel where she found the Larsen family. When her mother-in-law saw her, she "almost screamed" in a rude tone, "Oh have you come back to put my boy in the pen?" Lorena would later write that she felt indignant over the whole situation in Manti. She had once "opened the door to salvation," as another polygamous wife once described it, for Bent and Julia by joining their family as a second wife, and it had come to this. She was somewhat relieved, however, when she went to visit her friends at the Manti Temple later that day, and the temple president sat her down and in a "low" voice confidentially told her, "There is no law but the law of God for you" and told her "just how to live." When he told her she could continue to have children, she was surprised but considered his voice the voice of authority. Lorena would explain that the secrets he told her had helped her "bear up under the trials of the years which followed"—about this time, she got pregnant again.

Aggie McAllister, after her husband got out of prison around 1889, got pregnant again, too. After their "joyful" secret reunion in the temple, Joseph had gone his way, and Aggie had gone hers, and "then commenced the sneaking again." She would explain what the other two already knew: "He wasn't supposed to live with me if he was to obey the law." She was able to disguise her pregnancy until the last month, when she had to go into hiding. Her sister's husband refused to let Aggie and her four children stay with them, so Aggie ended up going to Santa Clara, outside St. George, and staying with an older couple, a "dutchman" and his Swiss wife. Aggie wrote that she would "never forget that ride" as she sat on the sloping seat (presumably driving the horse) with "a can of coal oil to hold," her children under cover in the back with her husband. Her husband helped her that night but had to "go back to work" the next morning.

Only a few days later in March 1891, she went into labor and couldn't get a nurse from St. George in time, so the "dutchman's" wife delivered a "big fine boy" that "took cold and cryed and wouldn't nurse." Aggie was disgusted with her nurse who "threw" her baby "on her bed on the floor" because it was "blue with cold," and she had given up. Aggie said, "Give that baby to me," and he lived "until three in the morning, then died." They laid the baby out and "put it at the foot" of Aggie's bed until the "little black coffin came at last." She had to "cover" her head—she couldn't "stand it any longer." She sent for her husband, who took the baby back to St. George to bury it, and then returned. Aggie wrote, "No one ever knew how I felt. Not one of my people there. Mother was in California. We didn't let my sisters know, didn't dare to. It was awful to go through." While trying to recover, she was neglected, "took cold," and "sores broke out" on her mouth." She was "sick and lonesome."

After three weeks, she went home to St. George and immediately got pregnant again, then had her fifth boy, Ralph, the following January in 1892. Evidently, her husband was again sent to prison the next year, but Aggie would eventually have ten children, and her aunt remarked, "If Aggie and Joe have many more babies they would have to take them to the bug house, they are so crazy over them."

In about 1895, after ten years of marriage and ten different homes, Aggie's husband "bought the Farnsworth place" in St. George and told her she could have it and that he would "never ask" her "to give it up." There were five rooms in it. As soon as he got the deeds settled, however, she wrote, "he told me Mollie was to have the place and I was to take her home with two rooms in it." Aggie admitted, "I suppose it was right, she had the largest family. I felt awful about it. What he should have done was to tell me at first." But Aggie obviously resented getting Mollie's old house. Hopefully she was exaggerating when she wrote, "I moved to Mollie's home. It was the dirtiest place I ever cleaned. It was alive with mice and bed bugs, human manure all around the house, no screens at the doors except on the board shanty on one hinge. Everything looked like her. I hated the place." She finished, "After awhile I got over it. We always had a good garden." Her husband earned seventy-five dollars per month, but twenty-five of it went to pay for Mollie's five-room home—"there wasn't much left for two families to live on."

As for Lorena, when she got back to Monroe in 1891, Bent told her she would have to help support herself, and she started "dressmaking" to "keep the children in clothes." This was tough going because other dressmakers were "working so cheap" that "it didn't pay very well." Bent furnished "bread, potatoes, wood, and hay for one cow, and sometimes a few other things." She had tried to hide her pregnancy and keep it a secret, but as she began to show, she had to face her critics. Her sister told her that "a pregnant plural wife was equal to an adulterer." Her mother visited and told her that her brother was "almost apostatizing on account of" her "condition." Lorena knew what people thought: "the whole people felt that the Manifesto almost automatically divorced men and their plural wives, that their family ties, their marriage relations were dissolved." She depended on the temple president's secret advice but could not "explain" it to "a living soul."

When Lorena's husband came that evening to chop wood in women's clothing so "any passer by would think" it was her, afterward he came in for a chat. She told him what her mother had told her that day about a pregnant polygamous wife being an adulterer, and to her surprise, he agreed with her family. He told her that he and two other polygamous husbands had "a consultation" and decided to take their "first wives and live with them for this life, and the rest must keep themselves pure for them in Eternity." Lorena was "almost struck dumb" because he had "repeatedly" told her that "although the whole world turned in the opposite direction," he would not "forsake" her. Here she was almost ready to give birth again and felt that now that her "husband had turned," she didn't know if she had "an earthly friend"—only God knew what she "suffered that night." They talked, and she wept "until the day was breaking." Lorena wrote, "he told me I had wept rivers of tears since he married me, but weeping didn't change his plans, but the dawn was here and he must go."

At this point, Lorena "plead with the Lord" to give her "strength and wisdom" and at sunrise went "crosslots" to where Bent was feeding stock at Aunt Julia's place. She told him "with dry eyes" that "he had got to stand by me until baby was born, and then he could go where he wanted to go." The days leading up to the birth were "almost blighted hope concerning" her husband, and she worked to exhaustion on the dressmaking that was "piled high" until she couldn't stand up straight. In good faith, she had trusted her husband, and when he had seemed "a bit partial in his family dealings," she had overlooked it. She felt that he had "loved his two wives as a mother loves her children." But now that he had made a choice between them and was "willing for me and mine to be sent adrift," she had lost "confidence." She did not know that he would soon change his mind.

Phrasia's experience was similar, and her heart ached to explain the decline of her marriage after the Manifesto. In November 1892, she wrote in her diary that she was "a widow now" because the Manifesto was "real." She wrote that Church President Woodruff had said in court that they should "never" hope to see "plurality revived" and that she would have to "gather faith to stand alone in the Church and all other things." Phrasia was just grateful for the "bright, noble spirits" she had been able to bear before she and Day "ceased living together."

In 1893, her husband helped get her little house, but it was discouraging having to "fight in words" for her "rights" vis-à-vis the other wife, Eliza. Phrasia had been aggravated that she didn't get the chickens or milk that were owed her—and that she had to ask Eliza for them herself—and mostly that her husband had "by word and deed acknowledged that he dared not do what his conscience told him" was "just and right" for her. Phrasia even wrote that it had been "the town talk" for years that Eliza "bosse[d]" both Day and Phrasia, and Phrasia was disgusted that her husband lacked "firmness of will." She didn't blame Eliza, because it was just "her disposition to look out for herself and really she cannot see as others see or feel for others woes." She finished by writing that she shouldn't have recorded all this, but she "guessed" that "no eyes" but her own would see it.

Over the next several years, her husband came down from the pedestal where she had once placed him ("king of my heart, and man among men"), and she wrote that he would "have to climb back himself" if he could. She compared her "old love" for him with the "frozen condition" of her heart. One day he swore at her, and she forgave him, but later wrote she realized that over the years she had been a "visionary castlebuilding thing." Her romantic notions were typical of American wives of the period who believed that a "true woman" was rewarded with "a noble manly man," whom Phrasia had formerly believed Day to be. Lisa Olsen Tait explains that in the nineteenth century, "Romanticism dies a hard death for most American women" and that "in some ways, Mormon women were working out the same things that any nineteenth-century American woman was working out" as the realities of marriage struck against romantic notions.

Unlike Aggie and Lorena, who continued having babies during the 1890s, Phrasia believed she should not have sexual relations with her husband. After their failed trip to Colorado, he went to prison, and she didn't want more problems for him. Phrasia started teaching school again, which she called "dreadful hard work," and she became soul mates with the out-of-town "talented Journalist, and gifted speaker" Ellen Jakeman, who sometimes stayed weeks with Phrasia. Her long visits with Ellen made her feel "for the first time...fully appreciated." Phrasia went to "the summer school in Manti" with her husband, but her "pulse remained dormant."

But for years she had been "reflecting and praying" on whether she should have more children. After her baby girl Elva had died, she had Rye in 1892, so she was raising three children but didn't know if she was "doing right" by not having more.

In 1896, she was thirty-two and "concluded to give nature (or God) one chance, while there were virtually no laws" being enforced against polygamists, and, anyway, Utah was almost at the point of being accepted in the Union. While under this line of thinking, she wrote, "Dec 30 the chance was taken and nature profited by it," and she got pregnant for the last time. In the margin of the journal, she later wrote that this pregnancy was the "Beginning of the end." Once pregnant, she sent in her resignation as a teacher. She had failed her last teaching exam and asked her principal four times for a recommendation to take the teaching courses she needed, but he had never come through. She decided to switch directions and "take a course in obstetrics" in Provo, and felt badly that Day had not helped her prepare to go to Provo or "make it easy for her" to "help herself."

Like Lorena, Phrasia suffered humiliation during her pregnancy. When her husband found out she was pregnant, he was embarrassed. He "began being overbearing" and started making Phrasia subservient to Eliza, or even worse, to Eliza's daughter Estella, through whom Phrasia was supposed to get "money and provisions." Phrasia was often in a bind "waiting [Estella's] will of delivering money," making "rent run over due," and borrowing "coal by the bucketful." When Phrasia returned from Provo, she made a "declaration," one that would have sounded familiar to Lorena. Phrasia told Day, "I always had been and always expected to be second to Eliza in his consideration, but that I absolutely refused to come under her children." He responded, "You are in no condition to leave me now." She replied that she was "in the best condition [she] ever had been" and that if he did not treat her "nearer and dearer than her children he could go to them and remain!" She was "in suspence from April 10 until May 22," when, after Day returned from a trip to Provo, "a complete change had come over him." Phrasia wrote that the change came about by "whose means I do not know," but afterwards, "from that time until after baby was born he tried almost all the time to make life easy for me to be patient and kind, and do whatever lay in his time and means to lighten the work on my shoulders."

Phrasia carried on by studying hard and had a baby girl in October 1897. She named her Ellen after her dear friend, and the baby was "blessed at 8 days old by her father in the ward." Phrasia wrote that Ellen was a "sweet attractive babe but not so much as Elva [was]—every body calls her pretty." This was one of the last things she wrote in her diary, so it's unclear how much contact Phrasia and Day had after this—in 1900, Phrasia moved to Provo to take classes, and in 1903 she divorced Day. Phrasia's oldest son Orville's autobiography confirms that they were "very poor" while he was growing up, and when he was eighteen, he sent thirty dollars a month to his mother in Provo. In 1906, Phrasia briefly married and divorced another man named Mormon Miner. Her last little daughter, Ellen, her only girl (since Elva had died), would be a companion and friend to Phrasia. In 1920, they were living together alone in Highland, Utah—at the north base of Mt. Timpanogos—where Phrasia's oldest son, Orville, and his family had a farm. Phrasia would have been fifty-five and Ellen twenty-two by then. It was there one Sunday that Phrasia wrote that Ellen was always "teasing" her to write in her diary, but Phrasia felt "mostly too blue" to do so.

Although she had succeeded in learning obstetrics and was working as a "nurse" midwife for "private families," and Ellen was a student, she wrote that Sunday, "My life has been such a failure. I am ashamed to write more here. Let future generations forget if they can, the present generation remembers it too well." In 1920, Phrasia told the census taker that she was a "widow."

Phrasia, Lorena, and Aggie all died within a few years of each other in 1944, 1945, and 1947. In 1927 at age sixty-three, Phrasia moved back down to Manti, near Fairview, where she shared a house with her sister Pheenie and worked at the Manti Temple. She would write that the intervening years had been "overflowing with sadness and joys," and, finally, in her own words, "All my sorrows seem in a dim and mysty past, and I am more thankful than words can tell." In 1929, two years later, she "lovingly" gave her diary to her daughter "Ellen Heloise."

In 1944, Phrasia died suddenly at age eighty. Her last twenty years, she had liver and gall bladder trouble. In October of that year, she had visited Orville's family in Highland. Her other two sons had farms in Camas, Washington, and Ellen was stationed in Roswell, New Mexico, in the Women's Army Corps. Phrasia hadn't felt well while she was in Highland, and Orville's family begged her to stay with them, but she wanted to go home. The day she came home to 144 East Fifth South, Manti, she asked the doctor for an "opiate" for pain. A dozen friends came over in the evening to see how she was; some of them wanted to stay up and watch her, but she said she was too tired and could rest better alone. She died at 2 a.m.

In the coming days, a local news reporter wrote the details of her sudden death and reflected on her life in a long obituary that belied her 1915 feeling that her life had been a "failure." It noted that in 1888 she'd published in the *Juvenile Instructor*, and that she was known for the many stories, poems, articles, songs, dramas, plays, cantatas, farces, pageants, poems, histories, and stories she had created. Her songs had been performed at the temple, the church, reunions, and celebrations. She worked many years as a teacher and a midwife. But her detailed obituary said nothing about having been a polygamous wife, did not mention Day or Mormon Miner; it did not mention any marriage at all.

In 1944 when Phrasia died, Lorena was still living in Monroe, although her health was failing. After that awful night in 1891, when Lorena was nine months pregnant and Bent had told her they would no longer live together as husband and wife, something changed. In 1892, the marshals served papers on Bent again, as he feared. But as time went on, the government realized that the Mormons were (for the most part) no longer forging new polygamous marriages and lifted the pressure. Thus by 1900, Bent was living with her again in her adobe house, along with all eight of their children, aged eighteen, fifteen, thirteen, ten, eight, six, four, and one.

In 1901, an earthquake destroyed most of Lorena's adobe house, and Lorena and her children moved to a wooden granary until Lorena's oldest son, B. F. Larsen, "spent the summer of 1904 working at a sawmill in exchange for lumber." The next year, the "entire family worked together to build a new home for Lorena." That same year, in 1905, B. F. became principal at Monroe Elementary School. In 1907, Lorena was called as the Relief Society president in Monroe where she served her Mormon sisters for ten years. By 1910, she was alone with her children again: Bent was living with Julia and five of their children, and in 1919 when Julia died, Bent lived out his life with some of her grown children. As Lorena got older and her children married, she often helped her grown children "when she thought they needed help." In 1918, Lorena helped when her daughter Ida died and left "a family of young children." Later, Lorena lived with her divorced daughter and her two children. Finally, Lorena gave up her home in Monroe and went to live in the Provo apartment above her daughter Ella and her husband Taylor Turner's home at 620 East 800 North where she died in 1945 at age eighty-four.

The text of Lorena's funeral, while full of admiration, does not compare with the lively details and wisdom she exhibited in her autobiography. Only one funeral speaker briefly mentioned that Lorena had been a polygamous wife, and no one mentioned Bent. In 1930, Lorena, too, had told the census taker that she was a "widow," even though Bent would not die until 1946, a year after she died, in Salt Lake City at age ninety-eight.

Early in their marriage, Lorena wrote a poem to Bent titled "The Future," in which she wondered if he would still love her when she was old. She had written:

> Oh canst thou love me in old age
> Though sorrow, or misfortune may us befall?
> Can thine eyes trace my wrinkled brow
> or gaze upon my feeble form
> With that same tenderness and love
> As they did in youth's bright morn?
> And when the winter's chilling blasts
> Have outside all things frozen
> Will there still be a true fond heart
> Beating within each bosom?

Lorena knew that she and Bent would face "sorrow" and "chilling blasts" from the outside, in their case, the strong arm of the law, but she hoped on the inside their hearts would still beat for each other. In old age, were they torn apart by circumstances beyond their control, or did they choose to live independently?

When Lorena died in 1945 in Provo, Aggie was writing her autobiography. In 1900, she had told the census taker that she was a widow, too; in 1910, her husband was living with her and their children. Aggie wrote that after she quit as chair of the Republican Party in about 1906, "there was twenty years of my life I never went anywhere; but dashed up town on payday and back." She stayed home and raised her ten babies, born between 1886 and 1910, and enjoyed them "so much." Sometimes when she would get them all bathed and put their "little clean slip[s] on," she would say, "If anyone would ask me the prettiest thing the Lord ever made, I would say a baby." As her children got older and she was able to leave the house more often, she said it "felt funny," but she "soon got used to it."

Her twelve pregnancies took their toll on her body, however, and Aggie wrote that when her "last baby was born," she "went all to pieces" and never knew "a well day since" then. In 1925, she and her husband traveled to San Francisco to see a doctor about her diabetes and to see their daughter (whose husband had sent them the money for the trip) and their son Charlie, who was boarding with the doctor. She was annoyed with the Mormon doctor who would announce to people, "This is Sister McAllister, wife of Joseph McAllister, recorder of the St. George Temple, and had never seen a train until she was 56." Aggie wrote that everyone would look at her "so funny." During this trip, Aggie told her husband that "after 40 years it was our honeymoon"—they had such "a happy time" and, besides the doctor's comments, "everyone was so wonderful and grand to us hayseeds."

Then in 1930, her husband "took sick just a week and died." That year, the census taker had found Joseph, who was sixty-five, living with Mollie, who was sixty-two. But Joseph must have spent some time with Aggie, too, because she wrote that he "just wore [her] out by wanting so much waiting on." Just before he died, she overheard him tell Mollie's daughter Nemmie, "try and get Ma and Aggie together," since the two wives had never gotten along. Aggie thought "you never will. It is over now. I don't have to put up with her anymore." According to Aggie, Nemmie came in the kitchen and found Aggie crying. Nemmie put her arm around Aggie and said, "We all know how mother has treated you. I couldn't have treated a dog as she has treated you." Aggie was crying, "It wasn't my fault," and Nemmie told her, "We all know it." After the funeral, Aggie felt that Mollie didn't want to be friends, and Aggie felt, "Let things be as they were. I was very happy about it. No one could have made me be friends. I didn't have to put up with her any more."

In 1935, Aggie went to "Old Mexico" for a month to visit her daughter's family, and she traveled mostly by train, which she described thus: "Of all the ancient Noah's Ark things I have ever seen that was the worst." In her lifetime, Aggie had worked "in the Mutual, Relief Society, given lessons, given readings, and done everything they asked me to." She "did all the sewing" for her ten children, had made all her quilts, "sewed 40 lbs. of rags every year to make" her carpets, "did all the washing and never had a washer or wringer" till her aunt gave her an old one. She never had a "high chair or cradle." When she had her babies, she hired a girl for three weeks and would "then go at it again." She concluded with her trademark humor, "No wonder I am a wreck." When she wrote her autobiography, like Phrasia and Lorena, she was working in the temple. In 1944, Aggie wrote that she was glad polygamy was over: "I am glad those old polygamous times are over. I don't like to think about them." She died in 1947 at age eighty.

Lorena Washburn Larsen Reunion About 1936
Lorena is in the middle, seated, holding a baby.

FIGURE 9.7 Lorena Larsen and her posterity.

When Lorena Larsen was hiding from the law in the "barren" house she rented in Redmond, she had a significant dream. Probably thanks to her anxiety about leaving her "lovely little home" in Monroe, she dreamed that when she returned to her house, her "door-yard and front lawns were entirely overgrown with weeds, wild bushes, and vines." She "immediately went to work" pulling weeds and "digging out the rubbish." She was sad thinking of how her place had become rundown while she was "on the underground." While pulling weeds, she "suddenly" found herself next to "a beautiful tree completely covered with the finest fruit" she had ever seen. The tree "stood a few feet from the northeast corner of the house" and had been hidden "entirely underground." As she gazed at the beautiful tree, she heard a man near her fence say, "The underground tree brings forth very choice fruit too." She looked around and saw her grown children around her, and "the place filled with people." Her children brought her "dishes, bowls, and small baskets" that they filled with "that delicious fruit," and they "passed them around to the people"—her ancestors and her descendants.

Lorena's dream encapsulated the primary elements of "celestial marriage," timelessly connected as she was to all her people, yet, curiously,

Bent was not there. Her deep love for her husband had shifted to a deep love for her children. In the end, Lorena had created a beautiful family despite being separated from her husband, having to leave her home, living under assumed names, and enduring many other difficulties. Lorena and Phrasia must have wondered how their lives would have been different if their marriages had not been threatened and disrupted by the federal government and if they and their husbands had not been forced apart.

10

Interlude: The 1890 Manifesto

THE MORNING OF September 24, 1890, eighty-three-year-old Church President Wilford Woodruff started an intimate meeting with Church leaders by explaining that he hadn't slept well. Standing among oil paintings of dead Church presidents, he appeared "old and other-worldly" as he explained that he had been "struggling all night with the Lord about what should be done under the existing circumstances of the church" concerning polygamy. He then presented a draft of the Manifesto that would phase out polygamy and told the men how "strongly impelled" he had felt to write it. A few weeks later during the Church's semiannual conference in Salt Lake, the Manifesto was sustained, probably unanimously, by the Church members who were present. Some may have been surprised by Woodruff's announcement, given the Church's long-time resistance to the federal government's efforts to halt polygamy, but others saw the decision as a natural and welcome next step.

All three of President Woodruff's predecessors had struggled with polygamy. Joseph Smith's enthusiasm for the practice "wan[ed] during the last year of his life." After Smith's death in 1844, Brigham Young, perhaps blaming Emma Smith for poisoning her husband's experience with polygamy, encouraged the practice as a way to deepen the Saints' commitment and grow the Church. Young famously lived it himself, eventually marrying at least fifty-five women (some in name only). In the 1850s near the Salt Lake Temple block, his financial largesse and vision allowed him to build a potential polygamous family utopia. One of his residences, the still extant Lion House, was built to house up to twelve wives and their children and "consisted of twenty-five apartments or rooms." Next door, the still extant Beehive House had a family store where "each wife had a charge account." Behind the Beehive House and Lion House, the family could make use of "a carpenter shop, laundry house, pigeon house, shoe shop, blacksmith shop, flour mill, barns, corrals, and gardens. There was an orchard of fruit trees, raspberry bushes, blackberry, currant and goose-berry bushes, strawberry plants, and beehives."

Young started a silkworm industry on his property, too, to "provide fine clothing for his wives and daughters." He built a school and hired teachers. For outdoor play, he hired gymnastics, fencing, and dancing teachers for his children and constructed a gymnasium that included "horizontal ladders and straight ladders, horizontal bars, backboards to straighten shoulders, jumping ropes, hoops, roller skates, wooden swords, dumbbells, swings, and big balls to kick and roll about." There was also a twenty-by-five foot built-in swimming pool on his property for his children. The fifty Young family members, on average, who shared this compound, ate together at five every night. Shortly after dinner, the family listened to the children perform music or one-act plays or recita-tions, and then Young "read from the Scriptures," "presented a short homily," and prayed.

But during the 1860s and 1870s, some of his wives and their children moved out of the Beehive and Lion Houses. His first wife and other wives with large families, and some with small families, preferred moving to their own homes. Young's daughter Susa later wrote that her father re-gretted the way he set up his family and allowed his wives to leave if they wanted "to correct what he esteemed to be a mistake of his early judg-ment." Although he didn't doubt that polygamy was a commandment of God, he learned that it could create "considerable disharmony and finan-cial strain," and, in his case, was "only a mixed success."

Outside his family life, Young conducted Church business and re-ceived letters that disturbed him. He tried to encourage his people, but he became somewhat disillusioned with polygamy as early as 1858 when too many marriages that Church leaders had encouraged during the mid-1850s Mormon Reformation ended in divorce. At a December 1858 private meeting, he said that he "'did not feel disposed to do any sealing [for plural marriages]' after receiving a large number of requests for plural divorces," suggesting that he "at least considered the possibility of suspending the practice for a period of time." During the Mormon Reformation, Young wrote "President James Snow of Provo cautioning him that he should dis-courage such aggressive promotion of plural marriage," presumably be-cause zeal for the practice had hardly left a woman or girl over age sixteen unmarried. In October 1861 in the Salt Lake Tabernacle, Young told the crowd, "We are continually sealing women to men; and continually giving divorces." Although Young liberally granted divorces to women, he generally felt that divorces were the result of "blindness, ignorance, and hardness of heart," and he tried to explain that a divorce was just a piece of paper while a sealing was greater than that. During the last decade of Young's life between 1867 and 1877, his support for polygamy "was waning," and he focused more on other issues.

After Young's death in 1877, third Church President John Taylor, who served until his death in 1887, faced increasing pressure from the federal government to abandon polygamy, but he dug in his heels. Refusing to bow to the federal government, he spent the last two-and-one-half years of his life and presidency hiding "on the underground." Increasingly, during the 1880s, the federal government's polygamy raids were tearing Mormondom apart, and new laws allowed the federal government to confiscate Mormon property. But Taylor, who had been wounded by the Missouri mobs that killed Joseph Smith, said that he "would rather trust in the living God than in any other power on earth." As prophet, he directed his people to fast together and call upon God in one voice to rescue them from persecution. Some believed that God would literally come to their rescue, like the Israelites' God who had parted the Red Sea for their escape, confounding their enemies. Others believed they could usher in the "Second Coming" of Jesus who would save them.

Short of expecting a miracle, the Church's governing body, consisting of President Taylor, his counselors, and the Quorum of the Twelve Apostles, entertained various solutions. They knew they wanted Utah to gain statehood because it would "reduce federal control over their domestic affairs," but statehood could not be achieved while flouting polygamy laws. Church leaders rigorously worked their connections back East and in California to come to a compromise. But no Church leaders seemed to entertain the possibility of giving up polygamy. When Bishop John Sharp from Salt Lake renounced polygamy to follow his conscience and because "United States law forbids" it, he came under "intense criticism" from the *Deseret News* and Church leaders. Both polygamous husbands and wives were hiding from the law by now and husbands were going to prison. Rather than back down, more than 1,300 polygamists went to prison, most to the Utah Territorial Penitentiary where Salt Lake's Sugar House Park sits today.

In addition to outside pressure from the federal government, Church leaders heard rumors and received letters that indicated that the Saints wanted them to do something. Dan Bateman, who knew Taylor in 1886 and 1887, claimed that President Taylor was "almost driven wild" by the questions and letters he received about polygamy. For example, these lines from an anonymous letter from a Church member dated January 1886 were found in President Taylor's papers after his death: "You are hidden away and cannot know the true feelings of our people, and those that surround you are afraid to tell you if they know." The letter criticized him and other leaders who were hidden away while plenty of lesser men were going to prison, and it addressed conflicting opinions among the people. Probably because Church leaders had told their people that giving in would be tantamount to subordinating the laws of God to the laws of men, the letter writer told President Taylor, "you are setting one part of the polygamists who want to obey the laws of the land against those that will not obey them." The letter pleaded with President Taylor to tell the people to obey the law, gain statehood, and "stop all the wrangling and let peace come to so many unhappy families."

The letter writer still believed that polygamy was a law of God but was tired of "division and contention within [Mormondom] and reproach from without." This person felt that the great majority was suffering for the 2 percent of people who were polygamists and that it wasn't fair. Further, this person especially sympathized with polygamous wives: because God had been silent, He was "plainly" saying, "I have heard the cries of the daughters of Zion. I have counted the broken hearts of the many women who have been sent to their graves on account of Polygamy," ostensibly because they were overworked and downhearted.

Some Church members more openly questioned the doctrinal fitness of polygamy, specifically wondering whether or not living polygamy was necessary to "receive the greatest reward in the highest, or celestial, kingdom." If it were not necessary, the motivation to become a polygamist could be undermined. According to Kathryn Daynes, taken as a whole, Church leaders over the years were "ambiguous" on this point, but, "in general, those in polygamous marriages were told that they would have a greater glory than would monogamists, which implied that those with one wife could be exalted although with lesser glory." On the other hand, some sermons suggested that because not all church members had the means or opportunity to live polygamy, then monogamist members who believed that polygamy was a law of God and "desire[d] with all [their] hearts to obtain the blessings [of] Abraham" could receive great blessings in the afterlife, too.

Amidst the doctrinal "ambiguity," according to Carmon Hardy, "some church members began to waver" about how essential polygamy was, and in 1883 in Provo and American Fork, there was "widespread discussion" about "whether or not plurality was necessary for exaltation in the life to come." An 1878 "discourse" by Apostle Joseph F. Smith suggests that Church leaders were aware of this kind of talk. Smith said that some Saints "supposed" the doctrine to be "a sort of superfluity, or non-essential," and he went on to refute that. President Taylor also believed that polygamy was essential, but by 1887, some Church leaders were suggesting a return to Joseph Smith's original revelation, in which polygamy was only a possible ancillary to celestial marriage—not essential. All this is to say that the understanding of the doctrine seemed in flux.

In the 1880s, in addition to persecution from without and some doctrinal schisms within, demographic and cultural factors also impacted the practice of polygamy. Today we see how the practice seemed to be inherited. Polygamy was much more likely to continue within the same families—in other words, daughters from polygamous fathers were much more likely to become polygamists, and daughters from monogamous fathers were much more likely to become monogamists. Whereas earlier the greatest percentage of polygamous wives were women without fathers, after the frontier period had passed, the greatest percentage of polygamous wives in a study of St. George between 1861 and 1880, for example, were "polygamists' daughters," showing that "polygamous relationships were to some degree replicating themselves in the second generation." Evidence of this tendency plays out in polygamous wives' personal writings, as well. For example, as stated earlier, Lucy Flake wrote that her mother and sister were polygamists, and she thought she could "do as much as them." By comparison, Martha Cox's parents, who were monogamous, were horrified that Martha wanted to become a polygamous wife. In St. George where Martha Cox grew up, "monogamous parents raised monogamous daughters." Between 1861 and 1880 in St. George, less than 15 percent of polygamous wives came from a monogamous father. So there may have been a gap developing between polygamous and monogamous families, with both factions self-promoting.

The percentage of polygamous members was in decline, as well, partly because polygamy has "mathematical limits." During the Mormon Reformation of the 1850s when every available woman—young or old—seemed swept up into marriage, the "prevalence" of polygamy was "too high to be perpetuated." In other words, at first the practice ballooned not only because there were slightly more women than men, but because men married both women who were older than they were and girls who were much younger than they were. Once the female population of marriageable females was depleted, men only had so many women or girls whom

they could marry, and subsequently, the polygamous population by neces-
sity "declined to demographically sustainable levels." According to Davis
Bitton and Val Lambson, in any given population, polygamy by "more
than 20 percent of husbands and 30 percent of wives is on the high end of
what is mathematically plausible." Thus, even though statistically during
the 1870s and 1880s there were more polygamous wives because the general population was greater, polygamous wives made up a smaller percentage of the entire Mormon population. Perhaps inevitably, their
lifestyle became more specialized and obscure—polygamous marriages
were increasingly overshadowed by monogamous marriages.

Furthermore, in the 1870s and 1880s, the Utah Territory was not the
same isolated place it had been. In 1876, the English journalist William
Hepworth Dixon observed that polygamy among the Mormons was de-
clining compared with what he had observed before. He wrote, "the rage in
favour of plurality is past." When he told then-Apostle John Taylor his impression, Taylor gave a "weary shrug" and reportedly replied to Dixon that
perhaps in Salt Lake there were less polygamists due to the "Gentile influence," but "on the country farms and in the lonely sheepruns" there lived "a
pastoral people eager to fulfill the law." When the cynical Dixon asked Taylor
if he meant to say that "rich and educated Mormons [were] giving up polygamy, and the poor and ignorant brethren [were] taking to it," Taylor was
annoyed but answered that "some worldly men are weary of obedience"
while the "pure in heart and true in faith" are willing to "assume their cross."

In the late 1880s, younger Mormons were less interested in "assum[ing]
their cross." By then, young women had more opportunity for education
and, according to Kathryn Daynes, increasingly rejected polygamy "in
favor of romantic love." A generation gap appeared between the older generation that had participated in polygamy and the younger generation that
found it offensive. An 1888 *Exponent* article revealed that some young
women even tried to avoid polygamy by marrying young men who had
"bad habits," assuming that those young men wouldn't be worthy to become polygamous husbands. In 1889, female Church leaders launched a
periodical for young women titled the *Young Woman's Journal* to nurture
girls' relationships with the Mormon community and its values. According
to Sherry Baker, who analyzed the *Journal's* first five years, one recurring
theme was a retrospective idealized view of polygamy where, for example,
the first wife helped choose the second wife and they lived in harmony.
This theme was meant to reduce girls' "significant disenchantment" with
and "alienation" from polygamy, to help them understand why some

Mormon women had become polygamous wives, and to help the girls "come to terms with their history." The idealized view was meant to counter the negative observations that girls had grown up with.

Church periodicals from this time period illustrate this change in attitude. Between 1884 and 1890, the number of women who defended polygamy in the *Woman's Exponent* decreased, and their tone changed. Those who defended it tended to "reproduce the voice of their male leaders" rather than "fashion a voice of their own" or offer personal reasons for keeping the practice. Susa Young Gates, editor of the *Journal* even accused Mormon women of desiring the Manifesto. In 1893, she offered a retrospective view of women who had treated the "holy principle," plural marriage, with "neglect, sneers, mocking abuse and even cursing and railing" and went on to say that Mormon women collectively, herself included, should recognize their "sin." Her opinion was that "polygamy was abandoned by the Church because of negative attitudes toward it by the Mormon women themselves, including herself." She asked women to consider whether they knew women who, or if they themselves, had "said they would never consent to marry a man who had another wife" or "said openly or in private that not one of her daughters" should be a polygamous wife or "openly rejoiced when the Manifesto was issued"? Gates's accusations further illustrate the widening gap between Mormons who wanted to be done with polygamy and the "core of zealous Mormons" who without the Manifesto "would have continued the practice, at least for several more decades."

When President Taylor died in 1887, he at least partially understood the complexity of the situation. He also sympathized with polygamists and "acknowledged that the persecutions were growing intolerable." Although some of his advisors thought the Church should give up polygamy for, say, five years until Utah gained statehood, Taylor believed that "a political ruse" was "unacceptable" and did not want to pretend that Mormons would agree to abandon polygamy then not really abandon it. But while he was "outwardly gracious and appreciative" of feedback from the Quorum of the Twelve and members of the Church, "it seems that President Taylor's inward conviction was to find these efforts irreconcilably conflicting with correct principle." In the end, with no political solution and with polygamists increasingly leaving for Canada and Mexico, President Taylor encouraged the people to have more faith and be more obedient and wait on God.

Taylor's successor, Woodruff, inherited a mess: pressure from internal fanatics who saw Armageddon in what they perceived to be a fight between God's law and man's law; knowledge that polygamous families were suffering from polygamous raids; knowledge that most Mormons were not polygamists and yet were suffering for the practice of a few; the threat of losing Church real estate, including their sacred temples; and a culture shifting away from polygamy. Like President Taylor, President Woodruff was also "subject to intense solicitation from both Mormon and non-Mormon friends" to end polygamy. In addition, in 1890, Idaho Mormons were banned from voting whether or not they were polygamists, and the "Utah Commission annual report likely recommended that [Utah] Mormons be banned from voting," too.

In August 1890, while trying to negotiate with government officials, Woodruff traveled 2,400 miles to visit the Saints in Utah, Wyoming, Colorado, New Mexico, and Arizona, and "the eighty-three-year-old leader was able to see firsthand the terrible circumstances of polygamist Saints." As he considered what to do, he reasoned that the Church was on the verge of losing everything. He said, "The Lord showed me by vision and revelation exactly what would take place if we did not stop this practice." He saw that the Saints' temples would be confiscated, "many men would be made prisoners," and "trouble would [come] upon the whole Church." After engaging in "earnest prayer," he gradually came to the decision to abandon polygamy.

On September 24, 1890, in Salt Lake City, having just passed a sleepless night, he faced his inner circle with a draft of the Manifesto. He explained the situation the Church was in and told the intimate group of Church leaders that "with broken heart and contrite spirit" he had "sought the will of the Lord, and the Holy Spirit had revealed that it was necessary for the church to relinquish the practice of that principle." According to some who were there, Woodruff told them that "the Lord had made it plain to him that this was his duty, and he felt perfectly clear in his mind that it was the right thing."

Woodruff humbly told them, "The matter is now before you. I want you to speak as the Spirit moves you." No one spoke. When prompted, only his counselor George Q. Cannon supported him. Others, even in tears, asked questions and "protested." They insisted that they were "willing to suffer 'persecution unto death' rather than to violate the covenants which they had made 'in holy places' with the women who had trusted them." He would later explain, "I have had this spirit upon me for a long time. But I want to say this: I should have let all the temples go out of our hands; I should have gone to prison myself, and let every other man go there, had not the God of heaven commanded me to do what I did do; I went before the Lord, and I wrote what the Lord told me to write." As the aged prophet would later explain to some of his followers, "I am about to go into the spirit world, like other men of my age...and for me to have taken a stand in anything which is not pleasing in the sight of God, or before the heavens, I would rather have gone out and been shot."

In Salt Lake City that morning, the leading men of the Church eventually showed some willingness to go along with him. Woodruff wrote in his diary the next day that the "Proclamation" was "sustained" by his counselors and the Twelve Apostles. But about half of the Twelve saw the Manifesto as an "immediate expedient" and had "serious hesitations about ending a practice they thought necessary for exaltation." The other half were supportive or supportive with hesitations. A little more than a year later in November 1891, Woodruff admitted that there were still "a good many men, and probably some leading men, in this Church who have been tried and felt as though President Woodruff had lost the Spirit of God and was about to apostatize." Unlike average Church members, Church leaders probably lived in a world that was primarily polygamous. The Church was run by men who were polygamists, and they likely socialized with each other and with their many families that were polygamous. Over the years, these men also gave the speeches that promoted polygamy most strongly. Polygamy probably had come to seem normal and essential to some of them, and a few continued to secretly encourage polygamy until another Manifesto had to be decreed in 1904.

Not long after Woodruff read the Manifesto at the Salt Lake semiannual General Conference and it was accepted, people in outlying areas began to hear the news and tried to sort out what it meant. Some polygamous wives had to make some adjustments to their thinking. For example, second wife Annie Clark Tanner, who was married to the general superintendent of the Church Sunday school, and who had delivered her second baby alone on the floor while in hiding a month before the Manifesto was delivered, wrote that the Church's abandonment of polygamy initially disturbed her. She wondered if God were "the same yesterday, today, and forever" as she had been taught. Prior to the announcement, as a wandering polygamous wife who had fiercely hidden her identity to protect her husband from arrest, she compared her faith to the biblical "three Hebrews who were to be cast into a fiery furnace for their convictions." But for all her "earlier convictions, a great relief came over" her as she considered the news of the Manifesto. She compared her "feelings of relief with the experience one has when the first crack of dawn comes after a night of careful vigilance over a sick patient." She went on, "At such a time daylight is never more welcome; and now the dawn was breaking for the Church." She supposed that Church leaders realized at last that if "our Church had anything worthwhile for mankind, they had better work with the government of our country rather than against it."

Initially, the change may have been confusing to polygamous families. In the Manifesto, President Woodruff had written, "I now publicly declare that my advice to the Latter-day Saints is to refrain from contracting any marriage forbidden by the law of the land." At the same time that Woodruff declared that no further polygamous marriages would be sanctioned by the Church, Kathryn Daynes points out that Church leaders also "gave little guidance after the Manifesto was issued about what that statement meant for those already in plural marriage." Carmon Hardy believes that many Mormons during this time felt that "there was confusion as to what was and was not permissible."

Behind the scenes, President Woodruff privately felt that "polygamists should continue to support their wives" and told this to his Apostles within a month after the Manifesto had been voted on at October conference. The week after October conference, Church representative George Q. Cannon spoke with United States Attorney Charles S. Varian in Salt Lake City and explained polygamists' "reluctance" to abandon their families. Varian evidently understood this and "favored a suspension of the laws for a year or so for the purpose of seeing if Mormons would carry out the Manifesto in good faith." By this, he evidently meant that husbands could support their wives, but that husbands should only have sexual relations with first wives. While Woodruff defended the support of polygamous wives, he said in a November 1891 conference in Logan, Utah, that both new marriages and cohabitation with polygamous wives "should be halted." Woodruff himself had lived with only one of his wives since 1885.

Although the federal government had reconsidered how much money they were spending to spy on polygamists and had eased their efforts, even a few years after the Manifesto, federal agents continued to monitor whether polygamists were acting in "good faith." After the Manifesto, wives still feared the law and husbands could be pulled into court. For example, in the spring of 1891, Lorena Larsen's husband secretly sent for her to come to Manti, where he was living with his first family while working on the temple. When she arrived, she felt obliged to hide her identity and discreetly told some people to tell her husband that "a lady friend from Colorado" was there. Her husband chopped wood for her in a skirt and shawl to look like a woman and deflect suspicion. It seems they had reason to be cautious, because Phrasia Day was subpoenaed that same spring

(1891) to "appear in the case of EA Day," her husband. Her husband was arrested and agreed to appear in Colorado. In 1893 in Salt Lake, Florence Dean was awaiting the birth of her fifth child and wrote that it was "dangerous" for her husband to visit her. The danger he faced was probably the possibility of being caught coming to see a pregnant second wife.

When the federal government eventually became convinced that routine polygamous marriages were a thing of the past, they reduced their surveillance. In 1893, President Benjamin Harrison "granted amnesty to all Saints who had been in compliance with the law since the Manifesto." But "to marry polygamously or to cohabit with more than one woman continued to be a state crime." As time passed, "a tacit Agreement seemed to develop to let the passage of time and the death of the polygamous generation end the practice." For all its value, "the Manifesto was not a sudden turning point." Rather, reducing polygamy was a "slow process of yielding up the practice" rather than a "sudden moment of capitulation." Some new polygamous marriages were discreetly forged and some old polygamous families quietly continued. And although federal government attorney Varian had said that he did not approve of "criminal intercourse" between husbands and wives, some polygamous wives continued to have children. Of the thirteen wives in this study who wrote about this period, only three didn't have children after the Manifesto. Of the three wives in this study who didn't have children, one had left her husband, and the other two were first wives past childbearing age. Some who did have children did so with trepidation, however.

By 1890, the women in this study were generally weary of polygamy—of the thirteen women who wrote during this period, eleven did not even mention the Manifesto in their writings. Some of their husbands had spent time in prison; some of them had been chased by the law; and most of them had their own homes and were supporting themselves. Either they didn't feel that the Manifesto affected them or they silently endorsed the change. The isolated frontier existence that had perhaps made polygamy socially and economically attractive was disappearing, and Mormons had secured a base population of faithful children that assured their continued existence. If the process and products of polygamy were meant to lay a firm foundation for a growing church, then, arguably, this had been accomplished. After 1896 when Utah became a state, Mormons officially began to intertwine their own version of Manifest Destiny with the rest of America, even if polygamous wives still dotted the landscape.

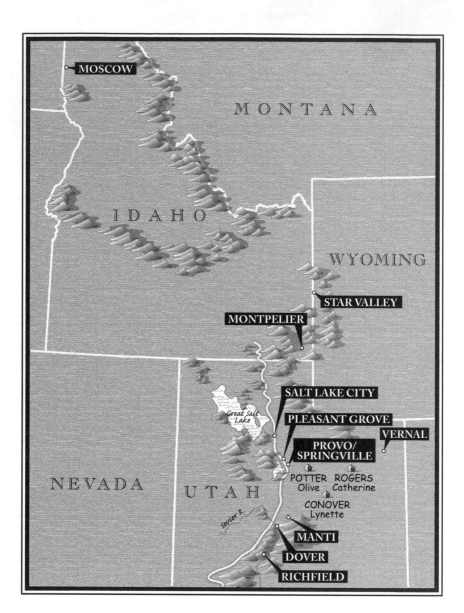

I grew rebellious

Catherine Rogers's Shop/House: 120 North Academy Avenue, Provo, Utah, in 1904

In 1904, third wife *Catherine Rogers* and second wife *Olive Potter* both lived in Provo, and both had stomach problems. By autumn, Catherine would die of carcinoma of the liver and intestines. If they had known each other early in 1904, they could have sat and commiserated in Catherine's fifteen-foot-wide dressmaking shop that abutted the sidewalk on Academy Avenue and attracted customers because of its print curtains and "fashion sheets" in the window. Mostly, they could have confided with each other that they had long ago left their husbands, not because of the Manifesto but to get the necessities of life for their children.

Fifty-five-year-old Catherine could have told thirty-six-year-old Olive that three years ago, when she moved to Provo, her dear old friend "Mother Bunnel" had let her stay in this shop. Catherine and her two youngest children, twenty-year-old Kate and eighteen-year-old Rudolph, still lived in the back of the twenty-five-foot-long shop, and Catherine worked in the front. Catherine had come to Provo so her children could continue their education; Olive would have understood because she moved to Provo for the same reason. Both of them worked with the determination characteristic of single mothers whose raison d'être was to feed, clothe, and educate their children in the hope that their children would have a better life than they had. To earn a living, Catherine had her dressmaking. When Olive first arrived in Provo, she had lived at 674 North 2nd East where she had taken in five student boarders, but then she moved to 911 East W. Center Street, located "too far from school to take in boarders," so she took in washing and ironing instead, as she often had during her life.

During early marriage, both Catherine and Olive had lived in Sanpete County, Utah, about sixty miles south of Provo. As Catherine was growing up there, her mother had been "ambitious" about her "education" and trained Catherine to be "quite a young lady." Catherine naturally assumed she would marry Pete, her "companion of whom [she] was very fond." As teens, Catherine and Pete talked "often" about polygamy, and one day Pete said that polygamy was "one law" he "never intend[ed] to live." When her father overheard Pete's comment, "from that time on there was no place in [her] fathers heart for Pete." Catherine explained that her father was not a polygamist himself, but he felt strongly that polygamy was a law of God. Although their home had never been "disturbed with this question before," her father began to insist that Pete was wrong. Even Catherine worried about "Pete's determination against" polygamy.

Her father's feelings made her anxious, and she prayed often about polygamy, but an answer to her prayer was "a long time coming." Then one night before bed, she saw a visionary man and woman who indicated that Catherine would go to heaven as part of a threesome. She had seen two people in a "clear light" and "one of them motioned" to her to "come near to them." She wrote, "It was so real" that she "took a step forward." The second person "raised his hand for [her] to stop and at the same time pointed to" her side. When Catherine "turned to look, a woman stood beside" her, and she "heard a voice say, 'If you would come with us you must take this woman's hand.'" Then "the light faded from [her] room and [she] stood alone in the dark." After this experience, she "knew the answer" to her queries about polygamy. The next morning, she told her mother about her experience, and her mother was very "affected" but "said nothing." Pete "didn't take it seriously" and "could not believe [she] would accept the law." From that point on, Catherine stated, "I could never explain my feeling just a calm knowledge that I would do my duty and God would lead me." Then an opportunity arose. And it didn't involve Pete.

In 1867 when Catherine was eighteen, a thirty-four-year-old Mormon medical doctor, who had graduated from McDowell Medical College in Missouri, came to live in Moroni with his family. Dr. Ruel Rogers was "about 5 ft. 8 in. in height," and "weighed about 165 lbs." with "gray blue" eyes and "light brown" hair. He and his first wife, Lovina, had three children. Catherine wrote that Lovina was "a woman of kindly grace and stately main" with "smiling eyes and a wealth of beautiful black hair"—Dr. Rogers referred to her as a "real pink of the South." The doctor had also married a second wife, Augusta, just before moving to Moroni.

After Dr. Rogers's arrival in Moroni, he "endear[ed] himself to the community as only a doctor can." Since Moroni was a small town and the people "quite a sturdy class" who didn't need a full-time doctor, Dr. Rogers taught school part time, and Catherine "came under his teaching." She wrote, "He was an intelligent and interesting instructor, but I was never quite sure whether fathers anxiety over the question of patriarchal marriage had reached the doctors notice for often I felt he displayed too much attention to me." At the end of the school term, Dr. Rogers "requested I meet him after class." She felt that "his business was in deed personal"—

FIGURE 11.2 Third wife Catherine Rogers.

he wanted "to know if I understood the order of patriarchal marriage. I was able to inform him I was very sure it was an order from God. This interview ended with an invitation to me to join his family and become Mrs. Rogers the third."

At first, Catherine "did not look with much favor on the proposition." She knew that her father "was entirely in favor of it" and that her mother "had very little to say" and was "worried." Catherine explained that when she "consented to marry Doctor Rogers it was not because of love for the man or even a feeling of companionship" because she had "built [her] future around Pete." He had been her companion "since childhood," and they "had learned to plan together and appreciate the same things." But she was influenced by her "fathers desires" and the answer she had to her prayers. So with her "fathers urging and the Doctors constant kindness and attention," she "finally accepted the offer," and she and the doctor were married in the Endowment House. As for Pete, their "parting...had been a sad one." Pete left Moroni, and Catherine "saw him only once again," when she lay near death after the birth of her sixth child.

Olive's husband had also been an older man whom she didn't really love, but in her case, her parents had discouraged her from marrying him and tried to talk her out of it. In about 1884, her family had moved to the farming community of Dover, twenty-five miles from Manti, and "a family named Potter were very sociable" with them. The husband, Edwin Potter, "eventually started paying attention" to Olive, and she thought "it was nice to be loved," as she

FIGURE 11.3 Catherine's husband, Dr. Ruel Rogers.

was "right in the boy-struck age." Her parents were "very much opposed to his attentions." Edwin was thirty-four and had five children, "the youngest just four years younger" than Olive, and his family lived in "two log rooms with a dirt roof." Olive explained, "Of course Polygamy was in vogue and I guess he wanted a nice young wife. If I had only realized it, it was the beginning of many and many a heartache and many trials."

Edwin, his first wife (Aunt Hattie), and Olive traveled by wagon in July 1884 to the Salt Lake Endowment House—Olive's parents did not accompany her, but if they would have, they might have been able to stop the ceremony. Olive was just under sixteen years of age, and she realized her mistake while she was still in the Endowment House: "I felt so terrible when we were going through, worse than if I had been to a funeral. My eyes were open then for the first time. I could have backed out then, but I was just a child and didn't have enough judgement." The day after the ceremony, in a telling move, Edwin's first wife "went to Idaho to visit her folks and was gone six weeks" while Olive went back "to keep house for [Edwin] and his children." The log house had one "fairly good size" room and a "small lean-to," which was Olive's room. Olive lived with the other seven members of the family until after her first baby was born.

Hearing this story would have brought back memories for Catherine, who right after marriage had moved in with her husband's other two families. She found the adjustment "very difficult" because she grew up in a "quiet home" characterized by "order and system," and life with the Rogers was "indeed changed." Each wife had a "separate apartment," but Lovina's and Augusta's children were like "brothers and sisters" to Catherine and "insist[ed]" on being "permitted to eat and sleep" in her apartment. Catherine remembered that Augusta's little girl would not leave her apartment even when her mother came to get her, calling her own mother "Aunt Gussie" and saying "I going to eat with my own mommie," as she called Catherine. Weighed down, Catherine felt that she could not confide in her own mother, who "already understood too much," but she could "pour out her soul" to Father in Heaven in prayer. After her first child's birth, she begged that God would send a feeling of "love and respect" she felt she needed "for the man who was [her] child's father," and her "prayer was granted." Dr. Rogers became to her "a man [she] was proud to say was [her] child's father. All his good qualities and abilities were magnified in [her] eyes and [she] found peace in [her] new home."

The Rogerses stayed in Moroni six years, where Catherine had a second baby, and then the family moved to Provo. Before leaving, since Catherine's father and mother had died, she "signed fathers and mothers property over to" her brother Christian, who had just married. During the four years the Rogers spent in Provo, Catherine was happier than she'd been "since [she] left her fathers home." In Provo, Lovina and Augusta each had a home, and Catherine's home was "in connection with" a drug store they established in 1873 called "The City Drug Store" on Main Street. Dr. Rogers "took special time to teach" her about the pharmacy, and the work "brought contact with new people." Karl G. Maeser, the president of Brigham Young Academy, "was a regular visitor" at their home, as were "many of the students and educators" associated with the Academy.

In Olive's case, though, life went downhill the longer she was married, as she moved from house to ramshackle house, each more impoverished than the last, as her babies kept coming. Her husband Edwin seemed unable to settle someplace where he could earn a living and just kept moving. First, Edwin built "one log room" for her that doubled as a "grainery" a half mile from the other family's house. Then the Potters moved five miles up the Sevier River, and Edwin constructed two houses a block apart" built in the "side hill—just one room each house." Olive wrote, "I cannot describe how terrible they were, and the rats were busy all night traveling around. . . . And the fleas. Oh my! How terrible! I had scabs on my back from scratching." Then Edwin got a job herding sheep and took his first family with him, so Olive was left alone but had a "light wagon" and horses so she could go see her parents from time to time, driving over "a steep hill" that required her to brake the whole way down, her baby lying alone in the back of the wagon. Then Edwin brought her to the sheep camp, as well, where both families slept "in tents right on the ground." The good part was that Edwin was "a good cook over the campfire and could make very good bread in the bake skillet," and they had "fresh mutton" whenever they wanted it.

But because of the polygamy raids, Edwin sent Olive to live with his sister and mother, Mother Brown, in Salt Lake. In retrospect, Olive thought she was "a fool" for all the work she did there, but she was "so conscientious" that she felt that she "had to do everything for [her] board." She got up at 6 a.m. to make "Uncle Hyrum's breakfast and put up his lunch," made breakfast again later in the morning for "Rosella and her mother," heated water for their baths, and even emptied the tub for them. In Olive's opinion, Edwin's sister and mother were "extremely lazy"; she added, "It is terrible for me to say it, but it is the truth." While living with them, she took in some wash because she "needed a little money and [her] husband was very poor."

In September 1887, when Olive had her second baby, her lazy mother-in-law was supposed to care for her but didn't manage to repay all the work Olive had done for her earlier. Olive had a midwife and "had a normal time and felt fine the first three days" but then "took a backset caused from neglect." Mother Brown was supposed to help her, but she didn't come over until late morning, wouldn't do anything unless asked, and made inedible food: "When she made gruel it was thick and pasty, and the dish would be covered with fly specks." Olive became more and more ill until her mother and father had to come: "I don't know what I would have done without my wonderful father and mother taking care of me so much of the time."

Catherine had better luck—at least at first. Even though her parents died not long after she was married, she was fortunate to have older friends, like Mother Bunnel, Martha, and Thomas Wooley, who helped her throughout her life. As a teenager, Catherine had temporarily moved to Provo to work as a spinner and met Mother Bunnel and her daughter Rosie when she boarded with them. When Catherine returned to Provo with the Rogers family, she renewed her friendship with Mother Bunnel.

Although Catherine loved life in Provo, Dr. Rogers, who was "an enterprising man," began "to look for greater opportunities" and decided to take his families to Pleasant Grove, fourteen miles north. In 1877, he "took up three quarter sections under the homestead right," at the base of Mt. Timpanogos in Pleasant Grove, "intending to make a beautiful farm home for each family." Dr. Rogers "sold all his belongings at Provo and established each family on a quarter section" while "carrying his practice on at Pleasant Grove and surrounding community." Lovina had the largest farm where "all stock, machinery and help" were kept; Augusta's land was next to hers; and Catherine's home was "on the higher land" where "in the dry season water was scarce." The doctor invested a lot of money with other landholders to bring water there, but "it was indeed pioneer farming," and she "grew discouraged." During this time, the doctor established "a drugstore in Pleasant Grove," and Lovina moved to town to help with it.

After Lovina left, the farms weren't the same, wrote Catherine. Lovina had been "a real mother" to Catherine and her babies and had "made sure [they] were provided for." When second wife Augusta "took control of all affairs at the farms," Catherine's "provisions ran short and the whole tone of the life changed." Catherine "talked to the Doctor about the condition," but it wasn't until Mother Bunnel and her daughter Rosie came to visit her that she realized how bad things were. They told Catherine what the government was proposing: that husbands would be "required to dissolve their relations with all plural wives," and that "any child born after 1883 would be...illegitimate" in the eyes of the law. Catherine's "first thought was to move to town" where she could "provide" for herself and her children. When she told her concern to the doctor, he told her he was worried, too, but, as she explained, "insisted I stay right where I was." He believed the government had no right to control his families.

As time went on, Catherine's life on the hillside got worse. Her provisions "grew very short," and "a great many times" her family was "without the necessary things to eat or wear." The doctor "reprimand[ed]" Catherine for "criticizing A[u]gusta" who had said they were "well provided for." Catherine's shoes "wore out," and Augusta wouldn't get her any, so she wrapped her feet in "gunny sacks."

In 1882, after five years on the farm, one day Mother Bunnel and Rosie paid Catherine "a surprise visit" and, after visiting for a while, Rosie asked Catherine for something to eat. Catherine only had "a little milk and some flour," so she "sent one of the children to get salt and baking powder" from Augusta "to stir up a cake." When Mother Bunnel and Rosie climbed in their buggy to leave, Catherine wrote, Rosie "threw me her dress and shoes saying, 'Catherine, wear these, I'll wear my coat home, and please get yourself and children off this farm into town where you can be fed and clothed.'" Catherine stood watching them "until they were out of sight" and then "cried until [she] was weak." After feeding her four children the leftover cake and putting them to bed, she "poured [her] soul out in prayer." The next day, she felt her prayer was answered.

When she woke up, the "way seemed clear," and she decided to move to town. By chance, Augusta's brother "came out to the farm and drove up" to Catherine's place. While they were talking, Catherine wrote, "it came to me that he had been sent in answer to my prayers. I asked him if he would take me and my family to town," and he said sure...he didn't know what he had come up for. Catherine threw her "few belongings" in the wagon while he put the children in, and "without regret" she "said goodbye to a place" where they lived for five years. She felt that she was "being guided by the spirit of the Lord and that he was answering" her prayers.

In town, she didn't go see the doctor or Lovina, but took her children to a friend while she went to find a place to live. A place "seemed to be waiting" for her because "a good man," Thomas Wooley, "had a small house unoccupied." He said Catherine was "welcome to it," and his wife Martha "volunteered to help make it ready." Before night, Catherine and her children "were located in a comfortable little house." The next day, she was not surprised when the doctor "drove up" to their door and was "greatly put out" that she would leave the farm without consulting him. He also told her that in town there were "government officials constantly on guard for men who even visited the homes of plural wives." She explained that she moved so that she could help support her family and that she thought it would be easier for him to send supplies to her there. She said that she "fully intended" to get sewing to help support her family. Indeed, she wrote that the people of Pleasant Grove gave her "sewing to do and by this means" she was able to get badly needed clothes for her family.

Catherine tried to explain to the doctor that, under the circumstances, she didn't want more children. She loved her five children and was "willing to work for them," but she felt "there would be much less suffering" if they "lived according to the law of the land and tried to feed the children" they had. The doctor disagreed and gave "no encouragement" for her point of view. Like "the authorities of the church," the doctor "felt Gods laws were greater than mans," and he felt it was their duty to "continue raising families." Men like Dr. Rogers did not back down to government pressure, and when Catherine seemed to be taking the government's side, he must have felt sure he was right.

The circumstances under which she became pregnant for a sixth time are not entirely clear, but reading between the lines, the reader can imagine Catherine's despair. When she learned that she was pregnant, she wrote, "I grew rebellious"—she had "suffered cold, hunger and had been without almost all the necessities of life and now" when she could finally "see [her] way to something better," she "did not have the courage and faith to meet" her pregnancy. In 1884, she delivered a premature seven-month-old baby girl, Kate, and Catherine "lay helpless" for weeks. She wrote that during this time a "heavenly messenger" came to "her bedside" and told her she would live, that "the Lord [was] pleased with her faithfulness" and that "in two years" she would "become the mother of a baby boy." In 1886, her son Rudolph was born, her youngest child. The same year, the doctor was taken to the penitentiary. These last two children, Kate and Rudolph, were the ones she would later take to Provo for an education when they were twenty and eighteen years old.

Olive understood this kind of situation all too well. When she was "with [her] husband," she "always had it so hard...for he was extremely poor." Her marriage was an endless routine of staying with her parents, going to her husband, getting pregnant, not having enough to eat or a decent place to stay, and returning to live with her parents. After a long stay with her parents when she was sick after the birth of her second baby, while Olive prepared to return to her husband, a neighbor told her mother, "Why did you let her go. She will just come back with another baby."

In the fall of 1888, after leaving her parents' house, riding in a wagon guided by Edwin's oldest children, getting lost then rescued by Edwin, and finally making it 230 miles to Vernal, Olive slept on the ground with her two babies outside first wife Aunt Hattie's house because "there was no room in the house." The next day, Edwin took Olive to the place he had rented for her. She was disappointed that the house was "quite aways from Vernal" in thickets and was "built in the side of a hill." She wrote, "It was the most terrible house." She could not remember if it was made of logs or willows and plastered over, but she remembered that it was "alive with bedbugs." In order to sleep, she had to "have the bed in the middle of the floor and have each leg in cans of water and then pour water all around on the floor." She had the "most terrible time" there but enjoyed the "nice patch of tomatoes and watermelons." One afternoon some Indians asked if they could have some watermelons, and she told them to help themselves. Hours later after dark, she could still hear them talking outside, and then a knock on the door—it was Edwin. She told him that "was one time" she was "glad to see him."

In about 1889, the Potters moved yet again, three miles outside of Vernal, where Edwin built "two log rooms a block apart" for each of his families—again, half of her room was "made into a grainery." Perhaps he thought he could avoid polygamy raids out in the country, but one day one of Edwin's boys came running to warn Olive that the marshals were coming, so she put her oldest daughter, Pearl, on her back and her second daughter, Myrtle, in her arms and, she wrote, "ran as fast as I could through fields and brush to some people I knew."

She stayed there a week, shared the only room with the people, and "had to sleep on a dirt floor." She was up all the time with her babies so they wouldn't disturb the people she was staying with, and she had a miscarriage

FIGURE 11.4 Second wife Olive Andelin Potter, her husband Edwin Potter, and their children.

two months along from the dashing run. She felt awkward taking the people's food because they were very poor, and she "couldn't eat what they did have on account of the flies." She thought her "stomach would turn inside out." No wonder that Olive had stomach problems. Edwin also hid for a week, and then the family moved fifteen miles out of town. Aunt Hattie watched Olive's children while Olive washed on a board for fifty cents a day. Olive returned to her cold house—that still doubled as a "grainery"—and started a fire before going to get the children. Once, when it rained for three days, she had to put the bed "in the middle of the floor" because that was the only dry spot in the house. In the spring of 1890, her third daughter, Mary Melvina, was born. That year Edwin left for Salt Lake to find work since they were "so extremely poor."

Catherine and her children were also "without the necessities of life" in 1886 when Dr. Rogers was sent to prison. Although she sewed to help support her family, she couldn't do it completely on her own, and she thought her best option was to stay with her brother Christian in northern Idaho. Catherine's Church leaders also thought this was a good plan. The Church was severely disrupted by the polygamy raids; the Church authorities were "suffering with the people" with so many confined to prison and the Church president himself on the underground. Christian, to whom she had given the deed to her family house, was living in Moscow, Idaho, with his family and urged her to join them. Sadly, while preparing for the trip, Catherine's oldest daughter, Victoria, who was eleven years old, was killed in a horse accident. Catherine, like other polygamous wives, had relied a great deal on her oldest child, so Victoria's death was almost more than she could bear—losing, as she wrote, "my support and my companion."

When Catherine arrived in Moscow, Christian met her and her children with "a buggy and a span of beautiful black horses" to take them to his farm. Christian had a "large timber claim," and his bins were "overflowing, there were cows, horses, chickens, turkeys," and "so much wood to keep the fires burning and such a freedom of want." Christian wanted to share it all with Catherine, to give her family "a home, and take care" of them. But Christian had a caveat: "he was not willing that [she] should belong to a church that, to him, was practicing an order contrary to the laws of the government." She was surprised that he had left their family religion and wanted her to leave also. She stayed with him "several months" until she could "control her grief," and then she told him, as she explained it, that "the Church of Jesus Christ with all its ordinances meant more to me than all else on this earth although I had been deprived of a husband, that my children had suffered hunger and cold, that the main support in my family had been taken away, yet I desired to remain faithful."

Her brother "would not or could not understand" and was "very angry" with her. She asked him to help her move to the town of Moscow where she could get a little house and sew until she had enough money to move where there was "an organization of Latter Day Saints." She was in Moscow for eighteen months, most of the time without a relationship with her brother. When she saved enough money to move, she and five of her children—the sixth, her oldest daughter, had stayed in Pleasant Grove but would eventually join them—ages twelve, ten, seven, four, and two traveled 700 miles south to Montpelier, Idaho.

In Montpelier, the bishop of the Church there took her and her five children "to his home and cared for [them] as he would have a dear sister." Within a few days, at the bishop's house, she met a man from Afton, Star Valley, Wyoming, who told her that his community needed a dressmaker. He also mentioned that Thomas and Martha Wooley were living there, the couple who had given Catherine a house in Pleasant Grove when she came down off the mountain. She decided to try to go there. The next morning, Catherine and her children traveled in the man's wagon to Star Valley, an idyllic "beautiful spot" where "a roaring, dashing stream" came from the canyon down into the valley, and where the surrounding mountains were "covered with heavy green pine and fir interspersed with juniper, birch, cottonwood and quaking aspen."

The man left Catherine and her children at the Wooleys' where Martha gave her a "joyful greeting" that warmed Catherine's heart. The Wooleys had a "large log cabin with a leanto on the back" where Catherine's family slept. After a good night's sleep, Catherine "enquir[ed] about a place to live and work to do," and Martha told her, "Why Catherine, I am sure God sent you" and told her she could stay there. The Wooleys never had children and were in their early sixties. Martha told Catherine that she had "to go back to Pleasant Grove for the winter" and was "worried about leaving Thomas" alone. Martha figured, "Now you can take care of him," and besides, Thomas needed a boy the age of Catherine's oldest son "to help him care for cows, sheep and horses" at his farm about a mile away. Thomas had a "nice cabin there where he stayed most of the time and would be glad for the boys help."

So Catherine's life in Star Valley fell into place. When she arrived, the first snows had fallen, and she compared the beautiful snow drifts that would build around their cabin to the "pure lives and serene spirit" of Thomas and Martha and the other good people of Star Valley. Being near them brought "peace to [her] soul" and a "haven of rest." Although the first winter she suffered from pains so severe in her neck and shoulders that she couldn't even dress herself, they decided it was "rheumatism caused from bad teeth." But when spring arrived, she felt better and "advertised for sewing and built up a very good business." During the fifteen years that she lived in Star Valley, she had "the children write to their father," but he "refused to give either supplies or money to support them unless [she] would come back." She replied that she didn't want him to "go back to the penitentiary" and felt that they "were much better off" in Star Valley.

So, it turned out that Thomas Wooley became a surrogate father to Catherine's children. In "jolly times," Thomas would let the children "[ride] on his knees" and "[let] them climb all over him until they were all tired out." Catherine thought it sad to see a man "who loved children so much" be "deprived of a family" since he had no children of his own. In an interesting twist on family life, Catherine made it possible for Martha to stay long periods of time in Pleasant Grove while Thomas stayed in Star Valley to care for their animals and farm. Thomas told Catherine that he loved her children so much that he would gladly have them "sealed" to him. He told Catherine, "if the Doctor would only give me these children I would be a happy man. If he does not want his family in this life or the eternities I would love to have them sealed to me. I have no children of my own so I would gladly accept you and the children." Thomas meant that Catherine could be sealed to him as a polygamous wife and have her children sealed to him, too. Although Catherine was flattered enough by his offer to write about it in her autobiography, it's unclear whether she was interested in his proposition. Besides, about this time, Martha (perhaps sensing Thomas' increasing interest in Catherine), sent a note that Thomas "had better return to Pleasant Grove" as he was "needed there." Before leaving, Thomas "deed[ed] the Star Valley home in town" to Catherine and her children. In May 1896, shortly after leaving Star Valley, Thomas caught pneumonia and died in Pleasant Grove.

While Catherine was being cared for by the Wooleys, Olive returned home to her parents again. The "first chance [she] got" to leave Vernal was with three teams taking wool to Provo, and she knew her father was working there on a new building, so she hoped to meet up with him. She sat in the front of the wagon "by the man, with [her] feet dangling," holding her baby, and her other two, Pearl and Myrtle, sat in the back on the wool sacks; Olive prayed they wouldn't be bumped out of the wagon. Without hats during the multiple-day journey, they got very sunburned and "blistered." When Olive arrived in Provo, she searched all afternoon for her father, and when he saw her, "he cried, 'My child, my child, where did you come from.'" He paid the men who had brought her, got her a place to stay and some hats, telegraphed her mother to expect her, and purchased train tickets for Richfield 120 miles away. Olive could not have made it without her parents who supported her "most of the time."

Olive finally concluded that she "couldn't be happy" around her husband or his family. She explained, "I didn't love him, getting married so young and him so much older and with a family already...I respected him and didn't have anything against him, for he was good and kind to us and loved us, but he had too much family and the other family was extravagant." Aunt Hattie had "cows and would buy butter, and chickens and would buy eggs, a garden and would buy vegetables. Didn't take care of anything." And Edwin was "so poor, he could not make the grade." Olive and her parents ended up "support[ing] her family most of the time." Olive had her fourth child, Ruby, while at home, fulfilling her neighbor's prophecy, and a little more than a year later, in January 1893, left her children in her mother's care and went to work 160 miles north in Salt Lake.

In Salt Lake, Olive eventually found a position at the Gilmers', on "Gilmer Drive on Ninth South and Eleventh East," where she earned twenty dollars a month and sent the money home for her children. Olive cooked, cleaned, canned "fruit, pickles, sauces, mincemeat, and every-thing." Every evening meal was "large enough for a banquet" served in three or four courses, and the Gilmers gave her their cast-off clothes and shoes. She stayed in Salt Lake five years, and during this time was offi-cially separated from her husband Edwin. Perhaps surprisingly, after a seven-year break from childbearing, in 1900, Olive had her fifth daughter, Myreel. When her baby was five months old, Olive moved to Provo so her girls could go to school "at B.Y.U.," even though Edwin didn't want her to go because he "didn't think girls needed an education." Olive insisted, and Edwin gave in and moved them to Provo traveling in "a hay rack." He gave them "kindling, a couple of sacks of coal and five dollars to pay the first months rent."

In 1901, settled in Star Valley, Catherine and her two youngest chil-dren, Kate and Rudolph, started moving south again, too, as they took a trip down to Salt Lake for conference. While there, she arranged for her children to meet their father in Pleasant Grove, "as they were too young when we left," she explained, "to retain any memory of him." When the time "drew near" for them to return to Star Valley, she instead felt "deeply impressed to go to Provo and send the children to Brigham Young Academy." She "sought the Lord in prayer" and refunded their return train tickets—she only had ten dollars and a suitcase. While her children were visiting their father, Catherine went to Provo to see her old friend, ninety-year-old "Mother Bunnel," who "welcomed" Catherine "as a daughter." While talking, Mother Bunnel offered her an empty "little building just near her home" to set up a dressmaking shop on Academy Avenue, now known as University Avenue. Catherine cleaned it up with a borrowed bucket and broom and bought a used sewing machine.

She had done the best she could for her children: her oldest four were mar-ried; her youngest two, Kate and Rudolph, now had some family connections in Provo. Their father, Dr. Rogers, died in 1903, and his first wife, Lovina, now lived in Provo. When Catherine first arrived in Provo, some of the Rogers fam-ily took Rudolph to work in the beet fields where he made enough money in a few days to buy "potatoes and coal for the winter." Mother Bunnel helped her borrow a stove and a bedroom suite from her granddaughter.

In 1901, Catherine's last entry in her autobiography reinforced her faith in God and in miracles. As a girl, she had a vision in her bedroom. When she needed help escaping her dreary life on the Pleasant Grove hillside, she found the Wooleys. When she was wandering in Idaho, she again found the Wooleys who with "pure religion" helped the "fatherless and widow[ed] Rogers in their affliction." And at the end of her short life, God helped her again when Mother Bunnell let her stay in the shop. Catherine needed help again. When the used sewing machine she bought was delivered, "for some reason it would not take the stitch," and as she "tried to right it," she became "discouraged and exhausted"; her daughter Kate was nearby to witness her trouble.

While they were struggling, a lady came into the shop and told Catherine she had seen the "fashion sheets" in the window and wanted her to make a blouse "like the pattern in the window," which had "tiny fine tucks across the front yoke and sleeves." The lady showed Catherine the "light blue silk" and thread she had just purchased for the blouse and asked if she could make it for her. Catherine "glanced at the stubborn machine standing there with knotted thread" and "turned to the lady and said, 'Yes, I would be glad to do it, could you call tomorrow to fit it?'" When the lady left, Kate said, "Mother why did you take it? What will you sew with? Look at the machine and thread?"

Catherine and Kate knelt down and prayed, and Catherine wrote, "I told my Father in Heaven he knew our needs. I thanked him for the work I knew he had sent. I asked him to help me run the machine and make the stitch perfect." By the time she was done praying, Kate was crying. Kate "watched breathless" as Catherine "straightened the silk, smoothed the pattern and cut the blouse." Then she "threaded the machine with the silk thread and ran the tucks with a perfect stitch, not one skip or loop." When the lady came the next day, she was "delighted with the beautiful work and fit." Afterward, like the manna God sent the Children of Israel, "sewing came" until Catherine was "crowded for time." Catherine's final words in her autobiography were, "Kate started to school but helped me evenings and mornings and when the harvest was over my boy also went to school and we were happy and very thankful for friends and the blessings given to us." In September 1904, Catherine died of "carcinoma of the liver and intestines." Her oldest daughter came from Idaho and signed the death certificate, and Catherine was buried in the Provo Cemetery. Not that many years hence, Lovina was buried next to Catherine.

Olive continued working in Provo. She worked until ten or eleven every night washing and ironing to earn five dollars a week and developed "a lame back" and stomach trouble. She lived in Provo for twelve years. In 1909 when Edwin died of "Heart Failure" in Vernal, she was too poor to attend his funeral. Around 1912, when Olive was fifty-one, she moved to Arizona where her sister lived and where her daughter Pearl was teaching school. They lived in a tent, but Olive wrote, I "enjoyed myself more than all my life. I was free and felt like a bird just out of a cage. The people were very good to us."

In 1904, if Catherine and Olive had shared all these stories in that dressmaking shop, there were surely other women who would have understood, too, such as sixty-three-year-old *Lynette Conover*, from Springville, six miles south. She didn't really like talking about it, but she had twice been a polygamous wife and hated it.

In 1853 at age eleven, Lynette and her family, she explained, Presbyterians at the time, set out for Oregon. They decided to winter in Utah, and her father found work at the Gardner Mill in West Jordan and subsequently converted to Mormonism with Lynette's mother. While working there, her father answered a call from Brigham Young to "help strengthen the settlement" of Manti farther south that was threatened by Indians. When Lynette's family and other new settlers arrived in Manti, having trudged through the snow to get there, the bishop asked the old-timers, "Who will take these people in?" A William M. Black said, "I will take one family," and Lynette's family went with him to Margaret Black's house, presumably the home of one of his wives. Lynette's family eventually permanently settled in Manti, in Sanpete County, where Catherine grew up, too, a little later.

When Lynette was seventeen, "her troubles commenced," and her trouble was exactly the same problem as Catherine's: her father insisted that she marry into polygamy, although, until then, her "father had always been good to [her]." Lynette went on, "I can now see that it was the pressure of the times that caused him to act as he did." Lynette explained that "some old fanatics were preaching" at the time that "a young man could not save a girl if he married her... that to be saved she must marry some old codger tried and true." In other words, to some, an older man who had demonstrated his faithfulness to the Church and his integrity to the community was preferable to a young man who hadn't yet proven himself. As Michael Quinn explains, some parents urged their daughters to marry "a seasoned man who'd been tried and tested" rather than become "a sole wife of a young stripling... who might not be as devoted to the gospel." Lynette explained that her parents embraced this persuasion, or "disease" as she called it, and, she wrote, "when one of the tried and true came our way I MUST marry him." Lynette talked back to her parents as Catherine had. Lynette "cried and begged, and begged and cried, but to no avail." She wrote, "I was forced to marry him and go into his family."

Like Catherine and Olive, Lynette ended up leaving her first "tried and true" husband, "a man by the name of DeMill." She had two sons with him, and when one of them died, she left DeMill for she "disliked" him "very much." Afterward, she became the polygamous wife of William M. Black, the man who had volunteered to take Lynette's family in that first cold winter night in Manti, and she had a son with him. Somehow, this four-and-a-half-year-old son she had with DeMill and the almost two-year-old son she had with Black died on the same day, a triple tragedy for Lynette; she left Black, too, because, as Lynette's daughter later explained, Lynette "could not stand polygamy." Despondent, sometimes she would go sit in the cemetery near her boys' graves for comfort. The only reason she mentioned these marriage troubles in her autobiography was so that readers would know that her dead sons were legitimate.

A few years later, at age twenty-six, as Lynette was riding a horse down from Salt Lake City, her married friend introduced her to an Overland stage driver, John Conover, who was headed in the same direction to see his sister in Provo. Later that year, Lynette and John married, started a family, moved south for a while, but then returned to Springville and settled there.

The autobiographies of Catherine, Olive, and Lynette reiterated their faith in God and their continued affinity for their religion, but through many wrenching details, it was made clear to their readers they could not defend polygamy and weren't sad it fell apart.

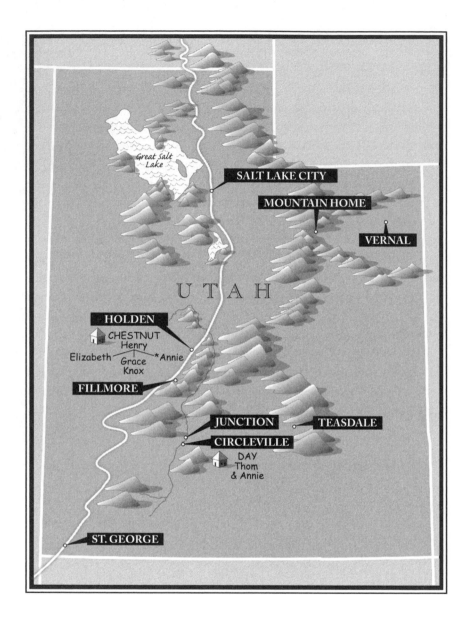

I heard a voice say you are away from Mr Chestnut

Annie Day's House: Junction, Utah, about 1907

On a small hopeful farm in the middle of southern Utah, forty-one-year-old *Annie Day*, who used to be able to outwork anyone, was feeling tired, and when she was tired, she wrote. In 1900, she started her life sketch after doing most of the work to harvest seventy-five bushels of wheat, which "done [her] up . . . so much [she] thot [she] was going to die." So she "tuck a note book and started to write down a sketch of [her] life that [she] could remember." On that August afternoon in 1907, she "cop[ied] what [she'd] started to write a few years" before and continued the story of her two marriages—her polygamous marriage to her stepfather at fourteen, their divorce, and her monogamous marriage to Thom Day. In sum, neither marriage was easy.

In 1907, Annie, Thom, and their seven children moved to Junction, a small farm town where in 1903 the Piute County Courthouse had been built, a significant red adobe brick building with a three-story corner tower. Annie's brother-in-law had gotten them a 20-acre lot there. She wanted a "nice foundation" under her new house, but the bid was fifteen dollars, which she thought was too high, so she got Thom to haul the rock, and she and her boys put it in. She wrote, "me and my boys could do aney thing." Soon after, they started building. Annie's father, who she reestablished a relationship with as an adult (he had abandoned her mother and gone to California when Annie was a child), came to Junction with his tools and helped them put up a "fraim house." Once they were settled, Annie and Thom ordered one hundred trees and, she wrote, "we dug holes at odd times and when they come we got them planted."

Annie's twenty-three-year-old oldest daughter, Melvina, from her first husband, was married and lived in Junction, too, and, Annie wrote, "we all was having the happiest times in our lives." She felt that "the people were so good and kind" to them, and they were "envited out to parties." Annie played the accordion and would sit on her front step and play, and "people could here [her] and come to visit and sing." The Days "always went to Sunday school and meeting," and Annie went to Relief Society. Besides helping her boys herd the town cows, doing outside work on the farm, and keeping house, Annie wove rugs for a living. Perhaps she was finally overcoming the disappointment and resentment that had shaped her prior life and affected the tone of her writing.

She had had a weird experience in polygamy. In 1876 when Annie was eleven, her twice-divorced mother married a widower named Henry Chestnut (Mr. HC), and Annie felt that when they moved to his house, they were "treated pretty good to what [they] had bin," since her mother's first husband abandoned them and her second husband treated them badly. But then her forty-six-year-old stepfather Mr. HC started to show a romantic interest in Annie. That first winter after moving to his house, Annie spent hours watching "Mr H. C.," who had emigrated from Scotland, weave cloth. While she sat there "he would say you will be my little wife wont you get older." She would "get of the bench" and say, "no you bet I wont Marrie a old man" and get her sister to sit next to him instead.

But Mr. Chestnut really did intend to marry Annie, and when she was just past fourteen, he laid out his plans. He and Annie's mother, Elizabeth, would travel by wagon to the St. George Temple in December 1879 where Mr. Chestnut planned to be sealed to both Annie and his dead first wife's sister Grace. As his first wife was dying, he promised to marry her younger sister Grace. Instead of following through on his promise, however, he married Elizabeth (Annie's mother). This December he planned to rectify that situation by finally marrying Grace as a polygamous wife, and he hoped to marry Annie at the same time.

That December, at age fourteen, while Annie was working as a live-in domestic, the lady she worked for told Annie that she thought her mother was trying to get her to marry her stepfather: "the lady I was working for said that is a [sin] your Mother is going to get you a husband and said Ile bet it is your step Father." This woman did not approve of Annie marrying so young and seemed especially disgusted that it might be to Mr. Chestnut. And the lady's hunch was true. Annie's mother sent two urgent messages to come home immediately. When Annie got there, the adults—Mr. Chestnut, Annie's mother Elizabeth, and Grace Knox—were anxious, and the wagon was loaded for a trip to the St. George Temple. Annie was confused about why they wanted her to go since she usually stayed home

FIGURE 12.2 Annie's stepfather and first husband Henry Chestnut. From *On the Utah Frontier: The Story of Thomas Clark Day and Annie Eliza Berry*.

to babysit the younger children. Her mother told her that "Aunt Alace" was staying with the children, and, since Annie had never been out of town, she decided it would make a "nice ride." On the way, the adults argued, or as Annie described it, "O such talk." Her mother and Grace seemed angry at Mr. HC. One would say, "I wish I never had to marrie you," and the other "would wish they never had to marrie." Annie wrote that she wondered "what they was going to do" with her.

When they arrived in St. George, Annie helped "pa," as she called her stepfather, with the horses and asked him why he was taking her to the temple. He was in a bad mood because of all the arguing and "in a cross way" said, "I am going to Marrie you of corse if I can." Annie "felt horried" and thought "is that the way wiman gets Married." She thought a woman should "say who she wants," or at least she thought that later when she was writing her story, but she "went along listening to them." At this point, she had a few clues that he intended to marry her, but Annie had always "done as [she] was told never spok back." Perhaps she suffered from the muteness that characterizes some abused children. Perhaps she suffered from the neediness that characterizes some adolescent girls without fathers. Perhaps she felt so insignificant and inexperienced that a little part of her enjoyed the grown-up attention—it was her first time to take a ride to a bigger town. Whatever the psychology at play, the adults who should have protected her did not.

The next day, December 12, 1879, Annie did her temple prerequisites and saw "all the rooms," but when it came time for the sealing ceremony to marry Mr. Chestnut, the group was stopped in the temple, either by patrons or officiators. Mr. Chestnut and Grace Knox were allowed to marry, but not Mr. Chestnut and Annie because "some did not want to see us get Married." At this point, Annie's mother Elizabeth asked, because she was conflicted about it, "is it rite for a man to Marrie a woman and her Daughter"? A "Mr McCalester" who worked at the temple puzzled it out saying, "well I have a Mother and 2 Daughters sealed to me but our recommends had to go to SL to John Taylor," the new Church president, for permission. Sometimes men were sealed to other members of a wife's family in name only, with the hope that they would all be together in the eternities.

Lightly regulated Mormon polygamy could be a little like the Wild West—polygamous wife Annie Tanner wrote of those times, "there were no fixed rules by the Church pertaining to" the practice of polygamy and "perhaps no two cases were alike." The system depended in large part on the "integrity of those involved," and Mr. Chestnut may have been lacking integrity—in a few years, he would be excommunicated from the Church. Brigham Young had both denied and approved requests to marry teenage girls—in one case, he gave permission for a thirteen-year-old girl to marry but said her husband must "preserve her intact until she is fully developed into Womanhood." During the Mormon Reformation when Young had received numerous requests to marry teens, he started granting "local leaders and families considerable latitude." In Annie's case, the St. George Temple officiators decided that they couldn't approve the union and sent a query to Salt Lake for permission. That December, when the message would have arrived in Salt Lake, President John Taylor, a polygamist, was hiding from federal authorities. It's unclear if he gave permission himself, but in about a week, word came back to St. George that they could go forward.

Annie was herding horses when Mr. HC came "in a hurry" telling her to "get the horses up and go to the temple." She did this "without saying a word." In her writing, Annie created a scene that juxtaposed an impressionable girl beside a muscular adult world. Annie insisted that she didn't know what she was doing. She wrote that she was "looking at the pretty rooms" and remembered "kneeling on the Alter and a man talking." She didn't remember the words he said but that "Mr H. C. said Yes and after they said to me say yes." She wrote, "I whispered yes not noing what I was saying." On the way home in the winter mud, Annie and Mr. HC walked to lighten the wagon. He put his arm around her and said, Annie wrote,

"O bless my little wife." She was "struck for a minit than said why, be I your wife?" He said, "yes," and she said, "well I never new that." He said, "didnt you hear that man Marrie us." She said, "no," and he said, "don't tell a sole or we will half to be put in prison for living in poligmey." She wrote, "I did feel so bad I wondered if all girls got married that way and would liked to run a way and in to monthes I come neer running a way."

Annie insisted that she didn't know she was marrying her stepfather even though there were numerous clues: he told her when she was eleven that he'd like to marry her; her employer said Annie's mother might be trying to marry Annie to her stepfather; Mr. HC himself told her on the way to St. George that he wanted to marry her if the authorities would let him; the family was held up in St. George waiting for permission for this marriage from Salt Lake; and in order to marry him, she would have been asked to kneel at an altar and say "yes." It was more likely that she felt powerless to stop it but at the same time didn't want Mr. HC to think that she believed she was married to him. And, of course, she didn't want to believe it herself. But right after leaving St. George on the trip home, he put his arm on her shoulder, and, subsequently, she wanted to run away.

Even though Annie and Mr. HC were married, her mother Elizabeth did not want Annie to get pregnant, at least not until Elizabeth was done having children herself. We don't know whether Annie had sexual relations with Mr. HC early on, whether they used some method of birth control, or whether they abstained. We do know that when Annie was about sixteen, she wanted a baby; when she was almost seventeen she got pregnant; and that her mother wasn't happy about it, in part because her mother just had a baby. According to Annie, a month before she delivered her first child, she asked Mr. HC if she could get some calico to make baby clothes. Annie wrote that she had given her work wages to the family and felt she had taken nothing out. So her mother and Mr. HC went four miles to the store and "baught things for nearly every one" and a "petticoat or under scirt" for Annie (she never had one), but "no clothes for baby." When they returned and Annie saw this, she cried and said, "ma why dident you get a little lite calico for 3 or 4 dresses"? Her mother answered, "well we have enough to buy for, you had aught to no better than to have children." Her mother reminded her that she herself was still nursing a baby and said, "you had aught to waight till I was done having children." Evidently, her mother wanted to force the point that Annie had gotten pregnant too soon and that it was inconvenient.

Annie was incensed! She wrote, "I had weighted nearly 3 years" to have a baby—she was almost eighteen. She asked Mr. HC if she could take the team back to the store herself, and he gave her permission. Eight months pregnant, with the determination that would become one of her defining character traits, she returned to the store, traded in her petticoat for twenty-five cents worth of calico, and "made 3 dresses for baby out of it." Her daughter Melvina was born a month later. Annie took Melvina with her to haul hay and passed her to the younger girls there who would bring Melvina to Annie to nurse, but it was really no place for a baby, and Melvina, the "poor thing," sometimes "cryed till she hurt."

Annie couldn't "enjoy" herself living "out on a farm all the time" with "ma" and "the old man." She loved to spend time with her friend Augusta who was her same age, who lived a mile away, and who was married to a young sheep herder named John. Sometimes when Mr. HC and Elizabeth weren't home, and when John was away, Augusta would visit Annie and cook a chicken and "danish dumplens" while Annie sewed for her. If Annie's mother were home—"o such frowns"—Augusta was not welcome, so the two friends would walk around outside and talk. Annie liked to stay at Augusta's sometimes, too, but this made Mr. HC "verry julic" because he "never wanted" Annie "away from the house." He evidently suspected (not without reason) that Augusta wanted Annie to leave him. Mr. HC had even forbade Annie to spend time there and threatened to kill her if she did.

One night when Annie was visiting Augusta and her husband John, Augusta begged Annie to stay with her overnight. Annie was scared, but Augusta didn't think Mr. HC would actually kill her. So Annie asked her sister Clara to get her baby Melvina, put "a clean apron" on her, and tell Mr. HC that Annie was staying at Augusta's house. Clara brought the baby without saying anything to Mr. HC, and soon after Mr. HC's "girl" went to fetch Annie to tell her to return home, but since Annie knew she didn't have work to do, she didn't go. Then Mr. HC himself came down and told John he was "julice of him" and wanted Annie home. Annie wrote that Mr. HC didn't need to be jealous of John, because John never suggested she leave Mr. HC when others had. When Annie refused go home, Mr. HC grabbed Melvina out of Annie's arms and left. Annie wrote that she "come neer leaving him that night," but the next day Mr. HC was "broken harted" and apologized to John, so Annie returned home, and subsequently had a second baby.

Annie knew in her heart that she should leave Mr. HC, all while continuing her outdoor farm work to support herself and two children, holding her second baby in one arm and a hoe in the other until her arm was swollen, or leaving her baby in a "dry ditch" while she worked. She wasn't happy. Even the male Church "teachers" who visited her house and her bishop said she should leave Mr. HC because he had been excommunicated from the Church—and besides, her situation didn't seem right. Annie wrote Church President John Taylor "through the bishop" and was advised to seek a divorce "through the proper chanel." She "didnent no what to do" because Mr. HC would "make such threts," so she let it be and became pregnant with her third baby. She prayed that if it were right for her to "live with Mr H.C.," then she would feel love for him, but that if it were right for her to go, then the "way be opened" so she could "leave him." She continued to pray earnestly "to the lord to no what to do" because she "always felt bad over being married the way" she was and her life continued to get "more misurabel." Then a way to escape came to her.

In October 1886, Annie was living with Mr. HC on the farm while her mother had gone to live in town so the older children could attend school (Grace Knox seems to have disappeared), and Annie's third child, a boy, was born. Around this time, Augusta told Annie that the Bible said in Leviticus 20:14 that a man who married a woman and her mother "should be burned," and Augusta had concluded that Annie was "doing wrong by living with" Mr. HC. Annie decided that very moment that she would "sleep alone" from then on—and she did for four months. This frustrated Mr. HC who didn't like her independent streak. On a Saturday morning in November when her baby was two weeks old, Mr. HC got in one of those "terebel spells as men have" and began to "swair at the way the house looked" and told her to clean the fireplace. She still felt weak from childbirth and had "the quinzy" and told him to clean it himself. This infuriated him, and she "tried to reason with him" but ended up going outside in the "snowing and blowing cold." Mr. HC went outside and took hold of her to get her to come in, but she pulled away and sat on the ground.

When Mr. HC's brother finally persuaded her to come in, Mr. HC asked where she wanted to go. Annie said she would go "aney where," such as to Augusta's or to the Riddles' where her mother was. When he realized she might leave, he "put his arms around" her, "kissed and begged" her to stay, and she was "over powered again." Annie made up her mind that she would "just do [her] work wich was to earn a living carding and spinning doing washings for others and earning me and my childrens clothes and shoes." When he asked her to clean the stable, she said no. When he asked her to do the milking, she said no. When he asked her to clean the privy, she said no. She told him that she had "always done it for you now I have 3 little ones to do for." By standing up for herself during those four months, she found that she cried less than she had during eight years of marriage and steeled herself "to meet anything" ahead. She knew she was in "truble and muss" and wrote that she had many a "lick and trubel" she was "not writing about" and would not "give up [her] thoughts or promptings" about separating herself from him.

One Wednesday morning, after an argument because Annie would not get Mr. HC's breakfast, he declared he was taking Annie to her mother to, he said, "see if she cant make you let me sleep with you." He proclaimed, "Ill see if I half to be treated this way." Annie wrote of that day, "Little did I think that would be my last sleep in that house or I would leave him that day." Mr. HC hitched up the team and wagon, and even though he told Annie to sit up front on the seat with him, she sat in the fresh hay in the back with her three children.

During the one-mile ride to town, Annie wrote that she heard "a voice say you are away from Mr Chesnut just as plan as I ever hear aney thing." She looked around because she "thought some one was neer" her, but she "could not see aney one and in a second a nother voice said that's a warning for you now take it." She wrote, "I never can for get the good feeling it left it was on the morning of March 16, 1887."

When they arrived in town, her curious mother came out to greet them with a smile, wondering why they had come to town on a Wednesday when they usually came on Sunday for church. Mr. HC explained that they had "a row." They shooed the kids away to school, and then he told Elizabeth, "she wont let me sleep with her and I am getting damed tired of it cant you make her treat me like a wife." Elizabeth said, "well no you [have] no business living with her the age you are and cut of the church and with me eather you never have treated her rite she should aught to have bin let a lone and Marrie [a] man of her age and you had aught to go and let us both alone." Mr. HC said, "all rite."

Elizabeth took charge and organized a separation for the family. She told Mr. HC that he should return to the farm to plant the grain, which would take two weeks, and then he could take the team of horses and leave the farm to them and presumably go his own way. He agreed to this, and said, "come on Annie lets go home." But Annie refused. He said, "for god sake are you going to leave me." She said she was, and he said, "well come and cook for me while I put in the wheet." She said no. He said it would only take two weeks, and her mother agreed: "go Annie it will only take 2 weeks." But Annie wouldn't, and said, "ma don't never advise me a gain look what I have sufferd now and always will for you taking me down to the temple and me doing as you have said all my life now ma you can go your way I will not bother you and pleas let me go my way." Her mother insisted, "o it wont hurt you to do the cooking 2 weeks." She said, "no I don't want to." Mr. HC, perhaps because Elizabeth was on his side, threatened, "well I will take your children the girls now and the boy when he is old enough." Annie replied, crying, "you cant get them neather by the church law or outside law for you have never treated me rite don't support me or them. Every rag we have on I have earned and even to there shoes...I even worked hard for what we eat and our beding." Mr. HC stepped to the door, Elizabeth decided to go with him to cook, and she asked Annie if she could finish sewing her sisters' dresses for the dance that afternoon, to which Annie replied that she would.

Mr. HC called to Melvina, perhaps feigning that he would take her, but Annie rushed out with her baby in her arms, and her two little girls, aged two and four, came from playing to join her, and the little family made a beeline for Augusta's house. Augusta said she would "scald" Mr. HC if he came to get Annie. In the afternoon, Annie went back to where her mother had been staying to finish making her sisters' dresses for the dance. Her mother and Mr. HC had loaded up their bedding to take to the farm, and Mr. HC was to bring Annie's bedding back, but when he came, he brought her mother's bedding back, which scared her. She wrote that he "alway" threatened to "kill" her if she "left him." He started "co[a]xing" Annie to come back to him, tried to kiss her, stood behind her and tried to kiss her and "co[a]x" her some more, but, she wrote, "I would not listen." She told him, "you have tuck me away now I am going to stay a way"—he finally left.

After separating from Mr. HC, Annie received both moral and financial support from her community. The next day she was "cleaning the door yeard" when the "teachers" from the Church came looking for her mother, but when they found Annie, they said, "well we want to see you aney way it was all the same." Perhaps unaware of the fear and danger associated with abusive husbands, they informed Annie that she would "half to leave that man or get cut of the church." Perhaps since the bishop had helped her write a letter about divorcing Mr. HC, the bishop had been waiting for her to follow through and sent the teachers to meet with her. She said, "Thank the lord I left him yesterday." She wrote that "they was shure glad and talked quite a while." Afterward, she "felt just like [she] had got out of a terebel muss or stinking dirty place." She "realey felt cleen and brighter and better."

A Sister Riddle invited Annie to stay in one of her rooms and work for her, and she did, but when Sister Riddle's husband returned after a week, he said that if they paid Annie the "upper valley ward [of the Church] wont help support her." When Annie's Aunt Alace heard this, she invited Annie to come stay with her. Annie's "uncle and Aunt Alace tried hard to get [her] in there family," presumably as a polygamous wife. Annie did the paperwork for her divorce and waited for it to be returned from Salt Lake. Then her cousin took her seven miles to get Mr. HC's signature. Mr. HC tried to coax her back and didn't want to sign it; she finally threatened, "if you don't I will go where you will never here or see me again," so Mr. HC said he would sign it the next morning. Predictably, he dragged his feet.

Evidently, Annie's mother also had divorce papers against Mr. HC but thought they shouldn't both divorce him. Elizabeth volunteered to divorce Mr. HC if Annie would stay with him, perhaps thinking Annie's marriage might be easier without her in the equation, or perhaps just wanting to get rid of Mr. HC herself, or perhaps knowing how much Mr. HC liked Annie. But Annie had made up her mind and didn't appreciate her mother's lack of support. Annie said, "O ma if you had just said live single till I was 15 I never would have had this to stand turned out with out a thing with 3 little ones." For a while, Annie lived with Augusta and John, and when Annie found work doing laundry for others, Augusta tended her children and nursed her baby for her.

Finally, Mr. HC and Elizabeth decided to move to Colorado, and before leaving, Annie helped her mother make quilts, and they had "quite a talking time." Her mother said it was "like pulling her heart strings out to go and leave [Annie] in such circumstances." Her mother apologized about the whole polygamous marriage mess. Annie wrote that her mother "wished I had Married a man of my own—sorrie it ever happened." Her mother told her that Mr. HC saw an old man hobble by and asked if he walked like that. When Elizabeth told him yes, he said he didn't "blame Annie a damed bit for leaving" him.

On June 7, 1887, Mr. HC, Elizabeth, and her children (who were Annie's brothers and sisters) cried and talked with Annie for an hour before leaving for Colorado. Elizabeth gave Annie a cow and a calf, but Annie cried when she found out that her mother had told Mr. HC to take the twenty-five dollars he made from selling another cow and "put it in the store for [Annie's baby] George" when he turned twenty-one because she needed the money then. Mr. HC offered Annie seventy-five dollars and "his best team wagon" if she would come with them. Four of Annie's brothers and sisters wanted to stay with her, but Elizabeth said that Annie would have enough trouble supporting her own children. Annie tried to get Mr. HC to leave her some "flour, meat money," and shoes for the children, but he only got a pair for George. Annie wrote, "That was the way I was searved for living 22 years with my Mother and step father." She could only "tell the truth": she was "glad when they left."

Elizabeth cried, saying it was "killing" her to leave Annie. Nevertheless, she tended to ask a lot of her: she told Annie that if anything happened to her (Elizabeth), she wanted Annie to raise her brothers and sisters. Elizabeth had specific instructions that if she died, Annie should not let Aunt Alace take Josephine for more than a week and not let Clara "have anay" of her children. Sadly, within two months, Elizabeth *did* die in Colorado, and Mr. HC wrote to Annie to come and raise her brothers and sisters: "for god sake come don't let any one talk you out of the notion for your sake for the children sake and your children sake and for god sake come to me I will send the money." Annie did not want to do that, and the bishop advised Annie that she should only help if Mr. HC sent the children to her. He never did.

For the most part, this ended her marriage and association with Mr. HC. Mr. HC exhibited characteristics of a domineering husband in the way he intimidated Annie, took advantage of her youth, and fluctuated between anger and affection. Annie's story provided many clues that her community found her situation pathetic and tried to help. In 1879, when she got married, Church leaders let her down, but in 1887 when she divorced, they worked to get her out of the mess—just as Brigham Young had a clear conscience when he introduced polygamy but had qualms after watching it unfold. The ideal of polygamy, as with most ideals, outdistanced the reality. When Mr. HC left for Colorado, he took with him the "motto" Annie had wrought with "a house with green trees all around & letters god Bless our home on it." He said he would "have that to remember Annie with or see her handwork all [his] life" as though the peaceful cross-stitch had been their reality.

As Annie tried to make ends meet, the Church helped support her family. Someone gave her "a milk pan full of Molases" and "a nother time a frunt quarter of mutton wich lasted [her] 2 weeks stuing a little peace most every day." A series of women invited her to stay with them and helped with her children. A series of three couples invited her to join their families as a polygamous wife. She considered joining the second family if she could have her own house, but when they explained she would be staying with them, and Annie "could not stand" the man anyway, she moved on. She was not going to repeat her mistakes. Annie complained once that when her children were sick "no help not one Elder ever steped on my door step" to bless her children, but she also admitted that she had not asked for help and that lots of people in town were sick and worried about their own problems. For a while, Mr. HC continued to write weekly letters which she ignored, unless to pen an angry reply. Annie asked the Lord to help her, and, she wrote, "I know he did but it was hard on me" working for medicines and "clothes and little things for sick ones to eat." Then one day someone told her about Thom Day.

Twenty-nine-year-old bachelor Thomas Day owned ranch land in Teasdale, Rabbit Valley, Wayne County, Utah. About a year after Annie's divorce, an acquaintance named Brother Isaac Riddle told Annie about Thom, saying that "he had a man working on his property" who was "a good man" and "had lots of property and lots of things 2 wards for him self." Annie told Brother Riddle that she would "stay as I be," probably meaning that she agreed not to have a relationship with anyone else until she met Thom. Thom wrote her "a small letter...that cheered" her "some," and at the end of July, he came to meet her. She later told her children that

FIGURE 12.3 Annie with her second husband, Thom Day, and Annie's children. From *On the Utah Frontier: The Story of Thomas Clark Day and Annie Eliza Berry.*

Thom was "tall, dark, and handsome" and that she "fell in love." In the meantime, she kept "working trying to get out of [debt] and earn clothes for winter." The second time he visited, he asked her to marry him. She wrote, "I told him I would be his wife I said if you promis to be good, to be good to my children and me I will." She wrote that she "took I J Riddles word" that Thom was a good man and asked "a few questions" which gave her some confidence to marry him. They were married in September 1888, partly rushing it, she said, because she didn't know what she was going to do for wood that winter.

Thom and Annie began their marriage with a two-week round trip by wagon to the Manti Temple without the children. On their way back, they spent five or six days with Thom's family, who were surprised to find out that he was married! Continuing home, Annie took sick with a cold, and each mile felt worse and worse until she was lying in the back of the wagon. In cases of illness, Mormons would often seek a "priesthood blessing" for better health by the laying on of hands, following the New Testament practice. As Annie suffered, and because they were alone, Thom told her, "I never did lay hands on aney one, but I will if you think it will do you aney good." Annie said, "all rite," and she sat on the spring seat at the front of the wagon. Annie wrote, "he put his hands on my head and said a few wordes in prare and befour [he finished] every bit of pain left me I was verry week but no pain and kept on till we got home." Soon after their return home, she received a letter from Mr. HC who heard she was "going to get married to a man by the name of Day but," he wrote, "for my sake and your sake and the children sake and for god sake don't do it." She must have chuckled and sighed with relief to "be out of his reach."

By April 1889, Thom made some trades so he and Annie could move to town, which was easier on her health and made it easier to get to church. In the complicated trades for stock, land, horses, grain, and labor, Annie felt that Thom was shorted and didn't get the grain owed him, and they had "nothing to eat but milk and butter." As their milk ran low, she tried to coax Thom to stop the calves from taking so much milk from the three cows, but he ignored her, so she decided to take matters into her own hands. Pregnant, one night she got inside the corral gate and "entended to put up the calves," but "Thom came running hit me a lick with his willow and shuved me in side the gate"; she "just ran down the inside of the fence jumped over and put up the calves aney way." She insinuated that after this she was "not well" and perhaps blamed the incident for causing the stillborn son she had in September. She also thought that Thom was taken advantage of in his railroad wages that year.

Over the next twenty years, it was Annie's right as an autobiographer to tell her story from her point of view. She consistently felt indignant about the amount of indoor and outdoor work she had to do while pregnant nearly all the time; yet, at the same time, she seemed proud of herself since if there was one thing she admired, it was hard work, and she knew how to do it. She wrote that a man told her once that he admired her work ethic and wished his wife had a taste for outdoor work. She insisted on putting in wheat acreage and a large garden, and she often felt that if she wanted something to be done, she had to do it herself. The way she told it, Thom was gone for long periods of time herding sheep and left her and her children on the farm to do the work. She had been in debt when they got married, so, she wrote, "it seemed like we never could get a head."

Like many couples, Annie and Thom had different ways of doing the same job. For example, she persuaded him to help her put in "a milk cellar." After she coaxed him for two weeks, he hauled the rock and sand, and he helped put up the rock wall. She wanted it "put up strait in side," but "Thom did not cair," so she spent hours redoing the placement of the rocks, turning "large rock and fix over what he did," which made her mad. She stayed with it even while it was raining and even though she was sick.

One afternoon, she saw him "standing under a shade tree down in the lot." She turned the irrigation water on her garden, and her little boys cleared the leaves so the water could flow. When she had two rows left to be watered, Thom told her "our time is up ma" because their water time was up (they probably shared with the neighbors). This made Annie mad, and she said, "you lazy son of a bitch I have put in every dam dam and tuck out every dam dam." Thom raised his shovel to hit her, and she raised her hoe, and Thom said, "crist couldent live with you if he come down now." After this argument, Annie cried "all day to think" she had "said such a thing" to him and stayed in bed sick three days. When she rose and saw the corral gates down, Thom said, "you think I am a lazy son of a bitch do you." She said, "yes," and he was going to hit her but she raised her "club." After that, "he slept by him self" for a while and "wouldnent speek for 2 monthes." Perhaps he never knew how sorry she was for what she said.

Thom sometimes treated her too roughly, and they had trouble communicating—Annie even considered leaving Thom, but a neighbor dissuaded her. Not long afterward, Thom went sheep herding for fifteen months and returned home only three times—once for three days, and the other times for only one day. During the winter of 1892–1893, "Thom had not spoke to [her] all winter only when he had to." She remembered that on New Year's Day, she decided not to speak either. Thom sat by the fireplace moving closer when the fire would get low, then Annie would "go and get chips and make a big fire," so then Thom would scoot back, "and as the fire would go down he would come closer up all day till sundown with out speaking." After twenty years of marriage, she could say, "I tuck it to heart them days worse than now." Over time, she learned to not take everything as hard and to cope better. By then she was tired and had probably lowered her expectations, but they had contented times, too. One winter she taught Thom to knit, and he helped her make stockings.

According to their daughter, her parents had both been deprived of an education and yet both loved to read.

Annie's monogamous marriage to Thom Day, like most marriages, began on a good note, but between 1888 and 1907 (she stopped writing her autobiography in 1907), Thom physically abused her from time to time. From what she chose to write, they had some terrible arguments they both regretted, leading to what appeared to be a calmer period in Junction and then Mountain Home where Annie died in 1928 at age sixty-three. Thom died in 1946 at age eighty-seven. Overall, Annie chose to portray herself as an anxious hard worker who bore fourteen children. She sometimes lost patience with Thom, whom she portrayed as a man who moved more slowly than she did, sometimes got taken advantage of in the marketplace, and seemed emotionally distant.

Only four of their fourteen children grew to adulthood, a sign of how remote and helpless their lives often were. When Annie and Thom's first biological son died at age four, she was afraid that Thom would die of sorrow himself. The boy's problems had started when Thom accidently "steped on his finger mashed it," which was followed by a four-week illness leading to his death. She got "all the help" she could from the doctor and medicine, too, but they still lost him. When he passed away, she explained, "for an hour or more Thom acted so I thought I would half to loos them both." Annie felt that she would rather give up the other four children than lose that "loving child and it was a long time befour [she] could console [her] self." Losing so many children must have added stress to their marriage.

Although her monogamous marriage to Thom Day had some serious problems, their children's personal writings suggest that they had a happy family life. Like many rural families, they had religious and seasonal traditions. The family sang a hymn and prayed over meals and, as their means improved, Thom wrote in his short autobiography, "Me and my family would go in a white top buggy to Sunday School 10 miles to Boneta every Sunday." According to their daughter, during spring cleaning, Annie took up the carpets that had been tacked down throughout the house, cleaned them, laid down fresh "sweet-smelling straw," and replaced the carpets— the children loved to wrestle and play other games on the "soft rugs." The family went berry picking together and dried corn for snacks. Annie had an accordion, an organ, and violin that she taught herself to play through correspondence courses, and the family sang together.

Like many long marriages, their marriage mellowed over time. At the beginning, Thom was willing to go from being a rural bachelor to the father of a family of five. He had taken on three children from Annie's first marriage and Annie's debt. Annie was feisty, beautiful, and hardworking, but she was from a dysfunctional family and had a previous bad marriage. She had a tendency to be mouthy and to think she was right. Thom had a tendency to brood and to feel henpecked, and he sometimes lashed out at her. His mother died when he was five, he was deprived of an education, and he spent lonely spans of time sheep herding as a boy. At eighteen, he sold some sheep and paid his own way to school, but the younger children there ridiculed him. At nineteen, he was in love with another girl, but a Church member advised him to keep his family blood clean, suggesting the girl was not religious enough. Subsequently, Thom disciplined himself to separate from the girl until she married someone else. He then waited until he was twenty-nine to marry Annie in the Manti Temple. In his autobiography, he clearly respected Annie's religiosity and faith. Over the years, the family attended church (Annie taught Sunday school for many years), gradually made financial gains and got out of debt, and built a satisfying family network. The independent willfulness of their early years slowly melted until Thom became easier for Annie to persuade.

After twenty years of marriage, however, they were still working things out. One day she and Thom had "words over watering cows" and "he hit [Annie] on the head," a blow from which she had a hard time regaining strength. No polygamous wives in this study wrote of being hit by their husbands. Annie and Thom's daughter Fannie, who was fourteen, witnessed the abuse, and Fannie "kicked" Thom and said, "don't you ever hit my ma again." Not long afterward, Annie had a dream that "seamed to real to be a dream." She was afraid she was going to die, and she "roused up" and "told Thom" that she thought that they should move to Junction. At first he "refused" but then they "talked it over and started to get reddy." Annie was sick, and Thom helped get the "bed chair and stove in the wagon," and he helped her "in on a bed" where she lay the whole way. They temporarily left their older children behind so they could continue school. Annie loved Junction and figured out how to get their log home moved so the family could relocate.

It was here that she felt happy for "the first" time in her life and where she finished writing her autobiography that detailed how hard both polygamous and monogamous marriages could be. Writing about what she had suffered, divulging family secrets, telling unflattering tales about her husbands, Annie wrote what came out of her. She rarely analyzed or even considered other perspectives and concentrated on telling it the way she saw it. Ultimately, Annie exacted revenge for how she was treated and thereby warned readers to behave themselves lest they also leave an embarrassing legacy.

But Thom left a short autobiography, too, as did some of their children, and their writings give the impression that Thom was consistently hard at work farming. Thom's personal writings briefly describe his work: moving; homesteading; farming; hauling; digging ditches; and building new cabins, houses, stables, chicken coops, and granaries. Near the end of his career, he noted with pride how much money they earned for their crops. Thom acknowledged how hard Annie worked, too: "She was a hard working helpmate and a wonderful mother in councling her children, & she was a faithful Latter Day Saint all her life." What if Thom had written a daily diary rather than a short autobiography as an older man? How would the story have changed?

And what about Annie's polygamous marriage to Mr. HC? He obtained permission to marry her, but their relationship illustrated the lack of civility and morality on the extreme edge of polygamy, where girls slipped through the cracks. Nineteenth-century Mormon polygamous marriages were not just one thing but an entire spectrum of north and south, horizontal and vertical, far and near, early and late, old and young, pleasure and pain, substance and poverty, compatibility and disappointment, children and illness, respect and disregard, companionship and loneliness, regret and gratitude. Did monogamy have as many variables or as many extremes? Was a good polygamous marriage superior to a bad monogamous marriage? Or is there something inherently wrong with polygamy that keeps it from falling short of its seeming possibilities?

Today more than 850 societies practice some polygamy, most of them located in Africa and Islamic countries in the Middle East. A 2002 overview of literature published in *Clinical Child and Family Psychology Review* compiled information from approximately 150 published articles on the effects of polygamy on families in some of these societies. Although the review cautions against drawing broad conclusions about the cultures studied or extending the findings to other cultures, still, the review offers valuable perspectives on the condition of women in polygamy.

According to the study, women generally suffer in polygamy. Polygamous families experience more "marital discord" than monogamous families, and monogamous husbands and wives are more likely to engage in "family planning." For example, in a Bedouin-Arab community study, first wives whose husbands marry younger wives feel they "failed" as wives and report physical symptoms such as "body aches, headaches, insomnia, fatigue, breathlessness," and anxiety. First wives who are "perceived as old by their husbands" suffer from low self-esteem.

Polygamous wives generally "experience limited economic resources" and "unequal treatment among wives" despite Islamic religious mandates of equity. American Muslim polygamous wives of various ethnic backgrounds are more likely to be abused. Although statistically, polygamous men will have more children than monogamous men, individually, polygamous women have fewer surviving children than monogamous women, and polygamous families are less likely to invest in healthcare for their children. Polygamous husbands are generally more interested in the children of junior wives.

In nineteenth-century Mormon polygamy, a 2000 study that compared what women published in the *Woman's Exponent* to what they wrote in their personal writings found that women generally insisted that plural marriage was God's will but offered little personal experience that suggested they enjoyed polygamy. When threatened with its demise, they did not mention "that they would miss the practice, for themselves or for their children." As Daniela Johnson-Bennion writes, "Truly, how could anyone argue with Mormon women if they had reasoned they enjoyed polygamy?" In her study, she found that wives "never recommended the practice based on positive personal experiences" and never suggested that they enjoyed it, that it was fun, or that it was desirable in any other context than to gain salvation in heaven.

Despite the negative findings in these studies, in America today there's a growing sense that consenting adults should have the liberty to decide what their primary relationships should look like, especially given the high failure rate of traditional monogamous marriages. In 1946, Supreme Court Justice Frank Murphy, arguing for the minority, wrote that although Mormon fundamentalist polygamy was "distasteful," polygamy was "one of the basic forms of marriage," the practice of which, historically, had "far exceeded that of any other form." In 2013, U.S. District Judge Clark Waddoups struck down anti-polygamy laws and "declared the cohabitation statutes of Utah's polygamy laws to be unconstitutional" in a case brought by the Brown family featured in the TV show "Sister Wives." As Kathleen Flake explains, it doesn't make sense that sexual activity between "those who simply have multiple partners" is more legal than sexual activity between those "who believe themselves to be married to multiple partners."

Should an enlightened society allow polygamy? Should societies protect women from perceived oppression and inequality? Or should women have the freedom and independence to make their own choices, even if their choices offend our modern sensibilities? Obscure nineteenth-century polygamous wives at least offer some detailed scenarios for our consideration.

Farewell

EVERY SUMMER VACATION starting in 1962, my parents, my younger siblings, and I left California at sunrise, endured the thirteen-hour car ride
east across the desert, then perked up at dusk when we saw the lights of
Salt Lake City come into view. My father would pull off Yalecrest Avenue
and in to his parents' narrow driveway where my well-groomed grandparents would brightly emerge in the twilight; my double-chinned Grandpa
Jack Kelly would gently pat my straight fine hair and softly say, "Hi honey."
Once tucked in bed, I could hear the crickets chirping outside the open
window and feel the cool Utah night air. I would be excited to help my
grandma the next morning. My Grandma Anne Naismith Kelly had a
sunny disposition accompanied by a musical speaking voice that made
even cleaning windows fun, using vinegar, warm water, and newspapers
as we got ready for backyard parties. On the back-porch swing, where we
spent a lot of time, sometimes she would tell me about the Kelly family
businesses, all the way back to John Bookbinder Kelly—whose first wife
Helena's heart broke, Grandma told me, every time her husband went to
work with his second wife.

Helena Quirk had married John Bookbinder Kelly in 1844 on the Isle
of Man, and, sometime before 1853, they joined the Mormon Church and
left for Salt Lake. Not long after embarking, Helena gave birth to her fifth
child, George, my great-grandfather, on board the ship *Camillus*, on the
Atlantic Ocean. Of five births, he was only the second living child. In the
new land, Helena and John with their little children made the trek toward
Salt Lake: Helena brought a trunk with "silk dresses, umbrellas, and fine
bolts of wool"; her husband John brought the "bare roots of fruit trees"
and the mechanical parts for book binding. After their arrival in October
1853, Helena bore seven additional children, and John Bookbinder was a
"progressive man" who started a printing business, was a foreman at the
Deseret News bindery, and acted on stage. They lived at 422 South and
2nd West, in the Great Salt Lake 7th Ward, in a white temple-form

FIGURE 13.1 The author (lower left) with her Salt Lake grandparents, Anne and Jack Kelly.

American Greek Revival home, currently on the National Historic Register and languishing in downtown Salt Lake City amidst hotel parking lots and fast food restaurants, next to the State Liquor Store.

In 1867, John Bookbinder made a controversial decision: he married a second wife, Emma Eliza Sims, who worked at his office with him. Emma's mother had died when she was a little girl, and she and her sister had been raised by her mother's friend. In 1865 when Emma was thirty-four, her father drowned in the Platte River on the way home from a Church mission in England. Two years later, records show that John Bookbinder and Emma, who "many people said looked like Queen Victoria," were married in the Endowment House on Temple Square—he was forty-three and she was thirty-six, and they had a daughter together. That daughter remembered standing on a chair to mix bread at Helena's while her mother, Emma, was at work with John. That daughter also remembered that Helena, who was "cultured and educated and could give the definition of any word," was "delicate having heart trouble and asthma." Helena died in 1877 at age forty-nine of "dropsy." In 1899 when Emma died of diabetes at age sixty-eight, outliving both John and Helena, she was living in John and

Helena's "old Seventh Ward home." In the Salt Lake Cemetery, John's first wife Helena was buried near John, while second wife Emma was buried on top of him in the same plot.

John Bookbinder's son George, my Grandpa Jack Kelly's father, was part of the family printing business. Evidently, George either disapproved of his father's new marriage or at least sensed his mother's displeasure when her husband spent every day at work with his new wife. Perhaps George didn't like what Emma had inherited from his father, either, and probably did not approve of her being buried so close to his father. All this darkened George's view of the Church.

To add to this, about the time that the Kellys were established in their printing business, the story goes, their major client—the Mormon Church—decided to do its own bookbinding. In the end, John Bookbinder's two sons, including George, were most affected by the financial loss, and George shut off any connection with the Church and never talked about it to my grandfather Jack.

In 1901 on the west side, my Grandpa Jack was born near a "working class ghetto" that sat near the railroad tracks. By then, Main Street was "a maze of wires and poles" with "an electric streetcar system" that "served 10,000 people a day." Brigham Young had not made a provision for a downtown business district in his original plan, but here it was—"full-time police and fire departments, four daily newspapers, ten cigar factories, and a well-established red-light district." Salt Lake City's population was only half Mormon, and, unfortunately, Salt Lake City's "most striking feature" became "the conflict" that "developed between Mormons and non-Mormons," and my grandfather's life was characterized by this schism.

Although Grandpa descended from Mormon immigrants, he wrote in his autobiography that he remembered "no church affiliation, no prayers of any kind, no blessings on the food, no mention ever made of any divine power" in his home. Growing up "absolutely devoid of religion" as the youngest child, my grandfather only knew a little about Mormons from his good boyfriends who were all devout. Against the wishes of Jack's parents, at one point he joined a Church-sponsored Scout troop. Then at age sixteen, the year his father died, one of his friends came to him with the group's ultimatum that, although all his friends liked him, he would have to be baptized Mormon to stay in their group. By then, with his father gone, his mother gave her consent, and he was baptized but didn't regularly attend church.

After graduating as his class valedictorian from West High but without the means to attend college, Jack was with a friend on South Temple Street in the crowds attending the Church's semiannual conference when he first asked my grandmother Anne for a date. Anne descended from Mormon Scottish parents and was about five feet two, her lithe frame topped by blue eyes and light wavy hair, and in personality fun and a little sly. She accepted his offer, and they eventually eloped one night and got married in Farmington, about fifteen miles north, near Lagoon Amusement Park. Six months after eloping, they were married in the Salt Lake Temple to please Anne's mother, but afterward they weren't church-goers. Jack, with glasses and a double chin, was humorous, fair-minded, and intelligent, and he worked at Walker Bank, downtown not far from Temple Square.

Anne and Jack's middle child, my father, grew up in Salt Lake City, where he and his older brother and their pals could leave their home on Harvard Avenue and walk to and hike the mountains—once taking such a long hike that their friend's dog collapsed and died. One day someone told his mother that Sister Stevenson was the teacher at Church and that she loved boys, so his mother sent my father to Church. He had a strong de-sire to "do right" and continued attending by himself. At one point when he told his mother that he wanted to know for himself if the Mormon Church were true, she replied in her beguilingly realistic way, "You can never find that out." He remembers being advised by her that the Church was "all right, but not to be a fanatic."

When my father was growing up, my grandfather Jack started drinking with clients and became an alcoholic. Sadly, my father remembered watch-ing every night to see if his father's eyes were glazed. Once he awoke in the night to hear his mother crying and his father promising to lay off drinking until the end of the month—"now that's a long time," he had said. As an adult, I remember my grandmother telling me on her back porch that once when my grandfather came home from drinking, she was so upset that she broke a bunch of dishes. Her revelation completely sur-prised me because I had never seen any evidence of her anguish or his drinking. He quit drinking before I was born, partially thanks to my dad.

In 1949 at age twenty-two, my father, having become a believer, left alone by train to serve a Church mission in Kentucky and Tennessee. In his Pullman berth, he fervently prayed, he wrote, "pouring out my heart to my Heavenly Father to bless dad that he would have the desire to give up drinking." Only two months into my father's mission, he received a letter from his father saying that he was giving up drinking. Jack Kelly wrote, "With you as an example, I decided to let up on one of my old time sins—the one where you crook your elbow frequently. So far this month my elbow has been straight and stiff and I have no desire to make it crooked."

Two years later, when my father returned from his mission, Jack proudly announced that he had not had a drink in six months and ushered my father to Alcoholics Anonymous where he introduced him around, and my grandparents returned to church for good.

In 1954, my father lettered in track at the University of Utah, graduated in chemical engineering, got a job, and then at twenty-eight married my mother—a spiritual yet savvy woman who grew up poor on a remote Idaho farm but who earned a college scholarship to San Diego State. She always insisted that neither her family's poverty nor her wearing of her cousins' hand-me-down clothes bothered her and that on the farm she learned to work—something she considered a great blessing.

My red-haired mother also believed in prayer. As a young adolescent, her mother would sometimes wake her in the night to help relieve her mother's "heart spells," a breathless, rapid-heart-beating condition. Sometimes for hours my mother would pray while working on her mother's back to calm her heart. My six brothers and sisters and I listened, enthralled by our mother's alarming stories, as we grew up in the carefree 1960s and 1970s suburban Bay Area in California, our Cabana Club membership for the pool down the street paid in advance. I pictured my mom, a young adolescent, praying with all her heart that her mother wouldn't die, with coyotes howling in the background, with God as her only helper—time after time, her mother lived.

My mother also had polygamous ancestors. Although my mother would never shake her children's faith in Joseph Smith by questioning polygamy, it was easy to see that she never felt comfortable with the practice, yet she embraced the deep Mormon heritage it signified. Her great-grandmother was the polygamous second wife of Edmund Ellsworth, who at age thirty-six was the first Mormon handcart company captain, leading 280 Mormons west from Iowa to Salt Lake in 1856. Like many of the staunch early leaders, Edmund Ellsworth married five wives and probably considered it a duty he could manage: his first wife was Elizabeth Young, the oldest child of Brigham Young, whom he married in New York in 1842; his second wife was my great-great-grandmother Mary Ann Dudley (born in New Hampshire), whom he married in Salt Lake in 1852; the third and fourth wives were nineteen-year-old Mary Ann Jones and twenty-one-year-old Mary Ann Bates, who traveled in his handcart company and who both married him the same day soon after arriving in Salt Lake in 1856; the fifth was Ellen, whom he married much later.

At age eighteen, my great-great-grandmother Mary Ann Dudley had no formal courtship with Edmund but respected him—they knew each other from church socials. She was five-foot-six, and slender with red hair, a "very fair complexion," and blue eyes. As Mary Ann told it to a granddaughter, after Edmund proposed to her, Mary Ann asked his first wife Elizabeth for permission to join their family, and Elizabeth said that she and Edmund had talked it over and she "very much approved" of Mary Ann. Mary Ann, a pragmatist, knew that Elizabeth was "his true love" and learned that Elizabeth "was recognized as the head of the family next to Edmund." Mary Ann and Elizabeth lived together early on while Edmund was away on a mission and "worked harmoniously" together doing two-week shifts and then switching: "one would do the cooking, dishwashing, scrubbing, housecleaning, and caring for the children"; the other would "sew, make soap, quilt, visit, or whatever." They both had baby girls at the same time, too, and "clung to each other as a sinking ship."

When Edmund returned, married two more wives, and in 1866 moved forty-two miles further north to West Weber to build bridges and road beds for trains, Mary Ann said that Elizabeth stayed in Salt Lake, but the 1880 census listed all four of his wives and twenty-eight children living in West Weber. According to Mary Ann, the wives in West Weber lived in houses side by side, and Edmund routinely spent a week at each house. In the 1880s, during the polygamy raids, the family split up—Edmund to Arizona with his two younger wives, and Mary Ann went to Idaho where she homesteaded near some of her grown children who were also home-steading. As she aged, she sold her land and bought a house in Rexburg, Idaho, where in 1916 she died of pneumonia at age eighty-two.

A couple of decades ago, when I first started studying polygamous wives, my mother asked and then answered her own question: "What did the wives think of polygamy?" Brief pause. "Probably not much," she stated as though the subject were closed. She seemed uninterested in my naive and enthusiastic reply that polygamous wives were independent women, feminists in some ways. Not long ago, when I again talked to my mother about polygamy, she told me that she believes she'll be living po-lygamy in the next life. She told me this in the resigned way that she once told me she assumed she would care for my father's sister who had Down syndrome when my grandparents passed.

Over the years, I've heard other Mormon women, old and young, say the same thing, having read pointed nineteenth- and twentieth-century pro-polygamy rhetoric that made the practice seem like a foundational principle of our faith, usually based on the notion that the Church gave up polygamy solely for political reasons as a temporary expediency, but that in the eternities, it would be practiced again. In 2012, Mormon Joanna Brooks explained during a national radio interview that polygamy is still a present issue for some Mormon men and women who believe "polygamy is the order of heaven and that they very well may be asked to live it and they're prepared to make that sacrifice." In that same year, in a Utah County hair salon, two spirited Mormon women attempted to convince me that in the next life they would willingly share their husbands with their "unmarried girlfriends." Conversely, in the blogosphere, some young women express angst over whether polygamy will be in force in the afterlife.

Such confusion and angst was present from the start, beginning with Joseph Smith's wife Emma. Amidst all the marvels of establishing the new church, Emma had acted as a scribe while her husband translated the *Book of Mormon* and, in the early 1840s, was president of the new female Relief Society that had more than a thousand members. But in the early 1840s, she vacillated in her feelings about "plural marriage." According to Emma Smith's biographers Linda King Newell and Valeen Tippetts Avery, "there is no evidence that [Emma] ever opposed [her husband] on any doctrine but plural marriage." Emma had found out that Smith had secretly married the admirable Eliza Snow. Smith knew that he had secretly married other women, as well, and felt that unless Emma became converted, their relationship was sunk. Between March and May 1843, Smith repeatedly tried to explain "plural marriage" to Emma, sometimes taking her alone on long buggy rides to discuss it.

Smith never recorded his personal feelings about polygamy but told some that he had received the revelation long before acting on it in the early 1840s. He'd had time to consider how new family forms and temple sealings fit together. According to Richard Bushman, when Smith pursued potential wives, "there was no romantic talk of adoring love" and he did not "court" them or try "to win their affections." Instead he spoke of family kingdoms and exaltation. Terryl Givens likewise sees Smith's primary motivation as an attempt to establish a "timeless and borderless web of human relationships" among adherents, just as the great appeal of first-generation Christianity in the ancient world was "the feeling of entering into an extended family community." Smith was even sealed to some *married* men and women. Early Mormons could be seen as horizontally sealed to each other through polygamy, whereas modern Mormons are often vertically sealed to their ancestors in temples. As Merina Smith explains, through polygamy, early Mormons "would not only see their descendants multiply, but they would gain kinship with multitudes of people." We don't know to what extent Smith pursued sexual relations with his wives. And although "nothing indicates that sexual relations were left out of plural marriage," Richard Bushman explains, "not until many years later did anyone claim Joseph Smith's paternity, and evidence for the tiny handful of supposed children is tenuous."

But he pursued enough to bother Emma, who apparently wasn't persuaded enough by all the high-minded talk of new family forms. After much convincing, in May 1843 Emma finally gave her consent to a polygamous marriage and participated in her husband's marriage to two sisters, giving her "free and full consent." Five days later, Emma participated in sacred rites with her husband and felt good. However, shortly after when she tried to enter a room where Smith was with one of the sisters, he held the door closed. After that, Emma's feelings "turned," and she was "more bitter in her feelings than ever before, if possible, and before the day was over she turned around or repented what she had done and kept Joseph up till very late in the night talking to him."

Not only that night but at other times, "Emma began to talk as firmly and urgently to Joseph about abandoning plural marriage as he had formerly talked to her about accepting it." In the spring of 1843, "the recovery of his domestic life" became "almost impossible." Smith's brother Hyrum suggested that Smith dictate the celestial marriage revelation to help convince Emma to believe it. Hyrum suggested that Smith use the "Urim and Thummim"—that he used to translate the *Book of Mormon*, but Smith declined, saying he knew the polygamy revelation by heart. The very day that Smith dictated the revelation in July, he was particularly "caught between the plural marriage revelation and [his wife] Emma's opposition." When Clayton presented it to Emma, he received a "severe talking to."

The written revelation that introduced polygamy was affected by Smith's conflicts with Emma. According to Smith's nephew, future Church President Joseph F. Smith, the revelation "took the form it did because of problems with" Emma. The revelation emphasizes the "eternity of the marriage covenant" and a "continuation of the seeds forever and ever"—

that a couple's marriage covenant "shall be of full force when they are out of the world." But while the revelation is beautiful in some ways, it's troubling in other ways. As if directed toward Emma, it explains that polygamy is a possible ancillary to eternal marriage, and that a woman who rejects her husband's teachings about polygamy shall "be destroyed" because God "will destroy her." This seems harsh compared to the *Book of Mormon* where the voice of God defends women: "the sobbings of their hearts ascend up to God against" their husbands. The *Book of Mormon* saves condemnation for polygamous husbands: "ye have come unto great condemnation; for ye have done these things which ye ought not to have done...And because of the strictness of the word of God, which cometh down against you, many hearts died, pierced with deep wounds." In the Bible, God's voice was also sympathetic to wives when He told Abraham to hearken unto Sarah and when He helped Hagar.

The day after Smith shared the revelation with Emma, and after hours of crying and talking together, Joseph and Emma called Clayton to help administer their "compromise." As Richard Bushman explains, "They were in impossible positions: Joseph caught between his revelation and his wife, Emma between a practice she detested and belief in her husband." Evidently fearing the legal and financial ramifications of many wives, Emma requested half ownership of a steamboat and "sixty city lots," and Joseph evidently agreed "to add no more" wives. If he did, he told Clayton, Emma "would divorce him." That winter before his imminent death, Joseph and Emma were reconciled and back to their natural conviviality.

Smith's revelation on celestial marriage was canonized in the *Doctrine and Covenants* in 1876. Today the verses that sanctioned polygamy, like the verses that sanctioned sacrificial burnt offerings in the Old Testament, lie dormant like an unfinished puzzle.

After Woodruff's 1890 Manifesto and the government's subsequent retreat, Utah gained statehood in 1896. Around the turn of the century, a "fracture line in the attitudes of lay members" broke between the majority who saw polygamy as an embarrassment, avoided discussing it, and believed it had come to an end; and a minority who felt that they were "purposely set apart to keep the principle alive." Between 1890 and 1910, 262 secret polygamous marriages were performed—about half in Mexico where some felt that the Manifesto was a political expediency that did not affect them. In 1904, Church leaders clarified their position that polygamy was over, including in Canada and Mexico, and subsequently new marriages sharply declined. And the doctrinal shift away from polygamy that had begun in the 1880s continued: "Celestial marriage" was defined as "marriage that survived death," and Church members were told that polygamy was not a "general command to the Saints" nor "obligatory upon members of the Church generally."

Between 1904 and 1907, Reed Smoot, who had been elected senator by Utahans but had yet to be seated in Washington, became the subject of the Reed Smoot U.S. Senate confirmation hearings that sought to determine if the Mormons, including Smoot, who was a Mormon but not a polygamist, were serious about dropping polygamy. Senators argued that as an apostle, Smoot was "a member of Mormonism's highest governing body," a governing body under which "polygamy and cohabitation were yet approved and practiced." During this intense time, two apostles who had added wives after the Manifesto were forced to resign. On the other hand, during the hearings, "respectable gentile citizens from both Utah and Idaho" testified that polygamy was "as dead as slavery," and it was "repeatedly stated that the younger generation of Mormons was overwhelmingly opposed to polygamy." In 1907, Smoot, "who had a reputation for being firmly against the practice," was finally seated. Also in 1907, at General Conference, President Joseph F. Smith "gave a lengthy" patriotic speech that asserted that Mormons gave up polygamy when "every means of constitutional defense had been exhausted" and reaffirmed that they desired to obey the laws of the land.

In 1910, a letter from the Church First Presidency to Mormon stake presidents asked them to "actively search out those who were actually performing plural marriages and had so far evaded detection." Those who entered new polygamous marriages were considered "disloyal to the Church" and disobedient "to the direction of the prophet." In 1911, President Smith directed stake presidents to direct Church courts to possibly excommunicate offenders. In 1912, the Mexican Revolution "forced hundreds" of polygamous Mormons north to the United States. They had established prosperous colonies in Mexico and saw themselves as Mormon "elites" because of the great sacrifices they had made to live polygamy and move to a new country, but as time went on, they were "routinely passed up for ecclesiastical advancement and were sermonized against." Polygamists had gone from being the Church elite to being an embarrassment. In 1935, Lorena Larsen's adult son Bent F. Larsen recalled that "after the Church renounced polygamy all the heroism was gone." Growing up in a polygamous family after the Manifesto, he felt his family was living on "a sort of extended underground" to hide his family's identity. He went on to explain that attitudes had "changed and in a way there was a stigma attached to polygamous families." By the 1930s, the Church had divorced itself from the practice and history of polygamy and had quit talking about it.

In the background, fundamentalists in Utah, Arizona, Mexico, and Canada, who were not accepted by regular Mormons, followed the practice of polygamy. In 1953, as the mainstream Church continued to be embarrassed by the polygamists, and as Utah and Arizona citizens complained to government officials that the illegal polygamists were soaking their tax dollars to educate and feed their children, Arizona government officials raided polygamist-enclave Short Creek, Arizona, arrested thirty-six men, and took eighty-six women and 263 children into custody. Emotional media portrayals of families being separated to do jail time and the ensuing relocations "to small towns throughout the state" to split up their community didn't play well "against the backdrop of the growing Red Scare—the threat of a totalitarian state's power over individual rights," as *Slate* writer Neil J. Young describes it. Public opinion went against the government, and "two years later, nearly all of the men, women, and children had returned to their town—and the already largely separatist fundamentalists further withdrew from the world."

During the last half of the twentieth century, the former practice of polygamy continued to be an occasional curiosity among mainstream Mormons. Since a minority of Mormons were polygamists in the nineteenth century, and since women were not particularly fond of it, and since the Church had widened its distance from fundamentalists who practiced it, polygamy might have remained as old as Abraham if not for Apostle Bruce R. McConkie's encyclopedic bestseller, *Mormon Doctrine*. Never out of print between 1958 and 2011, it was the go-to book used by Mormon families like mine to settle doctrinal matters. Under the "Plural Marriage" entry, McConkie controversially stated that polygamy would one day return: "obviously the holy practice [of plural marriage] will commence again." But, in retrospect, McConkie's point of view should not have been portrayed as Mormon doctrine since the Church president when McConkie first published *Mormon Doctrine*, David O. McKay, was not given the opportunity to review the book ahead of its publication. Furthermore, when he and his counselors did review it, they found the tone too authoritative, significant portions objectionable, and the title unfounded. Because their reaction was not known until 2005, McConkie's statement muddied the waters.

In the 1990s, Church President Gordon B. Hinckley spoke publicly about polygamy. He repeatedly emphasized that polygamy was no longer part of the Church. In response to increasing media depictions of Mormon fundamentalist splinter groups that practice polygamy, he wrote in 1998 in the official Church magazine *The Ensign* that "there is no such thing as a 'Mormon Fundamentalist'" because, to him, fundamentalists, who typically practice polygamy, aren't Mormons. He went on, "It is a contradiction to use the two words together." Further, "the Church teaches that marriage must be monogamous and does not accept into its membership those practicing plural marriage" and excommunicates any who are found practicing it.

When Larry King interviewed Hinckley on *Larry King Live* September 8, 1998, the Mormon prophet went further, explaining that polygamy was practiced "when our people came west" and that "they permitted it on a restricted scale." When pushed by King to clarify, Hinckley said, "I condemn it, yes, as a belief, because I think it is not doctrinal. It is not legal." Later in 2008, the Mormon prophet reiterated that for Mormons polygamy was "118 years ago—it's behind us."

Hinckley's remarks suggest a connection between polygamy and the Mormons' western migration; suggest that polygamy was "permitted" rather than commanded; suggest that it was "restricted" and not for everyone; and suggest that it is past and not in the future. His comment that polygamy is not "doctrinal" may be interpreted to mean that, even though canonical, polygamy is not doctrinal anymore, particularly given the *Book of Mormon*'s condemnation of it—polygamy was practiced temporarily, during a short but profound window of Mormon history.

To further clarify, in 2013, Mormon Church leaders posted "Plural Marriage and Families in Early Utah" on the official Church website. The post begins by affirming that Mormons believe in monogamous marriage and that the fifty-year period between the early 1840s and the 1890s was an exception to that. While admitting that "Latter-day Saints do not understand all of God's purposes for instituting...the practice of polygamy" in the nineteenth century, the post explains that the practice resulted in "large numbers of children within faithful Latter-day Saint homes" and helped "shape 19th-century Mormon society" by providing marriage for everyone; equalizing wealth; uniting "a diverse immigrant population," and strengthening "group identification." Nineteenth-century Mormon polygamy, it seems reasonable to assume, was meant to be a temporary social arrangement to grow a new religion and to accommodate religious immigrants on an isolated frontier.

As Mormons move forward today, the nineteenth-century practice of polygamous marriage will seem more exotic or will be left exclusively to Mormon fundamentalists, but maybe the polygamous wives who lived it will take a more prominent place in the Mormon imagination—after all, they did much to lay a foundation for the modern Church. As Mormons meet for weekly Sunday meetings, while singing some royal hymn, the afternoon sun sending light shards through the few remaining pioneer stained-glass windows, perhaps from time to time the congregants will see a few wise old polygamous wives, no longer bent over from backbreaking work, no longer suffering from loneliness and heartache, seated on the podium in front surveying what they helped create, patiently waiting to tell their stories.

Sources

ABBREVIATIONS

BYUL Brigham Young University, Harold B. Lee Library, Provo, Utah
CHL   Church History Library (Church Archives), Church of Jesus Christ of
      Latter-day Saints, Salt Lake City
DUP   Daughters of Utah Pioneers, Salt Lake City
USHS Utah State Historical Society, Salt Lake City

The sources listed are organized by chapter. Each chapter is divided into primary sources, secondary sources, and references to specific quotes. Primary and secondary sources are listed in alphabetical order and cited in full the first time they are used; thereafter, they are abbreviated. I do not cite page numbers from the twenty-nine polygamous wives' personal writings because I quote from them so frequently and because their stories are usually organized chronologically, making references relatively easy to find. Except for well-known scripture stories, I provide scripture references from the four books of scripture recognized by the Church of Jesus Christ of Latter-day Saints, or the Mormon Church: the Old and New Testaments; the *Book of Mormon*; the *Doctrine and Covenants*; and the *Pearl of Great Price*.

WELCOME
Primary Sources

Jane Charter Robinson Hindley, Diary, ms. Ms d 1964, CHL; Joseph Smith, "Joseph Smith—History," *Pearl of Great Price: A Selection from the Revelations, Translations, and Narrations of Joseph Smith First Prophet, Seer, and Revelator to the Church of Jesus Christ of Latter-day Saints* (Salt Lake City, 1988); and Mary Jane Mount Tanner, *A Fragment: The Autobiography of Mary Jane Mount Tanner*, ed. Margery W. Ward (Salt Lake City, 1983).

Secondary Sources

Thomas G. Alexander, *Great Basin Kingdom Revisited* (Logan, UT, 1991); James B. Allen and Glen M. Leonard, *The Story of the Latter-day Saints* (Salt Lake City, 1976); Leonard J. Arrington, *Brigham Young: American Moses* (New York, 1985), and *Great Basin Kingdom* (Lincoln and London, 1966); Leonard J. Arrington and Davis Bitton, *The Mormon Experience* (Urbana and Chicago, 1992); Ben Bennion, "A Geographer's Discovery of *Great Basin Kingdom*," in *Great Basin Revisited,* ed. Thomas G. Alexander (Logan, UT, 1991); Lowell C. Bennion, "Plural Marriage, 1841–1904," in *Mapping Mormonism: An Atlas of Latter-day Saint History,* ed. Brandon S. Plewe (Provo, UT, 2012); Richard Lyman Bushman, *Joseph Smith: Rough Stone Rolling* (New York, 2005); Todd M. Compton, *In Sacred Loneliness: The Plural Wives of Joseph Smith* (Salt Lake City, 1997); B. Carmon Hardy, "That 'Same Old Question of Polygamy and Polygamous Living': Some Recent Findings Regarding Nineteenth and Early Twentieth-Century Mormon Polygamy," *Utah Historical Quarterly* 73:3 (Summer 2005) 212–24; Linda King Newell and Valeen Tippetts Avery, *Mormon Enigma: Emma Hale Smith* (Garden City, NY, 1984); John G. Turner, *Brigham Young: Pioneer Prophet* (Cambridge, 2012); Harriet Sigerman, *Land of Many Hands: Women in the American West* (New York and Oxford, 1997); and Richard Van Wagoner, *Mormon Polygamy: A History* (Salt Lake City, 1986).

Specific Quotes

3   a little sparrow, Ward, 11.

4   remarkable movement, Sigerman, 339–40.

6   25–30 percent, Lowell C. Bennion, 124.

6   all things, Van Wagoner, 3.

6   familial plentitude, Bushman, 440.

7   wrecking, Bushman, 437–38.

7   sexual dalliances, Turner, 88.

7   drew criticism, Arrington and Bitton, 53.

7   nearly murdered, Arrington and Bitton, 44.

7   perfectly square, Arrington, *American Moses,* 146.

8   England, Scotland, Arrington, *American Moses,* 156.

8   people actually, Alexander, 13.

8   string of Mormon colonies, Turner, 281.

8   Idaho, Arrington, *American Moses,* 167.

CHAPTER I.   I WAS PERFECTLY WILLING . . . BUT STILL
IT WAS HARD
Primary Sources

"Alex Badger to Dear Mother, May 10, 1863," in *Doing the Works of Abraham: Mormon Polygamy, Its Origin, Practice, and Demise,* ed. B. Carmon Hardy (Norman,

OK, 2007); Tanner, *A Fragment*; "William Chandless, Visit to Salt Lake (1857)," in *Doing*, ed. Hardy; "Rachel Emma Wooley Simmons [Autobiography]," *Heart Throbs of the West* 11 (Salt Lake City, 1950): 153–208.

Secondary Sources

Stephanie Coontz, *Marriage, a History* (New York, 2005); Kathryn M. Daynes, *More Wives Than One: Transformation of the Mormon Marriage System, 1840–1910* (Urbana and Chicago, 2001); Michael Goldberg, "Breaking New Ground 1800–1848," in *No Small Courage: A History of Women in the United States*, ed. Nancy F. Cott (New York, 2000); Edward William Tullidge, *History of Salt Lake City* (Salt Lake City, 1886); and Sigerman, *Many Hands*.

Specific Quotes

11   fresh appearance, "Alex Badger," Hardy, *Doing*, 207.
13   ten-feet long, Sigerman, 56.
13   who didn't have, Sigerman, 95.
13   extensive beautiful, Ward, 48–49.
13   423 houses, Ward, 50, 54.
14   tramped, Hardy, 185.
14   frontier period, Daynes, 92.
14   27 percent, Daynes, 95–97.
15   tender romance, Tullidge, 762.
17   "Home," Dora Greenwell poem quoted in Coontz, 163.
17   more of a partnership, Goldberg, 180.
18   recipe, Coontz, 162.
20   12 percent, Daynes, 70.
20   happiest, "William Chandless," Hardy, *Doing*, 191.
20   tent, Hardy, *Doing*, 172.

CHAPTER 2. I HAD ADMIRED HIS CONDUCT ON THE PLAINS
Primary Sources

Martha Spence Heywood, *Not By Bread Alone: The Journal of Martha Spence Heywood 1850–1856*, ed. Juanita Brooks (Salt Lake City, 1978); Jane Charter Robinson Hindley, Diary, ms. Ms d 1764, CHL; "Jane Charters Robinson Hindley—1855, Autobiography," *Our Pioneer Heritage* 16, comp. Kate B. Carter (Salt Lake City, 1973), 529–31; Ruth Page Rogers, Autobiography, from diary and letters tx. Ms d 1854, CHL; "John Williams Gunnison, the Mormons, or, Latter-Day Saints (1852)," in *Doing*, ed. Hardy; and Annie Clark Tanner, *A Mormon Mother: An Autobiography* by Annie Clark Tanner (Salt Lake City, 1991).

Secondary Sources

Arrington, *Brigham Young;* Kathryn Daynes, "Striving to Live the Principle in Utah's First Temple City: A Snapshot of Polygamy in St. George, Utah, in June 1880," *BYU Studies* 51:4 (2012): 69–83; Jessie L. Embry, *Mormon Polygamous Families: Life in the Principle* (Salt Lake City, 1987); "Gardner Mill and the Birth of Salt Lake Valley's West Side," historytogo.utah.gov; Sigerman, *Land of Many Hands;* Turner, *Brigham Young.*

Specific Quotes

27   Mississippi, Brooks, 3.
28   cluster of small industries, "Gardner Mill."
30   long courtship, Tanner, 64.
33   small fraction, Embry, 76.
33   family heads, Arrington, *Brigham Young,* 168.
36   nontraditional tasks, Sigerman, 101–105.
37   hat-making, Brooks, 4.
38   1855 letter, Brooks, 134.
38   good adobe, Brooks, 5.
40   needed breadwinners, Daynes, "Striving," 73–74.
40   handcart sisters, Turner, 257.
40   wed more quickly, Daynes, 97.
40   15 percent, Sigerman, 278.
41   demand a man, "John Williams Gunnison" in Hardy, *Doing,* 188.

CHAPTER 3. INTERLUDE: JUSTIFYING POLYGAMY
Primary Sources

Tanner, *Mormon Mother.*

Secondary Sources

Allen and Leonard, *The Story of the Latter-day Saints;* Arrington, *American Moses;* Arrington, *Great Basin;* Arrington and Bitton, *The Mormon Experience;* Lowell C. Bennion, "Mapping the Extent of Plural Marriage in St. George, 1861–1880," *BYU Studies* 51:4 (2012); Daynes, *More Wives Than One;* Davis Bitton and Val Lambson, "Demographic Limits of Nineteenth-Century Mormon Polygyny," *BYU Studies* 51:4 (2012): 7–26; Omri Elisha, "Sustaining Charisma: Mormon Sectarian Culture and the Struggle for Plural Marriage, 1852–1890," *Nova Religio: The Journal of Alternative and Emergent Religions* 6:1 (October 2002):

45–63; C. Mark Hamilton, "Temple Square," *Utah History Encyclopedia*, ed. Allan Kent Powell (Salt Lake City, 1994); Hardy, *Doing*; Hardy, "That 'Same Old Question'"; Dean L. May, "Mormons," *Harvard Encyclopedia of American Ethnic Groups*, eds. Stephan Thernstrom and Ann Orlov (Cambridge, MA, 1980); Louis J. Kern, *An Ordered Love: Sex Roles and Sexuality in Victorian Utopias—The Shakers, the Mormons, and the Oneida Community* (Chapel Hill, 1981); Orson Pratt, "A Special Conference of the Elders of the Church," *Deseret News, Extra* (Salt Lake City, August 28, 1852); Peggy Fletcher Stack, "Scholars Size Up Mormon Moses," *The Salt Lake Tribune* (December 28, 2013) C1, C3; and Van Wagoner, *Mormon Polygamy*.

Specific Quotes

43	bowery, Arrington and Bitton, 116–17; Allen and Leonard, 274–75; Hamilton, 547.
43	sublime, Pratt.
43	cut off, Van Wagoner, 30.
44	filled with fire, Stack, C3.
44	ancient Patriarchal Order, Van Wagoner, 84.
44	"Revelation," Hardy, *Doing*, 80.
44	unwise, Hardy, *Doing*, 80.
44	clearly need, Hardy, "That 'Same Old,'" 217–18.
44	pronouncements, Daynes, 75–76.
45	God required it, Van Wagoner, 84–85, 90.
45	countered various, Van Wagoner, 84, 89.
45	exceeding fruitful, Genesis 16.
46	wandering Nomads, Tanner, 59–60.
46	be blameless, 1 Timothy 3.
46	do like unto them, *Book of Mormon*, Jacob 2.
46	on the high end, Bitton, 15.
47	fall behind, Hardy, "That 'Same Old,'" 218.
47	want hard times, Arrington, *Brigham Young*, 167.
47	unique aura, Elisha, 53.
47	native and indigenously, Thomas F. O'Dea qtd. in May, 720.
47	very committed Mormons, Bennion, 32.
47	church approval, Kern, 156.
48	charismatic legacy, Elisha, 58–59.
48	ritual activities, Elisha, 53.
48	fulfill its responsibility, Daynes, 188.
48	slightly more, Daynes, 112.
48	immigrants, Daynes, 104–5.

48   52 percent, Daynes, 119–20, 123–26.

49   renew members' dedication, Allen, 279.

49   flour rations, Arrington, *Great Basin*, 152 and 161.

49   Church authorities, Arrington, *Great Basin*, 152.

49   sixty-five, Stanley S. Ivins in Arrington, *Great Basin*, 459.

49   seen the sorrow, *Book of Mormon*, Jacob 2.

CHAPTER 4. IT IS A HEART HISTORY
Primary Sources

Elizabeth Graham MacDonald, Autobiography, ts. MAN A 2554, USHS; and Eunice P. Stewart, "A Record Kept by Eunice P. Stewart during Andrew J. Stewart's Mission with Br. Orson Hyde, One of the Twelve Apostles, to Carson Valley or Elsewhere," BYUL; and Tanner, *A Fragment*.

Secondary Sources

Kenneth L. Cannon II, "Provo," *Utah History Encyclopedia*, ed. Powell; Stephanie Coontz, *Marriage, a History* (New York, 2005); B. Carmon Hardy, *Solemn Covenant: The Mormon Polygamous Passage* (Urbana, 1992).

Specific Quotes

56   Mormon insurrection, Cannon, 447–48.

56   in 1903, Hardy, 169.

58   If you've ever, Coontz, 145.

CHAPTER 5. THE DRUDGE AND TAIL OF SUCH WOMEN
Primary Sources

Angelina Farley, Diary, ms. Ms f 262, item 2, CHL; "Nelle Spilsbury Hatch, Mother Jane's Story (1964)," in Hardy, *Doing*; Henrietta Elizabeth Crombie Williams, "A Sketch of Henrietta Elizabeth Crombie Williams," DUP.

Secondary Sources

Laura L. Bush, *Faithful Transgressions in the American West: Six Twentieth-Century Mormon Women's Autobiographical Acts* (Logan, UT, 2004); bell hooks, *remembered rapture: the writer at work* (New York, 1999); M.E.W.S, "New England Women," *Atlantic Monthly* (August 1878); Richard Roberts, "Ogden," *Utah History Encyclopedia*, ed. Powell; Sidonie Smith, *A Poetics of Women's Autobiography: Marginality and the Fictions of Self-Representation*

(Bloomington, 1987); Stack, "Scholars Size Up Mormon Moses"; Fanny Stenhouse, *Expose of Polygamy: A Lady's Life among the Mormons*, ed. Linda Wilcox DeSimone (Logan, UT, 2008); "Winthrop Farley Family," *Heart Throbs of the West*, vol. 3, comp. Kate B. Carter, 120–22 (Salt Lake, 1959).

Specific Quotes

61	specialized in, Carter, 122.
62	rural agricultural area, Roberts, 399.
66	New England Woman, M.E.W.S.
67	oneness, "Nelle Spilsbury Hatch," Hardy, *Doing*, 163, 167.
67	unique recounting, hooks, 83–84.
67	selected, deselected, Bush, 24.
67	ideal woman, Smith, 54.
69	given everything, Stack, C3.
71	transgressive writing, Bush, 16–17.
71	through and out of, DeSimone, 7.

CHAPTER 6 INTERLUDE: SOMETIMES SISTERHOOD
Primary Sources

Josephine Streeper Chase, "The Josephine Diaries: Glimpses of the Life of Josephine Streeper Chase, 1881–94," *Utah Historical Quarterly* 8 (Spring 1978); Florence Ridges Dean, Diary, ms. Ms d 1530 CHL; Ellen Albina Wilhelm Draper, "A Pioneer Mother Describes Life in Early Utah," in *Voices from the Past: Diaries, Journals, and Autobiographies*, BYU Campus Education Week Program, ed. Leonard J. Arrington (Provo, UT, 1980) 93–95; Caroline Christiansen Pedersen Hansen, "Autobiography," *Our Pioneer Heritage*, comp. Kate B. Carter, 12:71 (Salt Lake City, 1960); Mary Ann Maughan, "Journal of Mary Ann Weston Maughan," *Our Pioneer Heritage* 2, comp. Kate B. Carter (Salt Lake City, 1959); Ellen Elvira Nash, "Ellen Elvira Nash Parkinson [Autobiography]," in *Our Pioneer Heritage* 8, comp. Kate B. Carter (Salt Lake City, 1965): 202–18; Hannah Isabelle Fawcett Nixon, Autobiography, ts. MAN A 760, USHS; Laura Ann Keeler Thurber, Diary, ms. Ms f 4745. CHL.

Secondary Sources

Arrington, *Brigham Young*; Leonard J. Arrington and Susan Arrington Madsen, *Sunbonnet Sisters: The Stories of Mormon Women and Frontier Life* (Salt Lake City, 1984); Martha Sontag Bradley and Mary Brown Firmage Woodward, *4 Zinas: A Story of Mothers and Daughters on the Mormon Frontier* (Salt Lake, 2000); Vicky Burgess-Olson, *Sister Saints* (Provo, 1978); Martha Sonntag Bradley and Mary Brown Firmage Woodward, *4 Zinas: A Story of Mothers and Daughters on the*

Mormon Frontier (Salt Lake, 2000); Jill Mulvay Derr, "'Strength in Our Union': The Making of Mormon Sisterhood," *Sisters in Spirit: Mormon Women in Historical and Cultural Perspective,*" eds. Maureen Ursenbach Beecher and Lavina Fielding Anderson (Urbana and Chicago, 1987); Terry Eagleton, *Literary Theory: An Introduction* (Minneapolis, 1983); Susa Young Gates, "With the Editor," *Young Woman's Journal* 10 (May 1899); Kenneth W. Godfrey, Audrey M. Godfrey, and Jill Mulvay Derr, *Women's Voices: An Untold History of the Latter-day Saints 1830–1850* (Salt Lake City, 1982); Elizabeth Wood Kane, *Twelve Mormon Homes Visited in Succession on a Journey through Utah to Arizona* (Salt Lake City, 1974); Hardy, *Doing;* Carol Cornwall Madsen, "Emmeline B. Wells: Romantic Rebel," *Supporting Saints: Life Stories of Nineteenth-Century Mormons* (Provo, 1985); Mary F., "The Patriarchal Order of Marriage," *Woman's Exponent* 10: 16 (January 15, 1882): 121; Harriet Sigerman, "An Unfinished Battle 1848–1865," in *No Small Courage,* ed. Cott; Turner, *Brigham Young; Journal of Discourses,* vol. 9, reported by G. D. Watt, April 7, 1861, jod.mrm.org/9/31; Van Wagoner, *Mormon Polygamy.*

Specific Quotes

73   were we the stupid, Godfrey, Godfrey, and Derr, 289.

73   nucleus, Derr, 164.

73   companionable, Turner, 156.

73   shared bonds, Turner, 157.

74   female elite, Derr, 164.

74   spiritual commitment, Derr, 165.

74   separated geographically, kinship relations, Derr, 163.

74   elude simple, Turner, 157.

74   national stage, Arrington, 365.

74   brains and tongues, Bradley and Woodward, 340.

74   sphere, Arrington, 339.

74   perfect equality, Gates, 240.

75   equal pay for equal work, Arrington and Arrington Madsen, 135.

75   bossed, Hardy, 313–14.

75   come share with me, Mary F.

75   Ellis Shipp, Arrington, 338–39.

75   entrusted, Arrington and Arrington Madsen, 131.

75   unique opportunity, Kane, 5.

76   Miss Lucy, Kane, 8–10.

76   Steerforth, Kane, 48.

76   Mrs. Jane, Kane, 83–85.

76   finding one's soul mate, Daynes, 64.

77   to see any friend, Hardy, *Doing,* 164.

77   are you tormenting, Brigham Young, 37.

78   Cannon, Van Wagoner, 96.
78   Wells, Van Wagoner, 94; Hardy, *Doing,* 166; Madsen, 326.
78   Phoebe Woodruff, Van Wagoner, 101–2.
78   Zina Young, Van Wagoner, 102.
78   Sarah Pratt, Van Wagoner, 100.
78   Artemesia Snow, Van Wagoner, 100–101.
79   positive testimonials, Van Wagoner, 94.
88   exceed the individuals, Claude Lévi-Strauss, qtd. in Eagleton, 180.

CHAPTER 7 MANY NIGHTS MY PILLOW WOULD BE
WET WITH GRIEF
Primary Sources

Lydia Ann Nelson Brinkerhoff, Autobiography, ts. MAN A 1945, USHS; Lucy Hannah White Flake, *Diary of Lucy Hannah White Flake,* eds. Chad J. Flake and Hyrum F. Boone (Provo, 1973); Emma Nielson. Diary, ts, USHS.

Secondary Sources

Derr, "Strength in Our Union"; "Elizabeth Edwards on 'Facing Life's Adversities,'" *All Things Considered* interview, NPR (July 17, 2011); Chad Flake, "From the Diary of Lucy Hannah White Flake," in *Supporting Saints* (Provo, 1985); "To the Last Frontier: Autobiography of Lucy Hannah White Flake," ed. Roberta Flake Clayton (unpublished manuscript).

Specific Quotes

93   Prudence probably lived there, Roberta Flake Clayton, 56–61; Chad Flake, 237.
95   hide her true feelings, DiSimone, 7.
97   so conventional and ritualized, Derr, 165.
102   Prudence's four daughters, Chad Flake, 238.
102   exact nature, Chad Flake, 252.
104   putting together a home, Edwards.

CHAPTER 8 I COULD NOT SAY THAT I LOVED THE MAN
AS LOVERS LOVE
Primary Sources

Martha Cragun Cox, Autobiography, ts. MAN A 146-3, USHS; Mary Ann Hafen, *Recollections of a Handcart Pioneer of 1860: A Woman's Life on the Mormon Frontier* (Lincoln and London, 1983).

Secondary Source

Lavina Fielding Anderson, "Salt of the Earth Lady," rsc.byu.edu, 1985.

Specific Quotes

109   most harmonious, Anderson.
109   wanderings, Anderson.
117   scraped, Anderson.
117   month's wages, Anderson.
117   taught every year, Anderson.
117   Mexican, Anderson.

CHAPTER 9. WORD CAME THE MARSHALLS WERE COMING,
SO I HAD TO SKIP OUT
Primary Sources

Elvira E. Day Diary, Eli Azariah Day, and Orville Day, *Histories of Eli Azariah Day Sr and his family*, comp. Mary B. Larsen, BYUL; Loretta Evans e-mail in possession of the author; Lorena Larsen, *Autobiography of Lorena Eugenia Washburn Larsen* (Provo, UT, 1962), BYUL; Agatha Walker McAllister, Autobiography, ts. MAN A 723 USHS.

Secondary Sources

Allen and Leonard, *The Story of the Latter-day Saints*; M. Guy Bishop, "Monroe," *Utah History Encyclopedia*, ed. Powell; Daynes, *More Wives Than One*; Daynes, "Striving"; Lisa Tait Olsen, *Martha Hughes Cannon*, KUED PBS affiliate (Salt Lake City, July 22, 2012).

Specific Quotes

123   Monroe fields, Bishop, 371.
125   1856, Allen and Leonard, 297.
125   by sending federal marshals, Daynes, *More Wives*, 48–49, 206–207.
128   disguised, Allen and Leonard, 396.
129   on church leaders, Daynes, *More Wives*, 75.
129   practice without limit, George Q. Cannon in Daynes, *More Wives*, 75.
129   St. George Temple, Daynes, "Striving," 80.
136   92 percent, obituary of E. Euphrasia Cox Day.
141   opened the door to salvation, A. Tanner, *A Mormon Mother*, 62.
146   she divorced Day, 146.

146   thirty dollars a month, Orville Day.
147   144 East, obituary of E. Euphrasia Cox Day.
147   *Juvenile Instructor*, obituary of E. Euphrasia Cox Day.
148   summer working at a sawmill, Evans.
148   they needed help, Evans.

CHAPTER 10 *INTERLUDE: THE 1890 MANIFESTO*
Primary Sources

"Diary of Joseph Lyman Jessop, 1: BK. March 7, 28, 1923, 149–50," and "Discourse Delivered By Elder Jos. F. Smith," in *Doing*, ed. Hardy; *Proceedings before the Committee on privileges and elections of the United States Senate of the matter of the protests against the right of Hon. Reed Smoot, a senator from the state of Utah to hold his seat...[Jan. 16, 1904–]* Volume 3 (Google eBook) United States. Congress. Senate; A. Tanner, *A Mormon Mother*.

Secondary Sources

Tom Alexander, *Things in Heaven and in Earth: The Life and Times of Wilford Woodruff* (Salt Lake, 1993); Arrington, *Brigham Young*; Sherry Baker, "Creating a Shared History: Serial Narratives in the *Young Woman's Journal*, 1889–1894" (PhD diss., University of Utah, 1988); Bitton, *History*; Bitton and Lambson, "Demographic Limits"; Martha S. Bradley, "Changed Faces: The Official LDS Position on Polygamy, 1890–1990," *Sunstone* (February 1990); Drew Briney, *Silencing Mormon Polygamy: Failed Persecutions, Divided Saints & the Rise of Mormon Fundamentalism*, (n.p., 2008); Kenneth L. Cannon, "After the Manifesto, Mormon Polygamy 1890–1906," *Sunstone* 8:1–2 (January–April 1983); Daynes, *More Wives*; Daynes, "Striving"; Jessie L. Embry, *Mormon Polygamous Families: Life in the Principle* (Salt Lake City, 1987); Ann W. Engar, "Beehive and Lion Houses," *Utah History Encyclopedia*, ed. Powell; Hardy, *Solemn Covenant*; "John Taylor," lds.org; Daniela Johnson-Bennion, "Comparing Themes of Polygamy in Mormon Women's Public and Personal Writings As Found in the *Woman's Exponent* and Their Diaries During the Edmunds Act, the Edmunds-Tucker Act, and the Manifesto" (Master's thesis, Utah State University, 2000); "Mormon Bishop Deposed," *New York Times* (September 1886); "Mormon Bishop Sharp, He Tells about His Plural Marriages, Pleads Guilty, and Is Fined," *New York Times* (September 25, 1886) from *The Salt Lake Herald* (September 19, 1886); M.E. Teasdale, "Correspondence" *Woman's Exponent* 17: 3 (July 1, 1888) 19; Paul Thomas Smith, "John Taylor," *Encyclopedia of Mormonism*, ed. Powell; Van Wagoner, *Mormon Polygamy*.

Specific Quotes

153   September 24, 1890, Van Wagoner, 142.

153   waned, Van Wagoner, 113.

153   fifty-five women, Turner, 376.

153   charge account, Arrington 170, 333; and Engar, 38.

154   horizontal, Arrington, 330.

154   read from the Scriptures, Arrington, 170–72.

154   to correct, Turner, 381.

154   considerable disharmony, Turner, 382.

154   ended in divorce, Van Wagoner, 113.

154   disposed, Briney, 109 (Note 71: Historian's Office Journal, Dec. 17 and 30, 1858, FHL).

154   President James Snow, Daynes, "Striving," 70.

154   continually, Hardy, *Doing*, 180–82.

155   waning, Van Wagoner, 113.

155   underground, Smith, 545.

155   would rather trust, "John Taylor."

155   reduce federal control, VanWagoner, 126.

155   John Sharp, "Mormon Bishop Deposed" and "Mormon Bishop Sharp."

155   1,300, Van Wagoner, 120.

155   almost driven wild, "Diary of Joseph Lyman Jessop" in Hardy, *Doing*, 381.

156   division and contention, Briney, 84–85; John Taylor Papers at U of Utah Library.

156   receive the greatest, Daynes, *More Wives*, 72–74.

156   waver, Hardy, *Doing*, 319.

157   a sort of superfluity, Joseph F. Smith quoted in Hardy, *Doing*, 113.

157   1887, Hardy, *Doing*, 321; Alexander, 250, 267.

157   polygamists' daughters, Daynes, "Striving," 72–73.

157   mathematical limits, Bitton and Lambson, 15.

157   too high to be perpetuated, Daynes, "Striving," 83.

158   20 percent, Bitton and Lambsom, 15.

158   1870s and 1880s, Daynes, "Striving," 82.

158   rage in favour of plurality, Dixon quoted in Hardy, *Doing*, 212–13.

158   in favor of romantic love, Daynes, *More Wives*, 173.

158   bad habits, Teasdale, 19.

158   disenchantment, Baker, 180.

159   reproduce the voice, Johnson-Bennion, 119.

159   neglect, sneers, mocking, Gates quoted in Baker, 111–12.

159   core of zealous Mormons, Brian Cannon note to author, 2013.

159   political ruse, Briney, 82.

160   intense solicitation, Hardy, *Solemn Covenant*, 130.

160   banned from voting, Alexander, 265.

160   2,400 miles, Van Wagoner, 141.

160   The Lord showed me, VanWagoner, 141.

160   with broken heart, VanWagoner, 142.

160   The matter, VanWagoner, 143–44.

161   sustained, Van Wagoner, 146.

161   immediate expedient, Alexander, 269.

161   a good many men, *Proceedings*, 556.

161   the same yesterday, Tanner, 130.

162   I now publicly, *Doctrine and Covenants*, Declaration 1.

162   gave little, Daynes, 184.

162   confusion, Hardy, *Solemn Covenant*, 133.

162   continue to support, Cannon, 28.

162   favored a suspension, Hardy, 142.

162   should be halted, Hardy, 144.

162   one of his wives since 1855, Alexander, 267.

163   granted amnesty, Bradley, 26.

163   passage of time, Embry, 11.

163   slow process, Bitton, 108.

163   criminal intercourse, Hardy, *Solemn Covenant*, 142.

CHAPTER 11. I GREW REBELLIOUS
Primary Sources

Johanna Catherine Nielsen, "Life of Johanna Catherine Nielsen," unpublished document in possession of the author, comp. Catherine Rogers Metcalf (1947), comp. Lucille Metcalf Harrison (1981), and ed. Robert Merrill Harrison (1983); Olive Andelin Potter, Autobiography, BYUL; Lynette Conover, "Autobiography of the Life of Emma Lynette (Richardson) Conover written by herself," USHS.

Secondary Source

Martha Hughes Cannon," KUED PBS affiliate (Salt Lake City, July 22, 2012).

Specific Quotes

180   A seasoned man, Quinn quoted in "Martha."

CHAPTER 12. I HEARD A VOICE SAY YOU ARE AWAY FROM MR CHESTNUT
Primary Sources

"Annie Eliza Berry (Day), 1865–1928"; "Record of Thos. C. Day, Jr., Myton, Utah, June 3, 1931"; "Annie's Account Book and Diary 1924–1928"; "Appendix A: Fannie's Biography of Annie Eliza Berry"; "Appendix B: Excerpts from Life Sketch of Zelma Eliza Day Lloyd"; "Appendix C: Comments by Daughter Fannie Day Harrison"; and "Appendix D: A Letter from Heber Day," in *On the Utah Frontier: The Story of Thomas Clark Day and Annie Eliza Berry,* ed. Clifford L. Stott (Orem, UT, 1994). Note: None of the children mention any abuse in the family, and Fannie wrote that her father lived with her when he was old. She wrote, "Father was a wonderful man, honest and honorable until his death"; "He was easy to get along with"; and "He was a grand old man. He was hard working and a faithful L. D. Saint and respected by all."

Secondary Sources

Cott, *No Small Courage;* Salman Elbedour, Anthony J. Onwuegbuzie, Corin Caridine, and Hasan Abu-Saad, "The Effect of Polygamous Marital Structure on Behavioral, Emotional, and Academic Adjustment in Children: A Comprehensive Review of the Literature," *Clinical Child and Family Psychological Review* 5:4 (December 2002): 255–71; Johnson-Bennion, "Comparing Themes"; Peggy Fletcher Stack, "Old Laws Lead to Win for Plural Marriage," *The Salt Lake Tribune* (December 15, 2013), A10; A. Tanner, *A Mormon Mother;* and Turner, *Brigham Young.*

Specific Quotes

186   no fixed rules, Tanner, 222.
186   preserve her intact, Turner, 257.
199   marital discord, Elbedour, 264.
199   family planning, Elbedour, 261.
200   American Muslim women, Elbedour, 261–62.
200   miss the practice, Johnson-Bennion, 119–20.
200   Justice Frank Murphy, Cott, 194.
200   U.S. District Court Judge Clark Waddoups, Stack, A10.

FAREWELL
Primary Sources

"John Willard Kelly," unpublished autobiography in possession of the author; "Life History of Mary Ann Dudley Ellsworth," unpublished document in possession of the author; "Memories of my father Bent Rolfsen Larsen, 1963," Bent Franklin Larsen, BYUL; and A. Tanner, *A Mormon Mother*.

Secondary Sources

Alexander, *Things in Heaven*; Bradley, "Changed Faces"; Joanna Brooks, "On Being," NPR (August 23, 2012); Bushman, *Rough Stone*; Terryl L. Givens, "'Lightning Out of Heaven': Joseph Smith and the Forging of Community," BYU forum address, November 29, 2005; John S. McCormick, "Salt Lake City," *Utah History Encyclopedia*, ed. Powell; Gregory A. Prince and Wm. Robert Wright, *David O. McKay and the Rise of Modern Mormonism* (Salt Lake, 2005); Merina Smith, *Revelation, Resistance, and Mormon Polygamy: The Introduction and Implementation of the Principle, 1830–1853* (Logan, UT, 2013); Newell and Avery, *Mormon Enigma*; and Neil J. Young, "Short Creek's Long Legacy," *Slate* (April 16, 2008).

Specific Quotes

205	a maze of wires, McCormick, 481.
209	the order of heaven, Brooks.
209	a thousand members, Newell, 117.
209	ever opposed, Newell, 142.
209	Eliza R. Snow, Newell, 134.
209	March and May 1843, Newell, 142.
209	new family forms, Smith, 4–5.
209	no romantic talk, Bushman, 439.
209	timeless and borderless, Givens.
210	extended family community, Elaine Pagels in Givens.
210	*married* men and women, Bushman, 439.
210	not only see their descendents multiply, Smith, 161.
210	sexual relations, Bushman, 439.
210	free and full, Newell, 143.
210	he held the door, Newell, 143–44.
210	Emma began to talk, Newell, 145.
210	the recovery, Bushman, 493.
210	Hyrum, Bushman, 495–96.
210	caught between, Bushman, 493.
210	severe talking to, Bushman, 496.
210	Joseph F. Smith, Hardy, *Doing*, 60–61.
210	continuation of seeds, *Doctrine and Covenants*, Section 132.
211	the sobbings, *Book of Mormon*, Jacob 2.

211   sixty city lots, Bushman, 498–99.

211   fracture line, Hardy, *Solemn Covenant*, 190, 170.

211   262 secret marriages, Hardy, *Solemn Covenant*, 183.

212   marriage that survived, Hardy, *Solemn Covenant*, 297–98; Alexander, 250, 267.

212   Smoot, Hardy, *Solemn Covenant*, 251.

212   two apostles, Hardy, *Solemn Covenant*, 265.

212   gave a lengthy, Bradley, 27.

212   actively search, Bradley, 27.

212   routinely passed up, Hardy, *Solemn Covenant*, 295.

212   after the Church renounced polygamy, Larsen, 301.

213   against the backdrop, Young.

213   David O. McKay, Prince and Wright, 50–51.

Image Copyright Permissions

Figure 6.7: Courtesy of International Society Daughters of Utah Pioneers.

Figure 7.2: Courtesy of Joanne Hadden, family descendant.

Figure 8.2: Courtesy of International Society Daughters of Utah Pioneers.

Figure 8.3: Courtesy of International Society Daughters of Utah Pioneers.

Figure 8.4: Courtesy of International Society Daughters of Utah Pioneers.

Figure 9.2: Courtesy of Christina Hullinger, family descendant.

Figure 9.3: Used by permission, Utah State Historical Society, all rights reserved.

Figure 9.4: Used by permission, Utah State Historical Society, all rights reserved.

Figure 9.5: Courtesy of International Society Daughters of Utah Pioneers.

Figure 9.6: Courtesy of International Society Daughters of Utah Pioneers.

Figure 9.7: Courtesy of Christina Hullinger, family descendant.

Figure 11.2: Courtesy of Katie Davison, family descendant.

Figure 11.3: Courtesy of International Society Daughters of Utah Pioneers.

Figure 11.4: Courtesy of Linda Orullian, Andelin descendant.

Figure 12.2: Used with permission of Clifford L. Scott, editor.

Figure 12.3: Used with permission of Clifford L. Scott, editor.

Acknowledgments

MANY PEOPLE HAVE helped me through the years. Sheila O'Brien at the University of Idaho first suggested that I research the lives of polygamous wives. I was subsequently awarded a University of Idaho English Department Thesis Grant and several research grants by the John Calhoun Smith Fund for Western Studies. The Charles Redd Center at Brigham Young University supported my work with two grants. Claudia Bushman, Barbara Meldrum, Maureen Ursenbach Beecher, Martha Bradley, Cheri Earl, Lisa Gosper-Espinosa, and Merina Smith read very early drafts. Kathryn Daynes generously shared additional polygamous wives' personal writings with me, researched their family histories, and encouraged me to complete my book. Cheryl Snapp Conner alerted me to Mary Ann Hafen's autobiography. Carole Hunt Kelly, Rick Kelly, Paul and Shirley Kelly, Cherilyn Harline, Julia Smoot, Nancy Lund, Fiona Givens, Merina Smith, Craig Harline, and Brian Cannon read and commented on later drafts. Julia Smoot also lent many books to me from her personal collection. Colleen Whitley suggested the historical interludes as an organizing device. My European-historian husband Craig Harline read every draft and helped with the index; most important, his own creative-nonfiction prose inspired me.

I wish to thank the Historical Department of the Church of Jesus Christ of Latter-day Saints, the Daughters of Utah Pioneers, the Utah State Historical Society, and Brigham Young University Special Collections for their excellent archival guidance, and I appreciate their helpful staff and volunteers. My brother Steven A. Kelly spent time in one archive to retrieve an autobiography for me. I also have deep gratitude for polygamous wives' descendants who provided me with additional information and photographs: Joanne Haddon, Reed Smoot, Brenda Bailey, Delia Madsen, Katie Davison, Linda Andelin Orullian, Christine Hulliger, Lisa Hoyt, and

Clifford Scott. Tireless research assistants Rachael Givens and Bradley Kime collected photographs.

I appreciate Oxford editor Cynthia Read for her immediate interest in my manuscript and for her professional expertise and guidance; editorial assistant Marcela Maxfield for answering my questions and helping with photographs; and senior production editor Joellyn Ausanka for her helpful advice and copyediting.

For all this help and much more, I am truly grateful.

Index

Note: American cities outside of Utah are organized by state.

Abraham (*Old Testament*), 6, 7, 43, 45,
    46, 89
alcohol, use and abuse of, 20, 21, 26
American Fork (Utah), 24, 27, 39, 156
Anderson, Lavina Fielding, 118
Arizona, ix, 4, 56, 103, 160, 208, 213
    Mesa, 104
    Mount Trumble, 80
    St. Johns, 92, 93, 98
    Short Creek, 213
    Snowflake, 92, 93, 102
    Sunset, 100
    Tuba City, 92, 93, 96, 97
Arrington, Leonard J., 49
Atlantic Monthly, 66
Avery, Valeen Tippets, 209

Bateman, Dan, 155
Beaver (Utah), 94, 132, 133
Benjamin (Utah), 54
Benson, George, 86
bishops, 28, 53, 64, 86, 96, 109, 126,
    134, 155, 175, 180, 189, 191
Bitton, Davis, 158
Black, William and Margaret, 180, 181
Blessings (Laying on of Hands), 94, 98,
    101, 103, 195
Book of Mormon, 7, 46, 49, 209–11
Boston, 61

Brigham Young Academy, 135, 169, 178
Brineholt, Anna, 134
Brinkerhoff, David, 92, 95–97, 104
Brinkerhoff, Lovina Lee, 92, 97
Brinkerhoff, Lydia Ann Nelson, 92, 93,
    95–97, 103, 104
Brooks, Joanna, 209
Buchanan, James, 19, 56
Bunnel, Mother, 165, 170, 171, 178
Bunnel, Rosie, 171
Bunnell, Romania, 16
Bushman, Richard, 6, 209–11

Caine, Joseph, 27
California, 8, 18, 19, 95, 142, 183, 203
    Gold Rush, 13, 14
    San Bernardino, 17
    San Francisco, 149
Canada, xi, 159, 211, 213
Cannon, Angus, 78
Cannon, George Q., 160, 162
Cannon, Martha Hughes, 78
Cannonville (Utah), 84
Cedar City (Utah), 94, 95
Chase, Josephine Streeper, 87
Chestnut, Elizabeth Cherrington, 182,
    184–88, 190–93
Chestnut, Grace Knox, 182, 185,
    186, 189

Chestnut, Henry (Mr HC), 182, 184–95
Chestnut, Melvina, 183, 188–93
childbirth and pregnancy, 19, 34, 65, 80, 83, 86, 89, 90, 96–98, 100, 137, 138, 142, 143–46, 163, 170, 172, 173, 177, 178, 187, 188
Circleville (Utah), 182
Colorado, 4, 118, 119, 136–38, 139, 141, 145, 160, 192
    Durango, 137
    San Juan County, 137
    San Luis Valley, 135
    Sanford, 138
Colorado Magazine, 119
Conover, John, 181
Conover, Lynette Richardson, 164, 180, 181
Coontz, Stephanie, 18, 58
Cox, Elizabeth (Lizzie) Stout, 106, 114–17
Cox, (Auntie) Henrietta James, 106, 115, 117
Cox, Isaiah, 106, 114
Cox, Martha Cragun, 106–13, 119, 157
Cumming, Alfred, 56

Day, Annie Berry Chestnut, 182–99
Day, Eli (Day), 122, 125, 135–37, 140, 141, 144
Day, Eliza, 122, 125, 135–36, 140, 141, 144, 146
Day, Ellen, 145, 146
Day, Elvira Euphrasia (Phrasia) Cox, 123, 125, 126, 130, 136–37, 138–41, 145–47, 162
Day, Estella, 146
Day, Orville, 146, 147
Day, Thomas, 182, 183, 194–99
Daynes, Kathryn, 40, 44, 156, 162
Dean, Florence Ridges, 81, 163
Dean, Joseph, 81
Dean, (Sally) Sarah Arnold, 81

death and illness, 19, 26, 38, 53, 70, 71, 80–82, 84, 94, 97–102, 104, 111, 112, 114, 140, 142, 147–49, 170, 175, 176, 179, 181, 195, 197
Denmark, 83
Derr, Jill Mulvay, 74, 97
Deseret Dramatic Association, 15
Deseret News, 37, 155, 203
Deseret, state of, 8
DiSimone, Linda Wilcox, 95
Dixon, William Hepworth, 158
Dover (Utah), 164, 167
Draper (Utah), 88
Draper, Ellen Wilhelm, 87
Draper, William, 88
Dublin, 26

Echo Canyon (Utah), 10, 21
economic conditions (general)
    famine and poverty, 27, 36, 69
    general housing conditions, 11–13, 18, 19, 143 (*see also* polygamy: housing and living arrangements)
Edwards, Elizabeth, 104
Elisha, Omri, 48
Ellsworth, Edmund, 207, 208
Ellsworth, Elizabeth Young, 207, 208
Ellsworth, Mary Ann Bates, 208
Ellsworth, Mary Ann Dudley, 207, 208
Ellsworth, Mary Ann Jones, 208
Embry, Jessie, 33
England, 8, 19, 204. *See also* Great Britain
Ensign, The, 214

Fairview (Utah), 122, 125, 135, 140
Farley, Angelina Calkins, 60–67, 71
Farley, (Mary) Ellen Reed, 60, 62, 64
Farley, Lydia Pons, 60, 62–68
Farley, Winthrop, 60–68
Farmington (Utah), 206
feminism, 73–75, 77, 79, 90

Fillmore (Utah), 182

Flake, Chad, 101, 102

Flake, Charles, 102

Flake, Lucy White, 92–95, 97, 98, 101–4, 157

Flake, Kathleen, 200

Flake, Prudence Kartchner, 92, 94, 97, 98, 101, 102

Flake, William, 92, 94, 97, 98

Gardner, Robert, 28, 30

Gardner Village (Utah), 28

Gates, Susa Young, 74, 154, 159

Gathering to Zion, 7, 8, 22

Givens, Terryl, 209

Goldberg, Michael, 17

Grantsville (Utah), 21

Great Basin, population of, 8

Great Britain, 48, 75. *See also* England; Ireland; Scotland; Wales

Green River (Utah), 137, 140

Hafen, Anna Maria, 106

Hafen, John, 108–10, 112, 119

Hafen, Mary Ann Stucki Reber, 106–9, 110–13, 118, 119

Hafen, Rosie Stucki, 106

Hafen, Roy, 118, 119

Hafen, Susette, 106, 108, 111, 112

Hagar (*Old Testament*), 6, 45, 138

Hansen, Andrew, 83–85

Hansen, Bengta Anderson, 83, 84

Hansen, Caroline Pedersen, 83, 85

Hardy, Carmon, 44, 156, 162

Harrison, Benjamin, 163

Hayes, Rutherford B., 75

Heywood, Joseph, 24, 26, 27, 30, 32, 34, 37, 38

Heywood, Martha Spence, 4, 24–28, 30–34, 37–38, 40–41

Heywood, Mary Bell, 24, 38

Heywood, Neal, 38

Heywood, Sarepta, 24, 27, 30–33, 38

Heywood, Sister Vary (Sarah Symonds), 24, 30, 32, 33, 38

Highland (Utah), 146, 147

Hinckley, Gordon B., 214

Hindley, Jane Robinson, 8, 24–27, 38–41

Hindley, John, 24, 26, 27, 38, 39, 41

Hindley, Mary, 24, 27, 38–40

Holden (Utah), 182

"Home" (Poem), 17

hooks, bell, 67

Huntington (Utah), 139

Idaho, 4, 8, 135, 160, 168, 179, 208

Montpelier, 164, 175

Moscow, 164, 174, 175

Oakley, 85

Preston, 86

Rexburg, 85, 208

Salem, 85

Illinois, 7, 62

Nauvoo, 27

illness. *See* death and illness

Indian relations, 13, 18, 180

Iowa, 7, 62, 136

Ireland, 8. *See also* Great Britain

Isaac (*Old Testament*), 45

Ishmael (*Old Testament*), 45

Isle of Man, 8, 26, 203

Jacob (*Book of Mormon*), 46

Jacob (*Old Testament*), 89, 90

Jakeman, Ellen, 145

Johnson-Bennion, Daniela, 200

Jordan Mills (also Gardner Village), 24, 28

Junction (Utah), 182, 183, 197

Juvenile Instructor, 147

Kane, Elizabeth Wood, 75

Kelly, Emma Sims, 204, 205

Kelly, George, 203, 205
Kelly, Helena Quirk, 203
Kelly, John Bookbinder, 203–5
Kentucky, 107
Kern, Louis J., 47
Kimball, Vilate, 76
King, Larry, 214

Lambson, Val, 158
Larsen, B. F., 124, 148, 212
Larsen, Bent, 122, 126–28, 131, 137–39,
    141, 143, 147
Larsen, Ida, 147
Larsen, Juliane (Aunt Julia) Sorensen,
    122, 126, 127, 128, 142, 144, 147
Larsen, Lorena, 122–28, 132–39, 140–45,
    147–51
Leah (*Old Testament*), 89, 90
Lehi (Utah), 24, 29, 30, 35
Lévi-Strauss, Claude, 88
Liverpool, 56
Logan (Utah), 162
    temple, 135
London, 44

MacDonald, Agnes Aird, 50
MacDonald, Alexander, 50, 55, 56
MacDonald, Elizabeth Atkinson, 50, 56
MacDonald, Elizabeth Graham, 50, 52,
    53, 55–57
MacDonald, Fanny Van Cott, 50
MacDonald, Sarah Johnson, 50
McAllister, Agatha (Aggie) Walker, 122,
    123, 128–33, 141, 142, 143, 145, 148,
    149, 150
McAllister, Joseph (Pa), 122, 129, 130,
    131, 132, 133, 142, 149
McAllister, Mary Ann (Mollie) Miller,
    122, 129, 131, 142, 149
McConkie, Bruce R., 213
McKay, David O., 213
Maeser, Karl G., 169

Manti (Utah), 48, 125, 140–141, 145, 146, 180
    temple, 133, 142, 146, 180
marriage, general
    abuse in, 195–98
    age at, 14, 126
    attitudes and ideals, 17, 18, 22, 58
    courtship, 14, 17, 33
    relationships with husband, 194–99
    wedding day and parties, 14, 15, 18,
        83, 96, 126
    See also polygamy
Massachusetts, 14
Maughan, Mary Ann Weston, 87
Maughan, Peter, 87
Mexico, xi, 36, 56, 84, 117, 138, 150,
    159, 211–13
Millcreek (Utah), 81
Miner, Mormon, 146
missionaries and missionary work, 8,
    26, 28, 29, 31, 32, 54, 69, 84
Missouri, 7
Moab (Utah), 138
Monroe (Utah), 122, 123, 126, 140, 142,
    147, 150
Mount, Joseph, 13, 16, 17
Mount, Elizabeth Foote, 13, 16, 17, 22
Mount Timpanogos, 3, 27, 146
Mormon Reformation of 1856–57, 48, 49
Mormons, The (PBS Series), 6
Moroni (Utah), 167, 169
Mountain Home (Utah), 182, 197
Murphy, Frank, 200
music, 118, 184, 197

Nebraska, 73
Nephi, 24, 25, 33, 34, 37. *See also* Salt
    Creek Settlement (Utah)
Nevada, 4, 8
    Boulder Dam, 118
    Bunkerville, 106, 107, 109, 118
New England, 48
New Jersey, 26, 29

New Mexico, 4, 103, 160
  Ramah, 99
  Roswell, 146
New York Herald, 74
New York State, 6, 7, 61, 62
  Buffalo, 25
Newell, Linda King, 209
Nielsen, Christian, 169, 174, 175
Nielsen, Johanna Catherine, xi
Nielsen, Emma Mecham, ix, 92, 93,
  98–104
Nielson, Frihoff (FG), 92, 98, 100–102
Nielson, Mary Everett, 92, 98, 100, 101
Nixon, Hannah Fawcett, 80, 81
Nixon, James, 80, 81
Nixon, Johanne Schultz, 80, 81
Nixon, Zephyr Kelsey, 81
Norway, 127

O'Dea, Thomas F., 47
Ogden (Utah), 60–62, 67, 70
Ohio, 7
Oregon, 8, 13

Panguitch (Utah), 85
Page, Daniel, 24, 28, 30, 35
Page, Mary, 24, 28, 35
Parkinson, Ellen "Nellie," 86
Parkinson, Louisa Benson, 86, 87
Parkinson, William, 86, 87
Parowan (Utah), 24, 35
Patriarchal blessings, 35
Payson (Utah), 18, 24, 35, 54
Pennsylvania, 75
personal writings, Mormon and
  American women, 3, 4, 25, 57, 58,
  67, 68, 70, 71, 79–81, 85–87, 97,
  100, 124, 145, 147, 154, 163, 183,
  197, 199
  letter-writing, 25, 29, 100, 101, 132, 133,
    140, 141, 155, 156, 194, 195
Pleasant Grove (Utah), 164, 170, 175, 176

polygamy, nineteenth-century Mormon
  abolition and waning of, and
    Manifesto, 5, 119, 123, 125, 126, 138,
    139, 143–46, 148, 153–63, 165, 181,
    184, 211–14
  age differences between spouses, 30,
    55, 88, 110, 129, 154, 157, 180,
    184–93
  American culture and government in
    opposition to, 4, 5, 12, 74, 81, 109,
    111–14, 123, 125, 128, 130–32, 143,
    153, 155, 158, 160, 168, 171, 172, 175
  autobiographical writings (*see*
    personal writings)
  and celestial marriage, 6, 12, 150
  ceremonies of, 6, 12, 32, 94, 129, 130,
    168, 186
  courtship in, 15, 16, 30–32, 34, 40, 78,
    82, 86, 87, 95, 96, 110, 111, 126,
    129, 166–68, 185, 187
  divorce and separation in, 16, 88,
    140, 146, 154, 155, 178, 183, 184,
    188–93
  educational and economic activities/
    conditions of wives, 11, 20, 21,
    34–38, 40, 54, 55, 69, 74–76, 81,
    84, 85, 93, 94, 102, 103, 109–11,
    113–18, 125, 127, 136, 140, 143–47,
    150, 154, 165, 169–72, 175–79, 184,
    187–90, 192–94
  expressions of happiness in, 112, 149,
    169, 183
  expressions of love in, 113, 116, 123,
    124, 126, 136, 137, 140, 142, 145, 149
  expressions of sorrow, anguish, and
    illness in, 12, 78, 86, 89, 93, 97,
    98, 100, 101, 104, 111, 138, 147,
    149, 181
  general attitudes in Mormonism
    toward, 40, 41, 44, 114, 128, 143,
    146, 154, 156–62, 166, 172, 175,
    180, 184, 188, 189, 194, 200, 209

polygamy, nineteenth-century Mormon
  (*continued*)
  God as comfort for wives (prayer,
    miracles, visions, dreams), 26, 27,
    40, 84, 94, 99–103, 112, 118, 126,
    127, 137, 139, 143, 150, 151, 166, 168,
    169, 171, 172, 178, 179, 190
  housing and living arrangements, 16,
    19, 20, 27, 28, 33, 36, 38, 39, 51, 53,
    63, 66–70, 76, 78–85, 88, 93, 98,
    100, 102, 107–9, 112–16, 123–25, 127,
    128, 130, 131, 134, 135, 138–40, 142–44,
    148, 150, 153, 154, 162, 165, 168, 169,
    171–76, 178, 183, 188, 189, 192–94
  imprisonment and prosecution of
    husbands, 82, 127, 129, 132–34,
    139, 141, 142, 148, 155, 156, 173
  justifications and doctrines of, 5–8, 17,
    40, 41, 43–49, 76, 79, 87, 88, 94,
    110–13, 126, 127, 138, 153, 156–58,
    160, 163, 166, 168, 177, 180, 209–14
  loneliness, ix, 26, 35, 37, 81–83, 98,
    99, 103
  marrying widows, 29
  marrying wife's sister, 16, 20, 21
  and monogamous ideals, 4, 5, 17, 18,
    22, 26, 31, 78, 86, 97, 113, 124, 126,
    145, 158, 193, 199
  motherhood in, 38, 115, 118, 133,
    142–46, 149, 150, 165, 172, 173, 175,
    178, 187, 189, 192–94
  old age in, 148, 149
  origins of, 6, 7, 12
  percentages of people living and
    demographics of, 5, 129, 157, 158
  pleasure trips and honeymoons with
    husband, 35, 85, 96, 111, 114, 127,
    130, 149, 168, 187
  preparation for, 111
  raids against, 84, 109, 123, 126, 128,
    132, 155, 160, 169, 171–74
  relationships among wives, 4, 5, 15,
    16, 19, 20, 30, 31, 38, 39, 53, 57,
    63–68, 70, 73–90, 93–95, 98,
    100–102, 109, 111–17, 128, 129, 132,
    133, 136, 140, 143, 144, 146, 150,
    154, 168, 171, 174, 177
  relationships with husbands, 12, 15, 16,
    19, 20, 32, 34–37, 40, 55, 57, 63–68,
    76–78, 81–90, 94–102, 104, 107,
    109, 112, 117, 123, 124, 130, 132–34,
    136, 137, 139–41, 143–46, 149, 151, 154,
    172, 173, 176–80, 187–93
  rumors and suspicions of, and
    secrecy surrounding, 7, 12, 26, 128,
    130–32, 134, 135, 140–43, 155, 162,
    163, 211
  social activities of wives, 33, 35, 36, 65
  social status of participants, 25, 26,
    33, 34, 38
  underground, hiding, 131, 132, 134,
    135, 137–43, 150, 155, 169, 170,
    171–75
  widows, 107, 119, 143
  wives posing as widows, 85, 146, 148
  See also childbirth and pregnancy;
    marriage
polygamy, other, 199, 200, 213–15
Potter, Edwin, 167, 169, 170, 173,
  174, 178
Potter, (Aunt) Hattie, 168, 173, 174, 177
Potter, Myrtle, 173
Potter, Olive Andelin, 164–70, 173, 174,
  177–81
Potter, Pearl, 173
Pratt, Orson, 43–45, 63
Pratt, Sarah, 78
pregnancy. *See* childbirth and pregnancy
Primary Children's Organization, 94
Provo (Utah), 3, 10, 11, 19, 22, 50, 51, 54,
  56, 75, 76, 147, 148, 149, 156, 164,
  165, 169, 170, 173, 178
  River, 28
  Woolen Mills, 53

Quinn, Michael, 180

Rachel (*Old Testament*), 89, 90
Reber, Aunt Barbara, 111
Reber, John, 110, 111
Redmond (Utah), 134, 136
Relief Society and women's church
    work, 4, 74, 101, 147, 150, 184, 209
Richfield (Utah), 82, 164, 173
Riddle, Isaac, 194
Rogers, Augusta, 166, 168, 171
Rogers, Catherine Nielsen, 164–79, 181
Rogers, Edna, 35
Rogers, Kate, 165, 172, 179
Rogers, Lorana, 24, 36
Rogers, Lovina, 166, 170, 172, 179
Rogers, Matilda, 24, 29, 30, 35
Rogers, Rudolph, 165, 172
Rogers, Ruel, 166, 168, 170, 172
Rogers, Ruth Page, 4, 24–26, 28–30,
    34–37, 40, 41
Rogers, Samuel Holister, 24, 28, 30, 34, 35, 41
Rogers, Victoria, 175
Romney, Miss, 107
Rouie, Peter, 17

St. George (Utah), ix, 24, 36, 56, 80,
    97–99, 107–9, 114, 122, 133, 142,
    157, 162, 184, 185
    Temple, 118, 127, 128, 130, 133, 149,
    150, 186
Salt Creek Settlement, 25, 33, 34.
    See also Nephi
Salt Lake, 13
Salt Lake City, 3, 7, 10–13, 17, 24, 35, 50,
    62, 69, 87, 111, 114, 126, 148, 154,
    160, 161, 177, 178, 187, 203–8
    Beehive House, 153, 154
    Bowery, 43
    City Hall, 11, 20
    Endowment House, 64, 83, 94, 111,
    114, 168, 204

Fort, 13
Lion House, 153, 154
Pioneer Park, 13
population, 13, 22
Social Hall, 15
Seventies Hall, 35
Sugar House Park, 155
Tabernacle, 43, 73, 154
Temple, 8, 11, 117
Temple Square (Temple Block), 13,
    40, 153, 204
Warm Springs Bath House, 14, 33
Salt Lake Valley, 7, 8, 13, 74
Sanpete County (Utah), 166, 180
Santa Clara (Utah), 107–9, 141
Sarah (*Old Testament*), 6, 45
Scotland, 8, 55, 184. *See also* Great
    Britain
Seer, The, 44
Sevier River (Utah), 123
Sharp, John, 155
Shipp, Ellis, 75
Sigerman, Harriet, 4
Simmons, Emma Bloxom, 10, 16, 21
Simmons, Frank, 21
Simmons, Joe, 10, 14–16, 20, 21
Simmons, Nett Woolley, 10, 16, 20, 21
Simmons, Rachel Woolley, 10–16,
    20–22
Smith, Bathsheba, 114
Smith, Emma, 112, 153, 209–11
Smith, Hyrum, 210
Smith, Joseph, 6–8, 12, 43–45, 48, 73,
    97, 153, 155, 157, 207, 209–11
Smith, Joseph F., 157, 210, 212
Smith, Merina, 210
Smithfield (Utah), 60, 61
Smoot, Margaret, 76
Smoot, Reed, 212
Snow, Artemesia, 78
Snow, Eliza R., 94, 95, 104, 209
Snow, Erastus, 78

Snow, James, 154
social life, Mormon, 14, 15, 25, 35, 36, 99, 100, 102, 126
Springville (Utah), 56, 180, 181
Stewart, Andrew, 50, 54
Stewart, Caroline Nickerson, 50, 54
Stewart, Catherine Holden, 50
Stewart, Eunice Quimby, 50, 54–55, 57
Stewart, Mariah Judd, 50, 54, 55
Steward, Mary Weir, 50
suffrage movement, 73–75
Summit (Utah), 132
Sundance Ski Resort, 3
Switzerland, 107, 111

Tait, Lisa Olsen, 145
Tanner, Ann Crosby, 10, 19, 22, 50, 53, 57
Tanner, Annie Clark, 46, 141, 161
Tanner, Mary Jane Mount, 3, 4, 10–14, 16–22, 50, 51, 53, 57
Tanner, Myron, 10, 17–19, 22, 50, 53, 57
Taylor, John, 155–60, 186, 189
Teasdale (Utah), 182, 194
temples, in Mormonism, 6, 104
Thurber, Annie Christensen, 82
Thurber, Laura Keeler, 82
Turner, Ella Larsen, 147
Turner, John, 44, 73
Turner, Taylor, 147

U.S. Supreme Court, 200
Utah Expedition, 18
Utah Territory and statehood, 37, 73, 74, 155, 156, 158, 160, 163, 211
    penitentiary, 155

Van Wagoner, Richard, 79
Varian, Charles, 162, 163
Vernal (Utah), 164, 173, 179, 182

Waddoups, Clark, 200
wagon train (1850), 26
Wales, 8. *See also* Great Britain
Walker, Ronald W., 44
Wasatch Mountains, 3
Washington
    Camas, 146
Washington, D.C., 75, 212
Washington (Utah), 24, 38
Wells, Emmeline, 75, 78
West, Mary J., 101, 102
West Weber (Utah), 208
Whitney, Horace, 16
Williams, Electa Jane Barney, 60, 68, 70, 71
Williams, Ezra, 60, 68–71
Williams, Henrietta Crombie, 60, 61, 68–71
Williams, Hyrum, 70
Williams, Rebecca Swain, 69
Winter Quarters (Iowa), 27
Woman's Exponent, 74, 78, 103, 158, 159, 200
Woodruff, Phoebe, 78
Woodruff, Wilford, 78, 138, 143, 153, 159–62
Wooley, Thomas and Martha, 170, 172, 175–77
Woolley, Edwin, 12
Woolley, Ellen, 13
Woolley, Mary, 12, 16
Wyoming, 4, 8, 74, 160
    Afton (Star Valley), 175
    Star Valley, 164, 176, 178

Young Women Mutual, 128
Young Women's Journal, 158, 159
Young, Brigham, 7, 8, 13, 14, 20, 31, 32, 35, 38, 40, 44–46, 54, 73, 74, 76–78, 153–55, 180, 205
Young, Neil J., 213
Young, Zina, 78